P9-CJL-648

VOLUME THREE

SACRED PLACES

OHIO AND ILLINOIS

A Comprehensive Guide to Early LDS Historical Sites

Series Titles

NEW ENGLAND AND EASTERN CANADA

NEW YORK AND PENNSYLVANIA

OHIO AND ILLINOIS

Other Titles Planned for the Series

MISSOURI

IOWA AND NEBRASKA

WYOMING AND UTAH

VOLUME THREE

SACRED PLACES

OHIO AND ILLINOIS

A Comprehensive Guide to Early LDS Historical Sites

LaMar C. Berrett
General Editor

Keith W. Perkins
Donald Q. Cannon

DESERET
BOOK

All photographs, unless otherwise indicated, by LaMar C. Berrett.

© 2002 Deseret Book Company

All rights reserved. No part of this book may be reproduced in any form or by any means without permission in writing from the publisher, Deseret Book Company, P. O. Box 30178, Salt Lake City, Utah 84130. This work is not an official publication of The Church of Jesus Christ of Latter-day Saints. The views expressed herein are the responsibility of the authors and do not necessarily represent the position of the Church or of Deseret Book Company.

DESERET BOOK is a registered trademark of Deseret Book Company.

Visit us at DeseretBook.com

Library of Congress Catalog Card Number 99-72525

ISBN 978-1-57345-657-9

Printed in the United States of America
Sheridan Books, Chelsea, MI

10 9 8 7 6 5 4 3 2

CONTENTS

Preface

When Moses came to the mountain of God and the burning bush, the Lord said to him, "Put off thy shoes from off thy feet, for the place whereon thou standest is holy ground" (Exodus 3:5).

Through the ages, the locations at which sacred historical events occurred have traditionally become holy. How holy or sacred a site is depends on the understanding of those beholding it. Elizabeth Barrett Browning wrote:

> Earth's crammed with heaven,
> And every common bush afire with God;
> But only he who sees, takes off his shoes—
> The rest sit round it and pluck blackberries.
> (*Aurora Leigh,* Book 7, 820–23)

The Church of Jesus Christ of Latter-day Saints has a long tradition of recognizing and recording sacred places and events. In 1838 the Lord said to Joseph Smith, "Let the city, Far West, be a holy and consecrated land unto me; and it shall be called most holy, for the ground upon which thou standest is holy" (D&C 115:7). Even earlier, when the Church was organized on April 6, 1830, the Prophet was told that "there shall be a record kept among you" (D&C 21:1). Since those early times, places and events central to the Church's struggles and successes have been sanctified and recorded. *Sacred Places* was written to bring the history and geography of the early period of the Church to life.

Following the history and movement of the Saints from their early days in New York to their settlement in the valley of the Great Salt Lake, this series will function as a valuable resource for academic historians and amateur Church history enthusiasts alike. *Sacred Places* provides detailed maps, interesting narratives, and numerous photographs in its effort to document the many places made sacred by the faith and testimonies of past generations of Saints. The comprehensive nature of this series encourages readers to follow in the footsteps of Joseph Smith, Brigham Young, and other Church leaders, or to seek out the paths of their own ancestors. The series also enables armchair tourists to vicariously visit the many magnificent places relevant to Church history.

Sacred Places is the culmination of more than 25 years of research and study. Its authors, all university professors, have devoted much of their lives to this work of preserving and documenting the legacy of our literal and spiritual ancestors. By purchasing and preserving many of these sacred sites, the Church has encouraged member and nonmember alike to visit locations important to our history. Visiting sites such as the Sacred Grove, the Hill Cumorah, Adam-ondi-Ahman, or Carthage Jail enables us to understand the history of the Church in terms of the real places and real people who witnessed the very real and sacred events of the Restoration.

Acknowledgments

Brigham Young University's College of Religious Education, Department of Church History and Doctrine, and Religious Studies Center have been instrumental in the realization of *Sacred Places*. Through various means—time, student assistants, secretarial help, research grants, and various other forms of financial aid—these organizations and the people associated with them have been indispensable.

Gratitude is expressed to past and present General Authorities of The Church of Jesus Christ of Latter-day Saints who have ensured that significant Church history sites have been purchased and preserved for the edification and enjoyment of future generations. LaMar C. Berrett, general editor, is particularly grateful to President Spencer W. Kimball, who told him that "we need to know and tell the truth about our Church history sites." President Kimball also related a fable concerning the Joseph Smith home in Palmyra, NY. "Some used to say that when the angel Moroni appeared to Joseph Smith the first time, it occurred in the Joseph Smith frame home, but we know that this is not true." This statement has impressed upon the editor the great responsibility he has in providing correct information regarding our tremendous heritage and its relation to these sacred sites. *Sacred Places* has been significantly affected by President Kimball's interest and encouragement. Special thanks are also given to those writers, researchers, journal keepers, Church historians, and others who laid the groundwork upon which *Sacred Places* has been constructed.

We are grateful to the staffs and administrators of the many repositories who have been so helpful in our research. The staffs of the Brigham Young University Harold B. Lee Library and the LDS Church Archives were especially gracious. We are also grateful for the efforts of archaeologists Dale Berge, Ray T. Matheny, and Virginia Harrington in conducting archaeological digs at various Church history sites.

We give special thanks to Wilford C. Wood, who spent much of his life purchasing and preserving sites and objects pertaining to the life of the Prophet Joseph Smith, and to James L. Kimball Jr., who provided invaluable help in researching property locations in Nauvoo.

The authors also acknowledge and thank Thomas S. Child for illustrating the maps.

We are grateful to the personnel at Deseret Book Company who have helped bring this series to publication. We especially acknowledge Cory H. Maxwell, Jana Erickson, Richard Erickson, Kent Minson, Sheryl Roderick, and Michael Morris for their efforts in editing and publishing this important information.

Finally we thank our wives and children for their patience and support over the past 25 years as we have labored to bring about this monumental work.

So many other individuals have contributed to the completion of *Sacred Places* that it is impractical, even impossible, to give personal credit to all those who deserve it. A blanket "thank you" is given to all who have helped in any way.

Information Contained in *Sacred Places*

Several symbols have been employed in *Sacred Places*. These symbols include small black squares ■ (both in text and on maps) indicating sites with direct ties to LDS history. Small black circles ● indicate important sites not directly related to LDS Church history.

Because of the voluminous nature of the bibliographical sources used by the authors, abbreviations were used in the text to identify those sources. Along with noting the sources used in preparing the book, the authors have also included many references for the reader who is interested in learning more about a particular event or Church history site. A complete bibliography with an alphabetic listing of abbreviations is included in the back of the volume. Also included is a list of abbreviations used to identify sources of photographs and other illustrations.

Many maps and illustrations, including photographs, have been included in an effort to help the reader to locate, visualize, and more fully appreciate the numerous sites identified in *Sacred Places.*

Ohio

Keith W. Perkins

OHIO

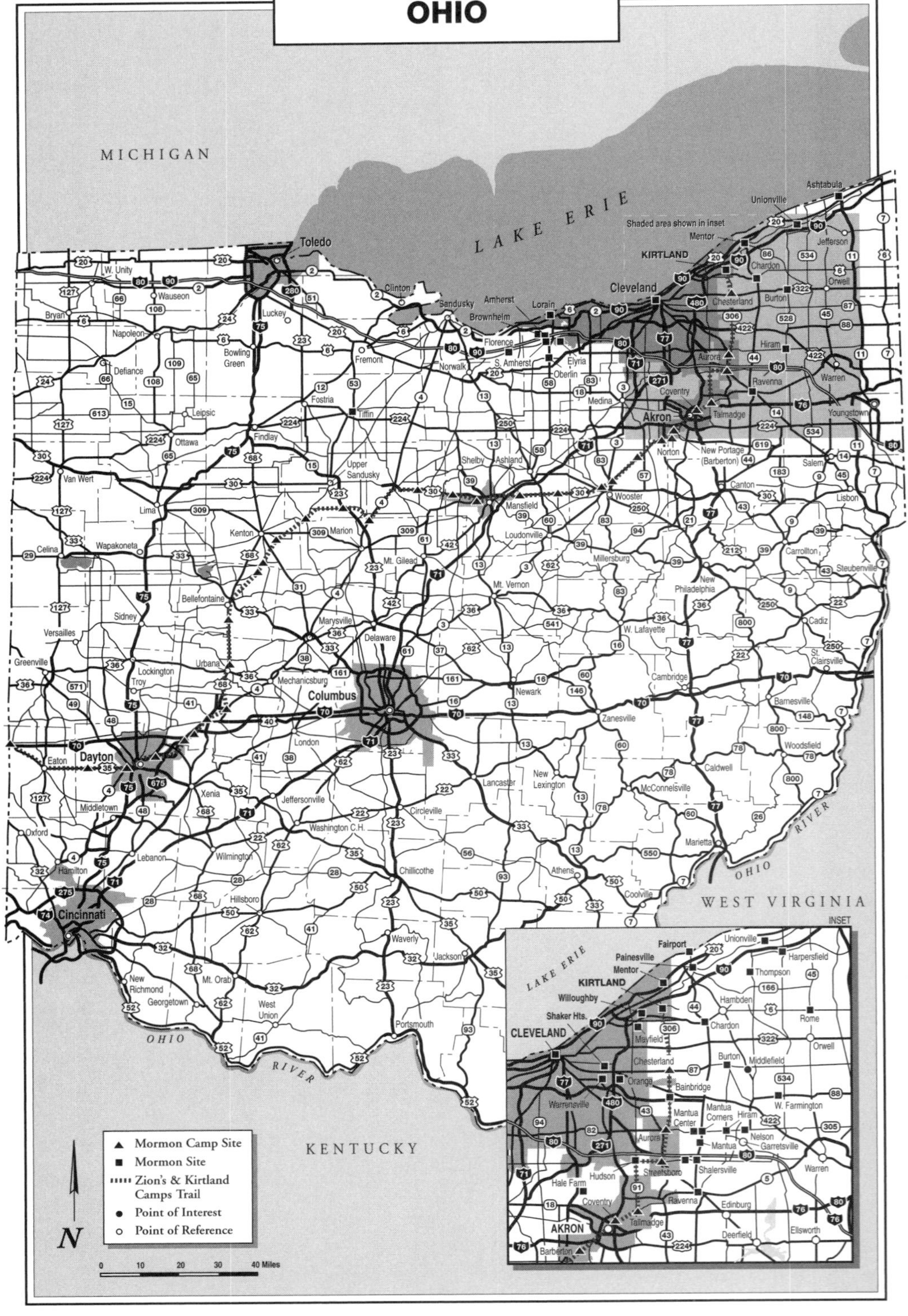
MICHIGAN
LAKE ERIE
KENTUCKY
WEST VIRGINIA
OHIO RIVER
Shaded area shown in inset
Toledo
Ashtabula
Unionville
Mentor
Jefferson
KIRTLAND
Chardon
Orwell
Cleveland
Chesterland
Burton
Amherst
Lorain
Brownhelm
Florence
S. Amherst
Elyria
Oberlin
Hiram
Aurora
Ravenna
Warren
Coventry
Talmadge
Youngstown
Akron
Norton
New Portage (Barberton)
Salem
Canton
Lisbon
Wooster
Mansfield
Ashland
Shelby
Loudonville
Millersburg
Carrollton
Steubenville
New Philadelphia
Cadiz
St. Clairsville
W. Lafayette
Cambridge
Barnesville
Woodsfield
Caldwell
Marietta
McConnelsville
Zanesville
New Lexington
Lancaster
Athens
Coolville
Newark
Mt. Vernon
Mt. Gilead
Marion
Upper Sandusky
Tiffin
Fostria
Fremont
Sandusky
Clinton
Norwalk
Medina
Luckey
Bowling Green
Findlay
W. Unity
Wauseon
Bryan
Napoleon
Defiance
Leipsic
Ottawa
Van Wert
Lima
Celina
Wapakoneta
Kenton
Bellefontaine
Sidney
Versailles
Greenville
Lockington
Troy
Urbana
Mechanicsburg
Marysville
Delaware
Columbus
London
Eaton
Dayton
Xenia
Middletown
Jeffersonville
Circleville
Washington C.H.
Oxford
Hamilton
Lebanon
Wilmington
Chillicothe
Hillsboro
Cincinnati
Waverly
Jackson
New Richmond
Mt. Orab
Georgetown
West Union
Portsmouth
INSET
Fairport
Painesville
Harpersfield
Thompson
Willoughby
Hambden
Shaker Hts.
Rome
CLEVELAND
Mayfield
Middlefield
Orange
Bainbridge
Warrensville
W. Farmington
Mantua Center
Mantua Corners
Mantua
Nelson
Garretsville
Streetsboro
Shalersville
Hale Farm
Hudson
Edinburg
Ellsworth
Deerfield
AKRON
Barberton
Mormon Camp Site
Mormon Site
Zion's & Kirtland Camps Trail
Point of Interest
Point of Reference
N
0 10 20 30 40 Miles

Introduction to Ohio

Ohio, "The Buckeye State," is a Midwestern state on the shores of Lake Erie. One of the leading industrial states in the United States, Ohio ranks 35th in size among all the states yet has the sixth largest population. It is named after the **Ohio River.** Ohio is an **Iroquoian Indian** term for "fine river" or "good river."

The Frenchman Sieur de la Salle was probably the first European explorer to reach the territory of the present-day state of **Ohio**. La Salle visited the area about 1670, and because of his discoveries, the French claimed the region. Britain claimed the same region as an extension of her colonies on the Atlantic Coast. Conflict over the region erupted in the **French and Indian War** (1754–63), which was actually a war between the British, including the North American colonies, and the French, who were allied with some of the American **Indian** tribes living in the Ohio area. In the peace treaty following the war, the French ceded to the British most of the land east of the **Mississippi River.**

The Americans took the region from the British during the Revolutionary War, and in 1787 it became the Northwest Territory of the newly formed United States of America. Ohio was separated from the Northwest Territory in 1800 and became the nation's 17th state in 1803. Lake Erie forms its northern boundary, and the Ohio River forms much of its eastern and all of its southern boundaries. The state's first capital was Chillicothe, but after being relocated several times, the capital settled in Columbus in 1816.

Natural resources have helped Ohio become a leading manufacturing state. It has an abundant supply of water, coal, salt, and other minerals. It is also centrally located near raw materials and major trading markets. The transportation industry, including the production of automobiles, airplanes, and motorcycles, is Ohio's most important manufacturing activity. Ohio also produces iron, steel, rubber, glass, and other consumer goods.

Part of the Midwestern Corn Belt's fertile soil stretches across central Ohio and provides for a successful agricultural industry. The chief crops are soybeans, corn, and wheat. Dairy goods, beef cattle, hogs, and fruit are also important agricultural products.

Ohio is sometimes called "The Mother of Presidents" because seven presidents of the United States have come from **Ohio,** including **Ulysses S. Grant, Rutherford B. Hayes, James A. Garfield, Benjamin Harrison, William McKinley, William H. Taft**, and **Warren G. Harding.**

Latter-day Saints in Ohio

In Oct. 1830, **Oliver Cowdery**, **Peter Whitmer Jr.**, **Parley P. Pratt**, and **Ziba Peterson** arrived as missionaries in northeastern[1] Ohio. They were headed to the frontier west of **Missouri**, which had been designated as **Indian Territory,** to proselyte. Along the way they stopped in the village of Mentor, Ohio, the home of influential **Reformed Baptist preacher Sidney Rigdon.**[2] **Parley P. Pratt**, who had been a member of Rigdon's congregation before his recent conversion to Mormonism, wanted to share his newly found religious beliefs with Rigdon. Rigdon questioned the authenticity of the **Book of Mormon** at first, but he allowed the missionaries to preach to his congregation after admonishing them to "prove all things; hold fast that which is good" (1 Thessalonians 5:21).

The missionaries also visited the hamlet of **Kirtland**, a few miles south of Mentor, where they contacted other Reformed Baptists who shared many of their beliefs. A group of these religionists had established a communal society on **Isaac Morley's farm** called "The Family." When the missionaries testified of the truthfulness of the **Book of Mormon** to this group, they met with unprecedented success in and around **Kirtland** and **Mentor.**

Parley P. Pratt said, "The people thronged us night and day, insomuch that we had no time for rest and retirement." Some came

---

[1] The northeastern portion of Ohio was claimed by the state of Connecticut and was known as the Connecticut Western Reserve. This area was developed at the end of the 18th century by the Connecticut Land Company.

[2] Sidney Rigdon and other "restorationist" preachers in Ohio during the early 1800s were seeking a restoration of New Testament Christianity. Their congregations were organized under the names "Reformed Baptist" (later "Campbellite"), and many of their beliefs harmonized with LDS doctrines, including faith, repentance, baptism by immersion for the remission of sins, and the gift of the Holy Ghost.

"for curiosity, some to obey the gospel, and some to dispute or resist it" (APPP 48). The Book of Mormon created so much excitement that there were not enough copies to go around; those eager to read it had to share. Before the missionaries left the area four weeks later, they had baptized more than 100 persons from the area, including **Sidney Rigdon**, and had organized a branch of the Church in **Kirtland** with **Sidney** in charge. He, **Newel K. Whitney**, **Frederick G. Williams**, and **Levi Hancock** were among the many new members of the Church from Ohio. **Edward Partridge** joined a short time later after meeting the Prophet in New York.

While the missionaries were having great success in **Ohio**, the Saints in **New York** were experiencing increased harassment from anti-Mormons. In two revelations received in Dec. 1830 and Jan. 1831 (**D&C 37–38**), the **Prophet Joseph Smith** was instructed to move the headquarters of the Church to **Kirtland** and have the Saints assemble in that region for the Church's "first gathering" in this dispensation:

> "That ye might escape the power of the enemy, and be gathered unto me a righteous people, without spot and blameless—wherefore, for this cause I gave unto you the commandment that ye should go to the Ohio; and there I will give unto you my law; and there you shall be endowed with power from on high; and from thence, whosoever I will shall go forth among all nations" (D&C 38:31–33).

Ohio was not intended to be the permanent headquarters of the Church. In 1831, the Lord said it would be a stronghold for "five years" (D&C 64:21). It was to be a place where the main body of the Church could develop in preparation for the move to the center of Zion in **Missouri**. Ohio was a natural location for the first gathering of the Church. Because of missionary success in Ohio, more Latter-day Saints lived there than in any other state, and growth was continuing rapidly. Ohio was also centrally located in the young nation and was accessible by water routes, the preferred method of transportation in the 1830s.

Joseph Smith arrived in **Kirtland** from **New York** in early Feb. 1831. Between Jan. and June of that year about 200 Saints sold their New York farms at a loss and migrated to Kirtland.

The seven years the Church was headquartered in Ohio were a

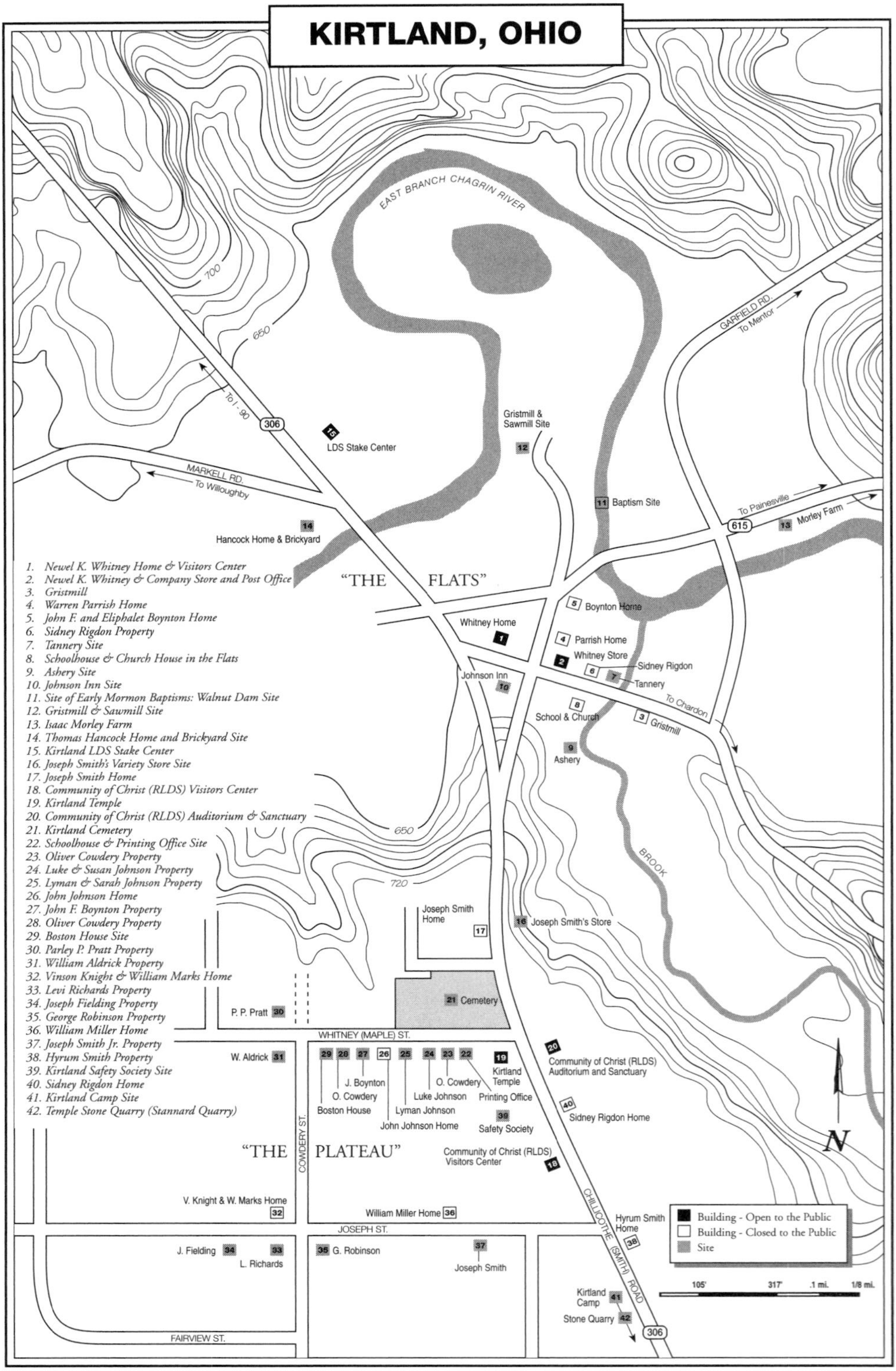
KIRTLAND, OHIO
EAST BRANCH CHAGRIN RIVER
700
650
To I-90
306
LDS Stake Center
15
Gristmill & Sawmill Site
12
MARKELL RD.
To Willoughby
11 Baptism Site
GARFIELD RD.
To Mentor
To Painesville
615
13 Morley Farm
14
Hancock Home & Brickyard
1. Newel K. Whitney Home & Visitors Center
2. Newel K. Whitney & Company Store and Post Office
3. Gristmill
4. Warren Parrish Home
5. John F. and Eliphalet Boynton Home
6. Sidney Rigdon Property
7. Tannery Site
8. Schoolhouse & Church House in the Flats
9. Ashery Site
10. Johnson Inn Site
11. Site of Early Mormon Baptisms: Walnut Dam Site
12. Gristmill & Sawmill Site
13. Isaac Morley Farm
14. Thomas Hancock Home and Brickyard Site
15. Kirtland LDS Stake Center
16. Joseph Smith's Variety Store Site
17. Joseph Smith Home
18. Community of Christ (RLDS) Visitors Center
19. Kirtland Temple
20. Community of Christ (RLDS) Auditorium & Sanctuary
21. Kirtland Cemetery
22. Schoolhouse & Printing Office Site
23. Oliver Cowdery Property
24. Luke & Susan Johnson Property
25. Lyman & Sarah Johnson Property
26. John Johnson Home
27. John F. Boynton Property
28. Oliver Cowdery Property
29. Boston House Site
30. Parley P. Pratt Property
31. William Aldrick Property
32. Vinson Knight & William Marks Home
33. Levi Richards Property
34. Joseph Fielding Property
35. George Robinson Property
36. William Miller Home
37. Joseph Smith Jr. Property
38. Hyrum Smith Property
39. Kirtland Safety Society Site
40. Sidney Rigdon Home
41. Kirtland Camp Site
42. Temple Stone Quarry (Stannard Quarry)
"THE FLATS"
5 Boynton Home
Whitney Home
1
4 Parrish Home
2 Whitney Store
6
Sidney Rigdon
7 Tannery
Johnson Inn
10
To Chardon
8
School & Church
3 Gristmill
9
Ashery
650
BROOK
720
Joseph Smith Home
17
16 Joseph Smith's Store
21 Cemetery
P. P. Pratt 30
WHITNEY (MAPLE) ST.
W. Aldrick 31
29 28 27 26 25 24 23 22
19
J. Boynton
O. Cowdery
Kirtland Temple
O. Cowdery
Luke Johnson
Printing Office
Boston House
Lyman Johnson
John Johnson Home
39
Safety Society
20
Community of Christ (RLDS) Auditorium and Sanctuary
40
Sidney Rigdon Home
N
COWDERY ST.
"THE PLATEAU"
Community of Christ (RLDS) Visitors Center
18
V. Knight & W. Marks Home
32
William Miller Home 36
JOSEPH ST.
CHILLICOTHE (SMITH) ROAD
Hyrum Smith Home
38
J. Fielding 34
33
L. Richards
35 G. Robinson
37
Joseph Smith
Building - Open to the Public
Building - Closed to the Public
Site
105'
317'
.1 mi.
1/8 mi.
Kirtland Camp 41
Stone Quarry 42
306
FAIRVIEW ST.

time of great growth and development. While living in Ohio, Joseph Smith learned much about the restored gospel of **Jesus Christ**. He received many important revelations, almost half of which are now part of the **Doctrine and Covenants,** pertaining to Church doctrine, policies, programs, and organization. In Ohio, the first bishop was called, the **First Presidency** of the Church was organized, members of the restored Church's first **Quorum of the Twelve** were called, members of the **Seventy** were selected, and the first **stake** and **high council** were organized.

The first edition of the **Doctrine and Covenants** was published in Kirtland, and the first temple built in this dispensation was constructed there. The Savior appeared to accept his temple, and the Father and the Son appeared to the **Prophet Joseph Smith** on at least four occasions in Kirtland (PJE 95–96, 99–100, 110–11). Other heavenly messengers delivered the keys of the last dispensation to the Prophet. Missionaries left Kirtland destined for many areas of the United States, Canada, and Great Britain. A **School of the Prophets** was organized in Kirtland to prepare the elders for their assignments in the Church.

Despite all the spiritual outpourings among the Saints in Kirtland, apostasy and persecution caused a mass exodus of the faithful Saints from Ohio in 1838. Though they had to abandon their temple, businesses, and homes, they knew they were not abandoning their commitment to keep the commandments of God.

The flats of Kirtland, OH. View to the SE with the east fork of the Chagrin River in the foreground and the Kirtland Temple on the Kirtland Plateau. (Photo by George E. Anderson, 1907; courtesy of LDSCA)

Kirtland, Ohio—Headquarters of the Church 1831–37

KIRTLAND

Kirtland is located on State 306 about one mile south of exit 193, on I-90 in the NE corner of greater **Cleveland,** and 10 miles south of Lake Erie. Kirtland was named after **Turhand Kirtland**, an agent of the Connecticut Land Company who owned property in Kirtland but never lived there himself. **Joshua Stowe** became the first settler in **Kirtland Township,** arriving in 1811. By the time **Isaac Morley** arrived two years later, Kirtland had a schoolhouse, a gristmill, and a sawmill. **Newel K. Whitney** built the first store in 1823.

The flats of Kirtland, OH, looking north across the business district.

The business district of Kirtland was at first located in the flood-plain of the east branch of the Chagrin River, an area known as the "flats." As the population increased and as construction began on the **Kirtland Temple,** settlement on the plateau south of the flats increased.

ENE aerial view of the flats of Kirtland, OH. (Photo by Keith Perkins)

Kirtland Flats

■ **1. Newel K. Whitney Home and Visitors Center.** The **Newel K. Whitney home** is near the intersection of State 306 and 615 (Chillicothe Road). This is the original home of **Newel** and **Elizabeth Ann Whitney**, but changes have been made in the structure over the years. Beginning in 1995, it served as the LDS Visitors Center in Kirtland until a new visitors center was built. The home, restored to its original condition, is a logical place to begin a tour of the area.

Newel K. and Elizabeth Whitney home, Kirtland, OH. This home serves as an LDS Visitors Center. (Photo by George E. Anderson, 1907; courtesy of LDSCA)

Before the gospel was introduced in Kirtland, the Whitneys had a spiritual experience that prepared them for membership in the Church. Elizabeth related:

> One night—it was midnight—as my husband and I, in our house at Kirtland, were praying to the father to be shown the way, the spirit rested upon us and a *cloud* overshadowed the house. . . . We saw the cloud and we felt the spirit of the Lord. Then we heard a voice out of the cloud saying: "Prepare to receive the word of the Lord, for it is coming!" At this we marveled greatly; but from that moment we knew that the word of the Lord was coming to Kirtland (WM 41–42).

Newel K. Whitney. (Courtesy of LDSCA)

The promise of the Lord to the Whitneys was fulfilled with the arrival of missionaries in the fall of 1830 and of the Prophet Joseph Smith in Feb. 1831. Upon their arrival in Kirtland from **New York** in Feb. 1831, **Joseph** and **Emma Smith** lived in the **Whitney** home, where the Whitneys and their five children kindly hosted them (HC 1:145; PJE 93–94). In the Whitney home, Joseph performed miracles, received revelations, and, for a short time, administered Church affairs.

In this home, Joseph healed **Alice Johnson** of chronic rheumatism in her arm after a group of inquirers asked, "Here is Mrs. Johnson with a lame arm; has God given any power to man now on the earth to cure her?" As the conversation shifted to another topic, Joseph crossed the room to leave. He paused on the way out and grasped Mrs. Johnson's hand, saying in a "solemn and impressive manner, 'Woman, in the name of the Lord **Jesus Christ** I command thee to be whole.'" She was immediately able to raise and use her arm, which had been disabled for years. Several people were converted to the Church as a result of this miracle (HC 1:215–16; HR 82–83; PJE 97).

While Joseph Smith was living in this home, the Lord called **Edward Partridge**, a man whose heart was pure "like unto Nathanael of old," to be the first bishop of the Church (D&C 41:11). Joseph may have received at least four revelations in the Whitney Home (D&C 41–44). Some laws of the Lord, including the law of consecration and stewardship and a reiteration of some of the Ten Commandments, were revealed in section 42, known as "the law."

Edward Partridge. (Courtesy of RLDSLA)

On Jan. 7, 1836, **Bishop Whitney** hosted a "sumptuous feast" at his home. Joseph Smith wrote that "this feast was after the order of the Son of God—the lame, the halt, and the blind were invited, according to the instructions of the Savior" (HC 2:362).

Newel K. Whitney Store, Kirtland, OH.

Newel K. Whitney Store, Kirtland, OH, with 11 leaders of the RLDS Church standing on the porch. Joseph Smith III, son of the Prophet Joseph Smith and president of the RLDS Church, was born in this building. The eighth person from the left, he has a white beard and is standing to the left of a pillar. (Courtesy of RLDSLA)

■ **2. Newel K. Whitney & Company Store and Post Office.** The **Newel K. Whitney Store** is located in the center of the **Kirtland flats,** near the intersection of state highways 306 and 615 (Chillicothe Road).[3] In the early 1980s, the Church purchased the store from Wilford C. Wood and restored it. Using original daybooks from the store, the Church stocked the restored store with the same kind of merchandise found on the shelves in the 1830s. In recognition of the Church's efforts, President Ronald Reagan awarded the Church the President's Historic Preservation Award in 1988 (ENS Jan. 1993, 31–37).

Newell K. Whitney Store, Kirtland, OH. (Courtesy of RLDSLA)

The Whitney store was the center of Church life in Kirtland (1831–37). Store proprietor Newel K. Whitney had been a successful merchant in Kirtland as well as the town postmaster

---

[3] President Ezra Taft Benson dedicated the store Aug. 25, 1984.

for seven years before Kirtland became Church headquarters. After **A. Sidney Gilbert** became a partner with Newel in the mercantile business, the store became the **N. K. Whitney and Company Store** until Sidney and his wife moved to **Missouri** in July 1831. Newel later became a bishop in Kirtland, and the store served as the bishop's storehouse while the united order was practiced.

An orderly sequence for visiting the storerooms follows:

(1) The store and post office room was in the west end of the ground floor. Customers came here to buy goods and to send and receive mail. It was here that **Orson Hyde**, a young store clerk and a **Reformed Baptist** preacher, came to investigate the **Book of Mormon**. He decided that he would disprove the book, but he became converted in the process.

When Joseph Smith arrived in Kirtland in early Feb. 1831, he "sprang from the sleigh and entered the . . . Whitney Store. Extending his hand to [Newel Whitney] as though he were a familiar acquaintance, Joseph said, 'Newel K. Whitney! Thou art the man!'" (HR 44–45). Astonished, Newel confessed that he did not know the stranger. Joseph responded, "I am Joseph the Prophet. You've prayed me here, now what do you want of me?" (ThC 6:125; HC 1:146).

Joseph Smith's family lived in the Newel K. Whitney Store for nearly a year and a half, from Sept. 12, 1832, to about Feb. 1834.

(2) The trading and supply room in the SE corner of the main floor provided storage for items like skins, sugar, and herbs. From this room the stairs led to Joseph and Emma's apartment.

(3) Emma's kitchen was located in the NE corner of the ground floor.

(4) Joseph and Emma's bedroom was located upstairs in the NW corner. Here **Joseph Smith III** was born Nov. 6, 1832. He was his parents' first surviving biological child and lived to become the first president of the **RLDS Church**, now known as the **Community of Christ**.

(5) The **School of the Prophets** room, in the NE corner upstairs, served as the meeting place of the first School of the Prophets in the winter of 1833. On Jan. 3 of that year Joseph received a revelation concerning this unique school (D&C 88:127–41), the purpose of which was to "teach one another the doctrine of the kingdom . . . of things both in heaven and in the earth . . . that ye may be prepared in all things when I shall send

you again to magnify the calling whereunto I have called you, and the mission with which I have commissioned you. Behold," the Lord said in the revelation, "I sent you out to testify and warn the people, and it becometh every man who hath been warned to warn his neighbor" (D&C 88:77–81).

Room of the School of the Prophets, Newell K. Whitney Store, Kirtland, OH. (1994)

The Newel K. Whitney Store was the missionary training center of the 1830s. As students in the school, the brethren were required to greet each other with "uplifted hands to heaven." They were received into the school through the ordinance of the **washing of feet,** symbolic of becoming clean from the blood and sins of their generation (D&C 88:135).

A revelation "regarded as a step toward the formal organization of the First Presidency"—**Joseph Smith, Sidney Rigdon,** and **Frederick G. Williams**—was received here Mar. 1832 (HC 1:334; CHC 1:307; D&C 81; 90:6). **Lucy Mack Smith,** the Prophet's mother, said at this time that she shared in the most glorious outpouring of the Spirit of God that had ever before taken place in the Church.

The Word of Wisdom (D&C 89) was revealed while the school was meeting in this small room. **Brigham Young** described the situation just before the revelation was given Feb. 27, 1833:

> The brethren came to [the Whitney Store] for hundreds of miles to attend school in a little room probably no larger than eleven by fourteen. When they assembled together in this room after breakfast, the first they did was to light their pipes, and, while smoking, talk about the great things of the kingdom, and spit all over the room, and as soon as the pipe was out of their mouths a large chew of tobacco would then be taken. Often when the Prophet entered the room to give the school instructions he would find himself in a cloud of tobacco smoke. This, and the complaints of his wife at having to clean so filthy a floor, made the Prophet think upon the matter, and he inquired of the Lord relating to the conduct of the Elders in

using tobacco, and the revelation known as the Word of Wisdom was the result of his inquiry (JD 12:158).

The Father and **the Son** appeared in this room during at least one session of the School of the Prophets. **John Murdock** testified that he saw the Lord (JJM 13), and Zebedee Coltrin said he saw both the Father and the Son:

> Joseph asked if we saw him. I saw him and suppose the others did and Joseph answered that is Jesus, the Son of God, our elder brother. Afterward Joseph told us to resume our former position in prayer, which we did. Another person came through; he was surrounded as with a flame of fire. . . . The Prophet Joseph said this was the Father of our Lord Jesus Christ. I saw Him" (ENS Jan. 1993, 37; PJE 111).

This room was built at the request of the **Prophet. Levi Hancock** did the remodeling of the store, including remodeling a room for the School of the Prophets.

(6) The upstairs room in the SE corner of the building doubled as Joseph's translating room and as the administrative headquarters of the Church. In 1833, the Prophet completed one phase of his inspired translation of the Bible in this room. It was probably in this room that Joseph received many revelations, including D&C 78, 84 (on priesthood), 85, 86, 87 (on war), 88 (the "Olive Leaf"), 89 (the Word of Wisdom), 90–98, and 101 (on Jackson County).

Joseph Smith's administrative headquarters and translating room, Newel K. Whitney Store, Kirtland, OH. It is believed that the table belonged to the Prophet Joseph Smith. (1990)

(7) The SW room of the upper floor probably served as a storage room for various sorts of merchandise.

■ **3. Gristmill (and Sawmill).** A gristmill and a sawmill (Site No. 12) were located north of the Whitney home on the west side of the east branch of the Chagrin River at a point west of the Walnut Dam site. They no longer exist, but a newly built gristmill south of the dam serves as a visitors center. This is the logical place to begin a tour of the area.

■ **4. Warren Parrish Home.** The **Warren Parrish home** is located immediately north of the Whitney store, on the east side of Chillicothe Road. Warren, one of Joseph Smith's trusted clerks, served many missions. Deeply involved in the **Kirtland Safety Society,** he was charged with embezzling $25,000 from the society and contributing to its downfall. He left the Church and became an active supporter of **David Whitmer,** president of the Church of Christ.

Wilford Woodruff, a missionary companion to Warren in the southern states, lived in this home both before and after his marriage to Phoebe Carter.

■ **5. John F. and Eliphalet Boynton Home. John F. Boynton,** one of the original Apostles of the restored Church, or his father, Eliphalet, or both, apparently lived in what appears to be a home dating to the 1830s. It is north of and behind the **Newel K. Whitney Store,** close to the SW bank of the east branch of the Chagrin River. John was disfellowshipped in 1837 and was finally excommunicated from the Church. He visited **Brigham Young** in Utah in 1872 but never rejoined the Church. For 20 years he traveled throughout the United State and lectured on various sciences. He died in Syracuse, NY, in 1890 (BiE 1:91).

■ **6. Sidney Rigdon Property.**

■ **7. Tannery Site.** A tannery was located on the lot just east of Sidney Rigdon's property, on the south side of a brook and on the north side of the road.

In the 1830s, animal hides were used to make everything from clothing to boats. The demand for tanned hides made the tannery an important part of the Kirtland economy. Tanneries usually consisted of little more than several poles that supported a roof to cover vats in which skins were soaked. It took nearly a year to tan a hide well.

The Church purchased the tannery in 1833 as a part of the **united order** in Kirtland, and **Sidney Rigdon**, a tanner by trade, was appointed as a steward over it (D&C 104:20; JSK 133). Nothing remains today of the original tannery, but a replica has been built.

■ **8. Schoolhouse and Church House in the Flats.** The schoolhouse that stands across the street from the Sidney Rigdon home near the intersection of State 306 and 615 (Chillicothe Road) is believed to be the original **Kirtland Schoolhouse.** Originally, it probably stood about 120 feet east of its present location; it was likely moved more than 100 years ago. Built in the early 1800s as an elementary school, it was used as a church house by the Latter-day Saints in the 1830s (HC 2:301, 316, 330, 345, 347).

■ **9. Ashery Site.** An ashery was located on the west side of a brook near the main intersection of state highways 306 and 615 (Chillicothe Road). The original ashery is long since gone but has been restored. As a frontier chemical plant it produced potash used to make soap, fertilizer, and glass. Potash was also used to make medicines and clean wool. The potash made at the ashery boosted the Kirtland economy. It was in demand as far away as the eastern United States because it was easily transported and lightweight.

The ashery was a simple structure constructed of four corner posts supporting a roof that covered a furnace and a vat. The ashes of hardwood burned in the furnace were mixed with water before being reheated. As the moisture evaporated, the mixture became potash.

When the Kirtland and Missouri united orders were separated and reorganized into two different orders on Apr. 23, 1834, the ashery was deeded to **Newel K. Whitney,** who had been the former owner (JSK 132–33). **Orson Hyde** assisted him in his work at the ashery as early as 1826.

■ **10. John Johnson Inn Site.** The **John Johnson Inn** was located on the south side of the road diagonally across the road from the **Whitney store** near the intersection of state highways 306 and 615 (Chillicothe Road). It stood on the triangular piece of ground enclosed by three roads. **Peter French** built the inn, which was the first brick building in Kirtland. The Church purchased it in 1833, and when the Kirtland **united order** was reorganized in 1834, **John**

The John Johnson Inn, Kirtland, OH.

Johnson was designated as the steward over the inn (D&C 104:34–38).

The inn provided lodging and served the Church as an office building and as the first printing office in Kirtland. The Kirtland edition of *The Evening and the Morning Star* was published here following the destruction of the press at **Independence, MO** (EMS Dec. 1833). It also served as a community hall and museum, displaying Egyptian mummies (HC 2:396). The original inn has been restored.

The **Twelve Apostles** left from the inn for their first mission on May 4, 1835 (HC 2:219, 222). Also at the inn, **Joseph Smith Sr.** was called as the first patriarch of the Church, although Joseph Smith Jr., in Dec. 1833, actually gave the first patriarchal blessing here (TPJS 38–39).

The Old Gristmill, WNW of the Walnut Dam site in Kirtland, OH, was in operation when the Saints lived in Kirtland. It was built in the 1820s and owned by Azariah Lyman. (Courtesy of LDSCA)

■ **11. Walnut Dam Baptismal Site.** A baptismal site on the east branch of the Chagrin River is located a block north of the **Newel K. Whitney Store.** A dam created a pool of calm water deep enough for baptisms (JJM 8; ThR May 1889, 74). Ice had to be removed for baptisms in the winter. On Dec. 31, 1836, **Brigham Young** baptized **Willard Richards** after some brethren "spent the afternoon in cutting the ice to prepare for the baptism" (HC 2:469).

The Walnut Dam in the east branch of the Chagrin River directed water to the Old Gristmill, located WNW of the dam (see map of Kirtland). The Saints used the pool of water formed by the dam to perform baptisms.

The practice of baptizing for the dead in the **Mississippi River** began in **Nauvoo, IL,** in the fall of 1840 (HC 4:206, 231) and during conference proceedings in Kirtland in May 1841, when "about 25 baptisms took place, the most of which were for the dead" (KEQR, May 24, 1841). These baptisms may have occurred at this site.

■ **12. Gristmill and Sawmill Site.** (See Site No. 3.)

■ **13. Isaac Morley Farm.** The **Isaac Morley farm** is located about one mile NE of the **Whitney store,** on the north side of State 615 (Chillicothe Road). Isaac, one of the earliest settlers in Kirtland, owned a large farm, which by 1831 comprised about 80 acres. A religious communal group of people known as "The Family" lived on the farm in 1831. Many early converts to the restored Church, such as the Wights, Billings, and Murdocks, had been members of

NW view of early 19th century home on the Isaac Morley farm, Kirtland, OH. (1977)

the group. **Joseph Smith** received revelations concerning the true order of communal living, including D&C 42, which explains Church welfare principles.

Isaac offered his farm as a settling place for Saints migrating to **Kirtland** from **New York**. In response to a revelation stating that "it is meet that my servant Joseph Smith, Jun., should have a house built, in which to live and translate" (D&C 41:7), Isaac began building a home on his farm for **Joseph** and **Emma Smith**, who lived there from Mar. to Sept. 1831, after which they moved to Hiram, OH. While on the farm, Emma gave birth to twins, **Thaddeus** and **Louisa**, who lived just three hours. Soon after these sad deaths, **John Murdock's** wife, **Julia,** died. **Joseph** and **Emma** adopted Julia's newborn twins, **Joseph** and **Julia** (HC 1:260).

The fourth general conference of the Church, and the first conference in **Kirtland**, was held June 3–6, 1831, on the Morley farm in an 18-by-20-foot log schoolhouse (JD 11:4; HC 1:175–76). Three years later, as preparations were underway for **Zion's Camp,** all priesthood members then in Kirtland gathered in this schoolhouse. According to **Wilford Woodruff,** during discussions here the Prophet prophesied:

> Brethren I have been very much edified and instructed in your testimonies here tonight, but I want to say to you before the Lord, that you know no more concerning the destinies of this Church and kingdom than a babe upon its mother's lap. You don't comprehend it. . . . It is only a little handfull of Priesthood you see here tonight, but this Church will fill North and South America—it will fill the world. . . . It will fill the Rocky Mountains. There will [be] tens of thousands of Latter-day Saints who will be gathered in the Rocky Mountains, and there they will open the door for the establishing of the Gospel among the Lamanites, who will receive the Gospel and their endowments and the blessings of God. This people will go into the Rocky Mountains; they will there build temples to the Most High (CR Apr. 1898, 57).

At this conference, the first high priests were ordained in the Church (HC 1:175–76), and many spiritual manifestations were given. The devil was revealed, and he bound **Harvey Whitlock** and **John Murdock** so they could not speak. Joseph cast the devil out of these brethren, and he stated that **John the Revelator** was then among the ten tribes of Israel. The Prophet proclaimed, "I now see God, and Jesus Christ at his right hand, let them kill me, I should not feel death as I am now" (LHJ 33).

During the seven months Joseph lived on the Morley farm, he received the revelations now found in D&C 45–50, 52–56, 63–64 (LHJ 33; PJE 95–96).

■ **14. Thomas Hancock Home and Brickyard Site.** The **Thomas Hancock home** and **brickyard site** are located just south of the intersection of State 306 and Markell Road. The structures stood on the north bank of the east branch of the Chagrin River, on the south side of Markell Road, south of the LDS stake center. Thomas Hancock was the father of **Levi W. Hancock**, one of the first seven presidents of the Seventy from 1835 to 1882 (BiE 1:88).

■ **15. Kirtland LDS Stake Center.** A modern LDS stake center is located on State 306, NW of the Chagrin River and directly north of the Markell Road intersection with State 306. It was originally built on this site in 1981 but was burned to the ground by an arsonist. Shared intolerance for such acts strengthened relations between Latter-day Saints and those of other faiths in Kirtland and the surrounding area, and a new building was speedily erected on the old foundation (ENS Feb. 1988, 74). This stake center was the first LDS Church building to be built here since the Kirtland Temple was completed in 1836. It houses a collection of records concerning early LDS families in Kirtland.

When **President Ezra Taft Benson** broke ground for the center, he said the scourge placed upon the people in the prophecy found in D&C 124:83 "is being lifted today" (JSK 247).

"On the Hill"

■ **16. Joseph Smith's Variety Store Site.** According to tax records, **Joseph Smith** had a **variety store** across the street from his home on a lot east of Chillicothe Road and south of the Newel K. Whitney Store. Joseph only operated this store for a short time. **Brigham Young** said Joseph needed the income from the store, but his role as president of the Church often caused him to allow Saints to buy goods on credit. Some patrons thought that a real prophet would

Aerial view of Kirtland, OH, flats and plateau, with the Kirtland Temple on the right. (1978)

let them off without paying. Joseph closed his store rather than let it cause ill feelings among members of the Church (JD 1:215).

■ **17. JOSEPH SMITH HOME.** Tax records show that the Prophet owned a lot on the west side of Chillicothe Road about .2 mile south of the Whitney store and the intersection of State 306 and 615 (Chillicothe Road) at number 8980. The lot and **Joseph Smith's** period **home** are about 100 yards north of the temple. Probably only the front portion of the house existed from 1835 to 1838, when **Joseph** and **Emma Smith** lived there.

Joseph Smith home, Kirtland, OH. (1980)

Frederick G. Williams Smith's birth of June 20, 1836, very likely took place in this home. Many Church meetings were held here, and **Zion's Camp** possibly was initiated here (HR 174).

Joseph and Emma Smith's Kirtland home was often filled with visitors who came to see the Prophet. **Michael Chandler** visited Joseph Smith here in July 1835 and sold four Egyptian mummies and two rolls of papyrus to the Saints. The book of Abraham was later added to the standard works as a result of this purchase (HC 2:235–36; ERA Feb. 1968, 40–41).

A facsimile from the book of Abraham, written on papyrus. (Courtesy of LDSCA)

The Kirtland Stake was more formally organized here on Feb. 17, 1834, with the selection of a 12-man high council. The council was presided over by the **First Presidency** of the Church, which in turn served as the stake presidency of the Kirtland Stake. This first stake of the Church was organized before wards were created (D&C 102; HC 2:28–33). Revelations found in D&C 102–104, 106, and 108 may have been received in this home. In addition, the Prophet received three unpublished revelations here on Jan. 12, 1838, one of which directed him and **Sidney Rigdon** to flee to Missouri "as fast as the way is made plain" (PJS 2:255).

■ **18. COMMUNITY OF CHRIST (RLDS) VISITORS CENTER.** The **Community of Christ Visitors Center** is immediately south of the Kirtland Temple, on the west side of Chillicothe Road at number 9020. The center shows a short film and sponsors guided tours of the temple, which start at the visitors center. Early artifacts, photographs, remnants of original temple stucco with bits of imbedded glass, and documents relating to early Church history are housed here.

■ **19. KIRTLAND TEMPLE.** The **Kirtland Temple**, the most prominent structure in Kirtland and the first temple in this dispensation, is located on the brow of the plateau on the west side of Chillicothe Road, on the SW corner of Chillicothe Road and Maple (Whitney) Street. The Kirtland Temple became the center of life for the Saints. It may be visited by going with a guide from the Community of Christ Visitors Center.

Aerial view of the Kirtland Temple, Kirtland, OH. (Photo by Keith Perkins, 1978)

The Kirtland Temple, with the east branch of the Chagrin River in the foreground.

In Jan. 1831, when the Church was beset by poverty and turmoil, the **Prophet Joseph Smith** received the divine command that led to the building of the **Kirtland Temple.** The Church then consisted of only a few hundred members—men, women, and children who labored together for the temple and contributed, according to **Eliza R. Snow,** "brain, bone and sinew" and "all living as abstemiously as possible" so that "every cent might be appropriated to the grand object" (WM 82). According to **Benjamin F. Johnson**, "There was not a scraper and hardly a plow that could be obtained among the Saints" to prepare the ground for the foundation of the temple (MLR 16).

The Kirtland Temple. (Courtesy of USHS)

Nevertheless, the Saints proceeded, bringing lumber from nearby forests and hewing stone from a local quarry. The construction of the temple slowed abruptly with the call of **Zion's Camp** to Missouri. **Sidney Rigdon**, then a member of the First Presidency, remained behind and recorded walking the walls of the temple "by night and day and frequently wetting the walls" with his tears, praying for the temple's completion (T&S 6:867). At other times, harassment and threats by enemies of the Church slowed the work. Elder George A. Smith recalled that sometimes guards attended the temple day and night and worked with a trowel in one hand and a sword in the other.

The women—who, Joseph Smith once remarked, were "first in temple labors"—did spinning, knitting, and sewing so that temple laborers would have clothes to wear. To give the exterior glaze a sparkling appearance, the women contributed glassware to be broken in bits and applied to the plaster. In his dedicatory prayer, Joseph referred to the sacrifice of the Saints: "For thou knowest that we have done this work through great tribulation; and out of our poverty we have given of our substance to build a house to thy name, that the Son of Man might have a place to manifest himself to his people" (D&C 109:5).

Just as the exact patterns of the Old Testament tabernacle and the temple of Solomon had been revealed from on high (Exodus 25:9; 1 Chronicles 28:11–12), so also the design, measurements, and functions of the Kirtland Temple were revealed. The temple was to be a house of prayer, fasting, faith, learning, glory, and order. It was to be a house of God (D&C 88:119) and a house

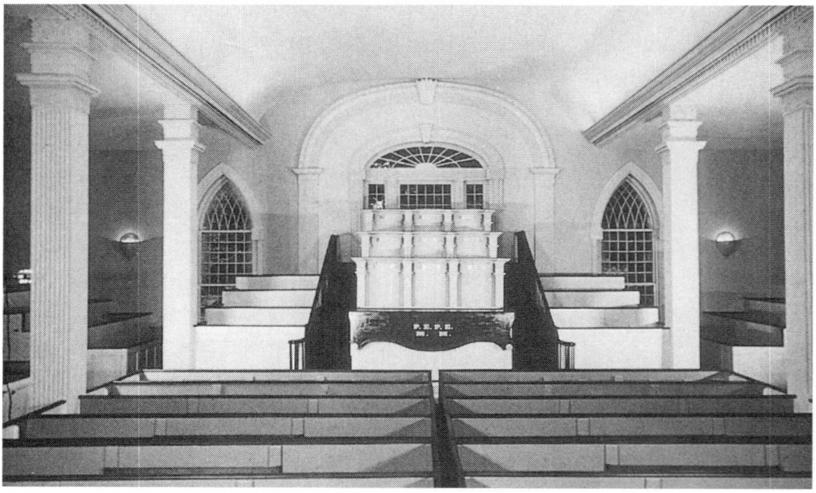

The first or main floor of the Kirtland Temple. The Melchizedek Priesthood pulpits in the west end, as shown in this photo, consisted of four tiers of pulpits. The bottom tier also served as a sacrament table. (Courtesy of RLDSLA)

wherein the Saints could receive their endowment (D&C 105:33). The **First Presidency—Joseph Smith**, **Sidney Rigdon**, and **Frederick G. Williams**—received a vision of the finished temple. Frederick G. Williams said that after they had viewed the outside of the temple in vision, the temple "seemed to come right over us," allowing them to see the inside in great detail (ERA Oct. 1942, 630).

Its interior was to be 55 feet wide and 65 feet long and have a lower and a higher court. The lower part of the inner court was to be dedicated "for your sacrament offering, and for your preaching, and your fasting, and your praying, and the offering up of your most holy desires unto me, saith your Lord." The higher part of the inner court was to be "dedicated unto me for the school of mine apostles" (D&C 95:16–17).

The cornerstone was laid on July 23, 1833. **Brigham Young** later explained that the first stone was laid at the southeast corner, the point of greatest light, and at high noon, the time of the greatest light (JD 1:133). This was a symbolic reminder that the house of the Lord is a center of light and truth.

The exterior of the temple measures 80 feet by 59 feet, with the walls being "two feet thick and more than sixty feet high" (HR 156). The 110-foot tower faces east according to the pattern given by revelation. The temple has a partly excavated basement, two full stories, and an attic. The exterior walls up to the cornice line are made of sandstone quarried two miles south of the temple. The walls were stuccoed and then painted with lines to simulate bricks. The walls were a faded bluish color.

The external design of the Kirtland Temple is typical of other contemporary houses of worship at that time, but the arrangement of the interior is unique. On each of the two main floors are two series of four-tiered pulpits, one on the west side, the other on the east. These are symbolic of the offices of the **Melchizedek** and **Aaronic Priesthoods** and accommodated their presidencies. The

Melchizedek Priesthood pulpits of the Kirtland Temple and curtains that were lowered from the ceiling to divide the room. (Courtesy of RLDSLA)

benches in the pews on the first two floors are reversible so that worshippers can face either direction. Choir seats were built in the four corners of the first two floors. Originally each of these two floors could be divided into four smaller rooms by lowering curtains, or veils, and each pulpit area could be divided by curtains.

The third floor, or attic, consists of five rooms that were used for offices, quorum and school meetings, and ordinances. Many of the brethren, including the **First Presidency,** received washings and anointings in these rooms. These ordinances were accompanied by solemn prayer, revelations, and great rejoicing.

The President's Room, or Room of the First Presidency, in the Kirtland Temple. (1978)

The room on the west end of the third floor, sometimes referred to as the **President's Room** or **Room for the First Presidency**, was especially important. This was the Prophet's translation room (the Egyptian mummies and papyrus were displayed on the third floor), and he received many visions here, including D&C 137. This was also the room in which **Joshua Seixas** taught the brethren Hebrew.

Jan. 21, 1836, **Joseph Smith** met on this floor with his two counselors and with bishoprics and high council members from **Missouri** and **Kirtland.** After the brethren received their anointings, Joseph testified that "the heavens were opened upon us" and that he "beheld the celestial kingdom of God, and the glory thereof." He saw "the blazing throne of God, whereon was seated the Father and the Son." In the celestial kingdom he saw "Father Adam and Abraham" (D&C 137:1–5).

In addition, he saw others who were then living (including his mother and his father, who was with him in the room), or who had died (including his brother, **Alvin**, who had passed away in 1823). When the Prophet wondered why Alvin, who died without baptism, was in the celestial kingdom, the voice of the Lord came to him, saying, "All who have died without a knowledge of this gospel, who would have received it if they had been permitted to tarry, shall be heirs of the celestial kingdom of God" (D&C 137:7; HC 2:380–81).

"The visions of heaven were opened to [the high council members from Missouri and Kirtland] also," the Prophet said. "Some of them saw the face of the **Savior**, and others were ministered unto by holy angels, and the spirit of prophecy and revelation was poured out in mighty power; and loud hosannas, and glory to God in the highest, saluted the heavens, for we all communed with the heavenly host" (HC 2:382).

According to the *History of the Church,* an estimated 900–1000 people attended the temple dedication on Mar. 27, 1836 (HC 2:410). A repeat dedication ceremony was held Mar. 31. It was a time of great rejoicing. Dedicatory anthems were sung, including "The Spirit of God," which was written for the occasion, and the sacrament was administered. The **inspired dedicatory prayer** became the pattern for all subsequent temple dedications. In it, the Prophet pleaded with the Lord for a visible manifestation of his divine presence (the ***Shechinah***), as in the **Tabernacle of Moses,** at **Solomon's temple,** and on the day of **Pentecost:** "And let thy house be filled, as with a rushing mighty wind, with thy glory" (D&C 109:37; see also Exodus 29:43; 33:9–10; 2 Chronicles 7:1–3; Acts 2:1–4).

Many Saints recorded the fulfillment of that prayer. Eliza R. Snow wrote, "The ceremonies of that dedication may be rehearsed, but no mortal language can describe the heavenly manifestations of that memorable day. Angels appeared to some, while a sense of divine presence was realized by all present, and each heart was filled with 'joy inexpressible and full of glory'" (WM 95). After the prayer, the entire congregation rose and, with hands uplifted, shouted hosannas to God and the Lamb.

The climax of the spiritual outpouring occurred Apr. 3, 1836, when the Savior appeared in the Kirtland Temple to **Joseph Smith** and **Oliver Cowdery** and said, "For behold, I have accepted this house, and my name shall be here; and I will manifest myself to my people in mercy in this house" (D&C 110:7). Three other personages of former dispensations then came and restored keys of the priesthood: **Moses** restored the keys of the gathering of Israel, **Elias** restored keys of the gospel of Abraham, and **Elijah** restored the keys of sealing. These keys represent the three different aspects of the mission of the Church: proclaiming the gospel, redeeming the dead, and perfecting the Saints.

Without the keys restored in the Kirtland Temple, Latter-day Saints would have no authority to perform temple ordinances in their temples. Washings and anointings had been given in Jan. 1836. After attending to the washing of feet, Joseph assured the quorums that he "had given them all the instruction they needed" to go forth and build up the kingdom of God, having "passed through all the necessary ceremonies" (TPJS 110). These ceremonies were preliminary to the fulness of the ordinances and the complete temple endowment later administered in the **Nauvoo Temple**.

The Kirtland Temple became the center of life for the Saints. Today it is in excellent physical condition and well maintained. A national historic shrine, the temple is owned and operated by the Community of Christ. Polite and knowledgeable guides at the Community of Christ Visitors Center are pleased to show the beautiful, sacred building to visitors. It is open year-round, and tours are conducted on a regular basis.

● **20. Community of Christ Auditorium and Sanctuary.** The **Kirtland Auditorium** and **Sanctuary** of the Community of Christ are located on the east side of Chillicothe Road across from the **Kirtland Temple.** They are used for worship and other services.

■ **21. Kirtland Cemetery.** The **Kirtland Cemetery** is located immediately north of the **Kirtland Temple,** on the west side of Chillicothe Road and on the north side of Maple (Whitney) Street. Many prominent Saints are buried here, including **Jerusha Barden Smith**, Hyrum's first wife and the mother of five children. She died Oct. 13, 1837, 11 days after giving birth to **Sarah**. **Hyrum** was in **Far West**, **MO,** on Church

Smith family plot in the Kirtland Cemetery at Kirtland, OH. Jerusha Barden Smith, Hyrum Smith's wife; and Mary Duty Smith, Joseph Smith's grandmother, are buried in the area shown in this photo.

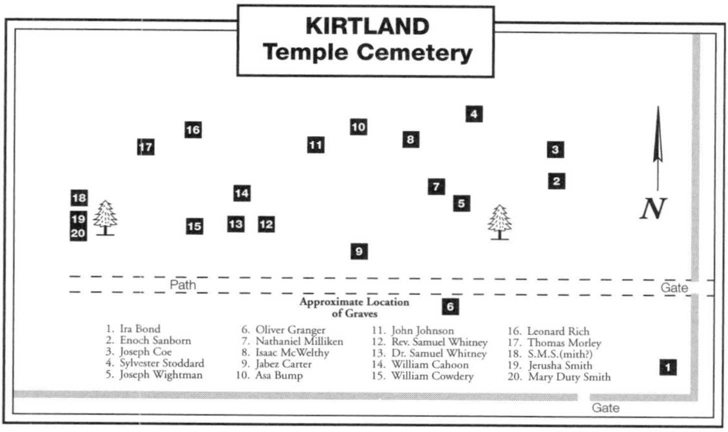

business at the time. **Mary Duty Smith**, grandmother of **Joseph Smith**, is also buried here. She came to **Kirtland** to see her family at the age of 93. **Thankful Halsey Pratt**, Parley P. Pratt's first wife, is buried here. Tradition has it that Joseph and Emma Smith's twins, **Thaddeus** and **Louisa,** might be buried here also. The accompanying cemetery map identifies burial plots of Latter-day Saints.

In the 1830s, a **Methodist** meetinghouse was located in the SE corner of the cemetery. It was north of the **Kirtland Temple,** facing the temple on Maple (Whitney) Street. **Sidney Rigdon** invited his friends to a meeting there about Nov. 14, 1830. He delivered a two-hour sermon that brought tears to himself and to the congregation. The next day **Oliver Cowdery** baptized him into the Church (HR 8). In 1838, arsonists burned the **Methodist** meetinghouse.

■ **22. Schoolhouse and Printing Office Site.** The first lot west of (behind) the **Kirtland Temple**, on the south side of Maple (Whitney) Street, is the site of a two-story, 30-by-38-foot building known as the **Schoolhouse** and **Printing Office.** Landscaping and a parking lot now cover the site. The Lord had commanded that two separate buildings be built, but because of the Saints' poverty, one building served both purposes (D&C 94).

The top floor served as a meetinghouse, **First Presidency** office, and Church printing office. The lower floor served as a schoolhouse. Following the building's completion and dedication in Dec. 1834, the **School of the Elders** (previously the School of the Prophets) was moved from the **Whitney store** and held in the schoolhouse during the winter of 1834–35 (HC 2:169–70). Besides receiving instruction through lectures on theology, such as the ***Lectures on Faith*** delivered by **Joseph Smith** and **Sidney Rigdon**, the elders studied penmanship, grammar, arithmetic, and geography. When the school was moved into the Kirtland Temple in Jan. 1836, a **Hebrew** class taught by **Joshua Seixas** was added to the curriculum.

It was a busy time in for **Joseph Smith**, and he remarked, "No month ever found me more busily engaged than November; but as my life consisted of activity and unyielding exertions, I made this my rule: *When the Lord commands, do it*" (HC 2:170).

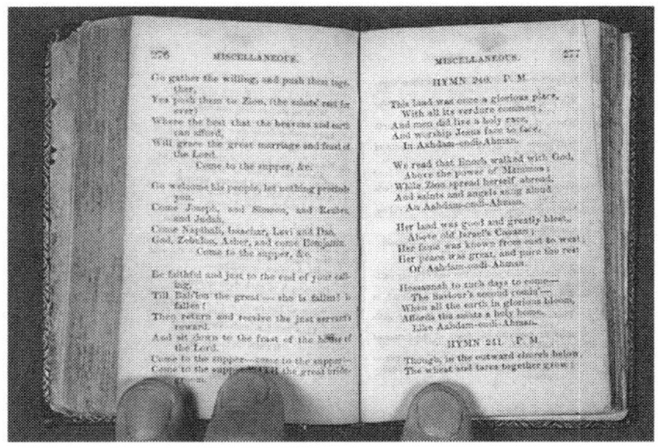

Emma Smith's personal hymnbook, which she edited and published in Kirtland, OH, in 1835. Emma's name is embossed in gold on the front cover. The hymnbook is opened to "Adam-ondi-Ahman," which the congregation sang at the dedication of the Kirtland Temple. (1970; courtesy of Wilford C. Wood)

Oliver Cowdery arrived in Kirtland on Dec. 1, 1833, with a new printing press. The Church's first press had been destroyed by a **Missouri** mob. In obedience to a revelation found in D&C 94: 10–12, Oliver set up the press in this building and printed the first edition of the **Doctrine & Covenants,** the second edition of the **Book of Mormon**, the Church's first hymn book (compiled by **Emma Smith**), and several Church newspapers: *The Evening and the Morning Star* (which was first published in Missouri), *Messenger and Advocate,* and *Northern Times* (HC 1:409, 448; 2:227).

Other rooms in the building served as offices for members of the **First Presidency** and as sites for conferences, which were also held in the schoolroom. At a conference in the schoolhouse Feb. 14, 1835, the **Three Witnesses** of the Book of Mormon chose the first Quorum of the Twelve Apostles in this dispensation. The Three Witnesses then ordained the Apostles who were present. **Oliver Cowdery** charged the Apostles with their duties, and the **First Presidency** laid their hands on the Apostles' heads to confirm their ordinations (HC 2:186–94).

On Jan. 21, 1836, the Prophet dismissed the school in the temple at about 3 P.M. so members of the First Presidency could retire "to the loft of the printing office," where their office was. There they "attended to the ordinance of washing [their] bodies in pure water, [they] also perfumed [their] bodies and [their] heads, in the name of the Lord" (HC 2:379).

On Jan. 16, 1838, this building and all of its contents were burned to the ground, apparently by faithful Saint **Lyman Sherman,** whose actions prevented enemies of the Church in Kirtland from obtaining access to the press (RPJS 321n6). Others blamed the Church's enemies for starting the fire (HR 350).

■ **23. OLIVER COWDERY PROPERTY. Oliver Cowdery** was appointed by revelation as the steward of several lots in Kirtland (D&C 104:28–34). He owned the first lot west of the Printing Office lot, and he owned the second to the last lot on the south side of Maple (Whitney) Street, east of Cowdery Street (see Site No. 28).

■ **24. LUKE AND SUSAN JOHNSON PROPERTY. Luke Johnson**, one of the original Apostles in this dispensation, and his wife, **Susan,** owned the second lot west of the Printing Office site, on the south side of Maple (Whitney) Street.

■ **25. LYMAN AND SARAH S. JOHNSON PROPERTY. Lyman Johnson**, an original member of the Quorum of the Twelve Apostles in this dispensation, and his wife, **Sarah,** owned the third lot west of the Printing Office site, on the south side of Maple (Whitney) Street.

■ **26. JOHN JOHNSON HOME.** After moving from Hiram, OH, **John Johnson** occupied the existing **home** at 7762 Maple Street (south side), across from the cemetery, on the fourth lot west of the Printing Office site.

Joseph Smith performed a wedding ceremony here for **John F. Boynton** and **Susan Lowell** on Jan. 20, 1836. Joseph wrote that the wedding was "conducted after the order of heaven," and it was a "time of rejoicing" (PWJS 143–44). Elder Boynton was called in 1835 as one of the original Apostles of the restored Church.

John Johnson's money made possible the purchase of land on the plateau and the flats, including the **Kirtland Temple** site.

■ **27. John F. Boynton Property. John F. Boynton,** one of the original Apostles in this dispensation, owned the first lot west of the **John Johnson** home, on the south side of Maple (Whitney) Street.

■ **28. Oliver Cowdery Property.** The second lot east of **Cowdery** (spelled Coudery on the street sign) Street on the south side of Maple (**Whitney**) Street was owned by **Oliver Cowdery**.

■ **29. Boston House Site.** The Boston House was on the SW corner of Maple (Whitney) and Cowdery Streets. It was so named because a wealthy sister named Polly Vose of Boston owned the property. The 53-by-32-foot house was three stories high. It is not clear whether Polly Vose ever moved to Kirtland. In 1844, she was still living in Boston, and in 1858 it appears she was living in Utah. She was generous with her means, sharing with the brethren and helping to finance **Zion's Camp** (JD 7:101).

Parley P. Pratt home, Kirtland, OH, according to photographer George E. Anderson. (1907; courtesy of LDSCA)

■ **30. Parley P. Pratt Property. Parley P. Pratt**, one of the original Apostles in this dispensation, owned the first two lots on the NW corner of Maple and Cowdery Streets.

■ **31. William Aldrick Property.** William Aldrick owned the lot on the NW corner of the intersection of Cowdery and Maple (Whitney) Streets.

Vinson Knight and William Marks home, Kirtland, OH. (Circa 1860; courtesy of LDSCA)

■ **32. Vinson Knight and William Marks Home.** The **home** of **Vinson Knight** and **William Marks** is on two lots at the NW corner of the intersection of Joseph and Cowdery Streets (number 7741 Joseph Street). The home is marked with a century home marker.

Vinson Knight was baptized about 1834 and ordained a counselor in the bishopric in Kirtland on Jan. 13, 1836 (HC 2: 365–66). He died a faithful Church member in Nauvoo on July 31, 1842 (RPJS 265).

This was also the home of **William Marks**, who was baptized before Apr. 3, 1835. He served on the Kirtland High Council and as president of the **Kirtland Stake** in 1838 (RPJS 230–31; OMKM 80). He was also president of the **Nauvoo Stake** until he was rejected in Oct. 1844. He then followed **James J. Strang** and, later, **Charles B. Thompson.** He assisted in founding the **RLDS Church** in 1860 and became a counselor to RLDS Church president **Joseph Smith III** in 1863 (RPJS 230–31).

■ **33. Levi Richards Property. Levi Richards**, a physician and brother of **Willard Richards**, was a member of the Church in Kirtland who eventually went west with the Saints after serving a five-year mission in England. He owned the lot on the SW corner of Cowdery and Joseph Streets.

■ **34. Joseph Fielding Property. Joseph Fielding** owned the third lot west of Cowdery Street, on the south side of Joseph Street. He was a brother of **Mary Fielding**, wife of **Hyrum Smith**. **Parley P. Pratt** taught and baptized him while serving a mission to the Toronto, Canada, area. **Joseph Fielding** was also one of the first missionaries to Great Britain, where he presided over the mission from 1838 to 1840.

■ **35. George Robinson Property. George Robinson** owned the lot on the SE corner of the intersection of Joseph and Cowdery Streets. A son-in-law of **Sidney Rigdon, George** succeeded **Oliver Cowdery** as general Church recorder and was also a clerk to the **First Presidency** part of the time from 1837 to 1840. During this period, he wrote "The Scriptory Book of Joseph Smith, Jr.," an important record book he started in **Far West** in 1838. He served as postmaster in **Nauvoo** in 1840, but by 1842 he denied the faith (BiE 1:252–53; EnM 2:589).

■ **36. William Miller Home. William Miller's home** probably still stands on the north side of Joseph Street, midway between Cowdery Street and Chillicothe Road. Miller was born in Avon, NY, in 1813 and died in Provo, UT, in 1875. He was baptized in **Kirtland** in 1834, married Phebe Scott, served a mission in England, was probate judge in Utah County and was president of the Utah Stake from 1860 to 1868.

■ **37. Joseph Smith Property. Joseph Smith** owned the three lots east of **William Miller's** property on the north side of Joseph Street and also the lot directly across the south side. There was a home on this site that appears to have been the Prophet's home.

Hyrum Smith home in Kirtland, OH. The back (right) part of this home was Hyrum's. It was moved so the newer home on the left could be built on the old foundation.

■ **38. Hyrum Smith Home.** At 9097 Chillicothe Road (State 306) (east side), and at a point where **Joseph** Street joins Chillicothe Road from the west, is the home of **Hyrum Smith**—older brother and close friend to the **Prophet Joseph**, second counselor in the **First Presidency**, Assistant President to the Prophet, and the patriarch to the Church (D&C 124:91–95).

The original home has been moved from its foundation and attached to the modern structure. The front part of the home is newer and stands on the original foundation. A marker in front of the home identifies the site.

Kirtland Temple, with the Kirtland Safety Society Bank on the left and the Teachers' Seminary building (site of an 1830s Methodist church) on the right. (Illustration by Henry Howe, 1846)

■ **39. Kirtland Safety Society Site.** The building that housed the **Kirtland Safety Society** stood on a lot south of and adjacent to the **Kirtland Temple**, about where the circular walkway is located. It was on the west side of Chillicothe Road, across from the **Sidney Rigdon** home.

Three-dollar Kirtland Safety Society note, 1837. (Courtesy of Wilford C. Wood)

In the 1830s, the number of banks in **Ohio** towns like Kirtland doubled. By 1836, Kirtland had grown to the point that it could "probably have supported a modest bank" (HR 315), and the Saints decided to establish one. When a petition for approval to incorporate a bank failed to pass the state legislature after all arrangements had been made to begin a bank, Church leaders decided to go ahead with

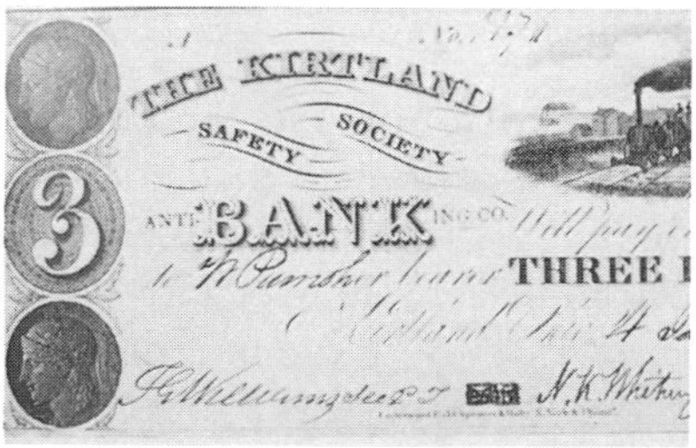

Three-dollar Kirtland Safety Society note, 1837.

the venture by changing the name of the establishment to the **Kirtland Safety Society Anti-Banking Company,** a practice that was not unprecedented in other **Ohio** towns (HC 2:470–73).

Not long after it began issuing its first notes in Jan. 1837, the Safety Society ran into serious problems and could not redeem its notes. Banking establishments throughout the whole country faced similar circumstances, and the banking industry experienced a general collapse. In Aug. 1837, **Warren Parrish** was caught defrauding the Kirtland Safety Society and counterfeiting the notes, a major cause of the institution's collapse after operating only about 10 months, Jan.–Nov. 1837 (HR 315–18).

The Kirtland Safety Society safe (according to the Western Reserve Museum), which was housed at the Hale farm and village near Hudson, OH, in 1989.

During the universal panic of 1837 in the United States, few remembered that **Joseph Smith** had cautioned the investors against excess and speculation. The failure by many to follow the Prophet's counsel led to the Society's failure, which was a cause of apostasy in Kirtland and of Joseph's flight from **Ohio** to **Missouri** (HC 2:487–88; 3:1–2).

In the darkest days of Kirtland, God revealed to Joseph that "something new must be done for the salvation of His Church" (HC 2:489). That "something" was the first foreign overseas mission in this dispensation. Under the leadership of **Heber C. Kimball**, the gospel was taken to England in 1837.

■ **40. Sidney Rigdon Home.** The restored and greatly enhanced **Sidney Rigdon** home is located on the east side of Chillicothe Road (State 306), across from the **Kirtland Safety Society** site and SE of the **Kirtland Temple**. It is a large two-story frame building with two columns extending the height of both stories.

Sidney Rigdon was a minister in the **Reformed Baptist** movement and very influential in preparing the way for the restored

The Sidney Rigdon home, Kirtland, OH, was probably the center section of the house that existed when this photo was taken in 1985.

gospel to be accepted by many in the Kirtland area. Sixteen months after joining the Church in Nov. 1830, he was called as a first counselor to **Joseph Smith.**

Stannard Stone Quarry, two miles south of Kirtland, OH, where sandstone for the Kirtland Temple was quarried. Note the drill holes. (1989)

Sidney requested that the Prophet visit his sick wife, Phebe, at this home on Feb. 25, 1836. Joseph wrote that he and his scribe "prayed for and anointed her in the name of the Lord, and she began to recover from that very hour" (PWJS 163; spelling and punctuation modernized).

■ **41. Kirtland Camp Site.**

■ **42. Temple Stone Quarry.** The **Temple Stone Quarry** (Stannard Quarry), where sandstone for the Kirtland Temple and other buildings was quarried, is two miles south of the **Kirtland Temple,** on the west side of Chillicothe Road (State 306). It is a part of the Chapin Forest Reservation Park. Public parking is provided in front of the small **Quarry Lake** near the park entrance. Conspicuous drill holes may be seen in the stones located in and near a small stream of water, about 200 feet down a path on the NW side of the lake. Workmen quarried the sandstone by drilling a row of two-inch holes 10–12 inches apart and then setting an iron wedge in each hole. As they struck the wedges with hammers, the rock would split.

Joseph Smith served as quarry **foreman** during the temple's construction (JD 10:165–66; T&S 6:868). The Prophet's cousin **George A. Smith** and **Harvey Stanley,** an English convert who later helped carve the Nauvoo Temple sunstones, hauled the first loads of stone from the quarry to the temple site June 5, 1833 (HC 1:353). Some of the sandstone blocks used in the doorways were up to eight feet long (HR 157).

A park, hiking trails, picnic tables, grills, rest rooms, and playgrounds surround the quarry.

North and Northeast of Kirtland

■ MENTOR

Mentor is on State 306 and U.S. 20, 3–4 miles NE of **Kirtland** and 1.5 miles north of I-90. It was one of the first settlements of the Western Reserve. **Joseph Smith** described Mentor and its surroundings as a "goodly land" with "wealthy" residents (HC 2:323).

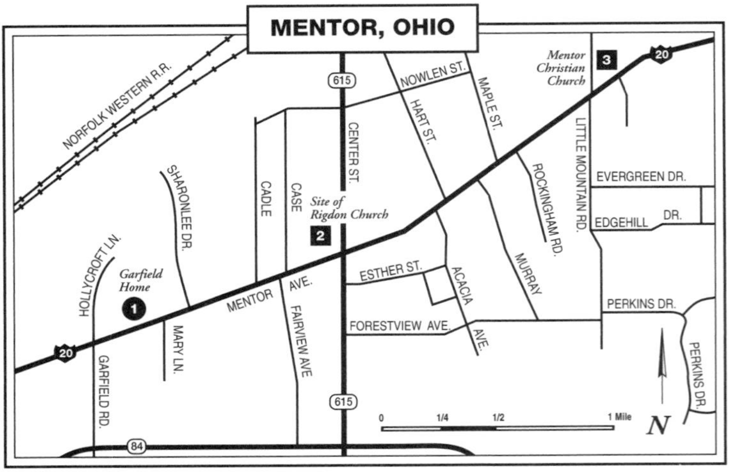

Sidney Rigdon, a minister of the **Reformed Baptist Society,** moved to Mentor in 1827. Members of his congregation, which eventually became one of the earliest **Disciples of Christ** congregations, were sometimes called **Campbellites** after **Alexander Campbell** (ARM 245). Sidney Rigdon and many members of his congregation were baptized into the restored Church when they heard the gospel in 1830 from Latter-day Saint missionaries on a mission to the **Lamanites. Parley P. Pratt**, formerly a Reformed Baptist, introduced Sidney to the **Book of Mormon**. Sidney was cautious, but, as Parley indicated:

> At length Mr. Rigdon and many others became convinced that they had no authority to minister in the ordinances of God; and that they had not been legally baptized and ordained. They, therefore, came forward and were baptized by us, and received the gift of the Holy Ghost by the laying on of hands, and prayer in the name of **Jesus Christ**.
>
> . . . The interest and excitement now became general in Kirtland, and in all the region round about. The people thronged us night and day, insomuch that we had no time for rest and retirement. . . . Thousands flocked about us daily. . . .
>
> In two or three weeks from our arrival in the neighborhood with the news, we had baptized one hundred and twenty-seven souls, and this number soon increased to one thousand (APPP 47–48).

Because so many in the Kirtland-Mentor area were prepared to receive the gospel, and because Parley P. Pratt, **Oliver Cowdery, Peter Whitmer,** and **Ziba Peterson** followed the promptings of the Holy Ghost in their labors, the scene of **Church history** changed from **New York** to **Ohio**. The Lord soon gave two revelations (D&C 37–38) indicating that the Saints in **New York** should sell their property and move to **Ohio**. This movement was the first "gathering" of the Saints in this dispensation. By early 1831, a branch was organized in Mentor (HR 42).

Mentor's location on the road between Kirtland and Painesville made it a crossroads for missionaries. Despite their great success, not all their experiences were positive. Parley P. Pratt wrote sarcastically of the "Christian benevolence" shown him by several Mentor residents who threw eggs at him before marching him out of town

(APPP 128–29). On Dec. 1, 1835, **Joseph Smith** took his family on a sleigh ride through Mentor (HC 2:323–24). He was disgusted with some of the residents, characterizing them as being "ready to abuse and scandalize men who never laid a straw in their way" (HC 2:323).

You may visit three interesting sites by traveling NE on Mentor Avenue (State 20) from the point where State 306 crosses Mentor Avenue:

1. **Lawnfield,** home of **James Garfield**, 20th president of the United States (1880–81). Garfield attended school in the **Kirtland Temple** and was a follower of **Alexander Campbell**. While serving as president of the United States, he was assassinated.

2. Site of Sidney Rigdon's church, on the NW corner of Mentor Avenue and State 615, where the Center Street School stands. Missionaries to the **Lamanites** preached here (HC 1:124; APPP 47–48).

3. The Mentor Christian Church, which traces its origins to **Sidney Rigdon**. This building dates to 1828 but is not the building in which Sidney preached. Because of his contributions to this church, his picture is displayed in the foyer, recognizing him as the first minister and founder.

■ PAINESVILLE

Painesville is 11 miles directly NE of Kirtland on State 20, between I-90 and Lake Erie. It was named after **General Edward**

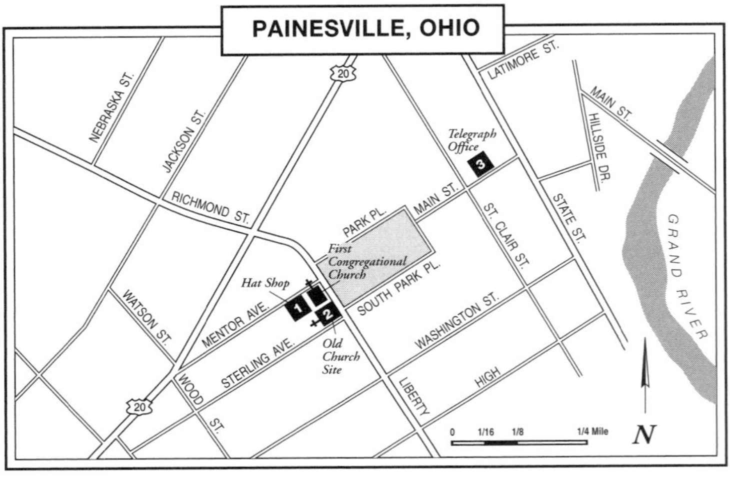

Paine. By 1820, Painesville had become one of the largest towns in the Western Reserve. It is the county seat of Lake County, which Kirtland has belonged to since 1840.

Edward Partridge, who became the first bishop of the Church, and his wife, Lydia, were living in Painesville when **Oliver Cowdery** and the missionaries to the **Lamanites** preached in the area in 1831. Edward operated a hat shop in Painesville, where he had been a practicing hatter since age 16 (see Site No. 1 on map).

The Partridges were members of Sidney Rigdon's congregation of Reformed Baptists when they first heard the restored gospel. Lydia Partridge recorded her husband's initial reaction: "He told them he did not believe what they said, but believed them to be impostors. **Oliver Cowdery** said he was thankful there was a God in heaven who knew the hearts of all men. After the men were gone my husband sent a man to follow them and get one of their books" (BYUS 11, no. 3 [1971]: 489).

Soon after their contact with the missionaries, and with questions still in their minds, **Edward Partridge** and **Sidney Rigdon** went to **Fayette, NY,** to meet the **Prophet Joseph**, who baptized Edward on Dec. 11, 1830, in the Seneca River. Joseph said Partridge "was a pattern of piety, and one of the Lord's great men" (HC 1:128), and the Lord said he was "like unto Nathanael of old, in whom there [was] no guile" (D&C 41:11).

While Edward and Sidney visited the Prophet, he received revelations concerning the two men (D&C 35–36; HC 1:128–31). The Lord told Sidney he could now give the Holy Ghost, which he could not do previously (D&C 35:5–6).

In July 1837, **Joseph Smith** set out on a mission to Canada, but when he got to Painesville, he was **arrested six different times** on charges brought by enemies of the Church. Every charge but one was shown to be trumped up, and on that one genuine charge the Prophet had to pay a few dollars on a debt.

Edward Partridge's home and hat shop site, Painesville, OH, was located on the right side of this photo and to the right of the First Congregational Church.

Painesville sites of particular interest include:

1. **Edward Partridge's home and hat shop site,**

located on the south side of Mentor Avenue (State 283), on the second lot beginning 100 feet west of the entrance to the First Congregational Church, which faces the town square. A sidewalk that leads to a classroom annex of a Methodist church marks approximately the eastern boundary of Edward's property.

2. A **Methodist** church once stood where another Methodist Church now stands on the west side of Liberty Street, facing the SW corner of the town square. "Malicious and vexatious law suits" were heard here (HC 2:502). While **Joseph Smith** lived in **Ohio** (1831–37), he was arrested several times on a variety of charges. Though some hearings took place in the church, most were held in the Lake County Court House in Painesville.

3. The 1830s office of the *Painesville Telegraph* was on the north side of Main Street in the center of the block between St. Clair and State Streets, currently two parking lots. In 1834, anti-Mormon articles began to appear in this newspaper. The **Prophet Joseph Smith** visited Painesville many times, drawing notice whenever he visited (HC 2:323–24, 502). That year Mormon- and Mason-hater **Eber D. Howe**, owner of the *Telegraph,* and apostate **Philastus Hurlbut** published *Mormonism Unvailed,* "the first book of any significance printed with the design of destroying the Church" (HR 207). Despite anti-Mormon sentiments, the Church took out a loan from the Painesville Bank in 1835 (PWJS 96).

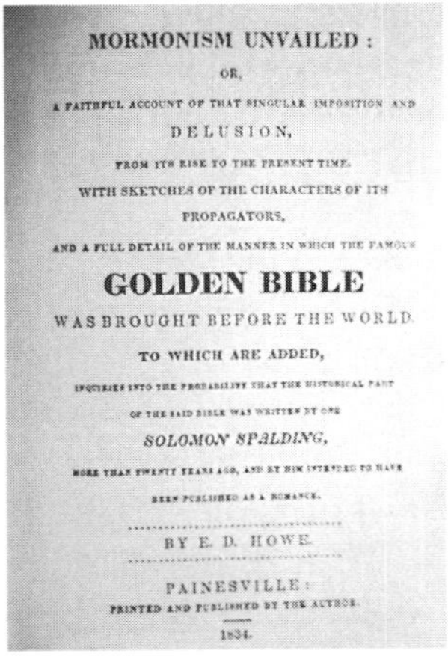
MORMONISM UNVAILED:

OR,

A FAITHFUL ACCOUNT OF THAT SINGULAR IMPOSITION AND DELUSION,

FROM ITS RISE TO THE PRESENT TIME.

WITH SKETCHES OF THE CHARACTERS OF ITS PROPAGATORS,

AND A FULL DETAIL OF THE MANNER IN WHICH THE FAMOUS

GOLDEN BIBLE

WAS BROUGHT BEFORE THE WORLD.

TO WHICH ARE ADDED,

INQUIRIES INTO THE PROBABILITY THAT THE HISTORICAL PART OF THE SAID BIBLE WAS WRITTEN BY ONE

SOLOMON SPALDING,

MORE THAN TWENTY YEARS AGO, AND BY HIM INTENDED TO HAVE BEEN PUBLISHED AS A ROMANCE.

BY E. D. HOWE.

PAINESVILLE:

PRINTED AND PUBLISHED BY THE AUTHOR.

1834.

Title page of the anti-Mormon book Mormonism Unvailed, *published in 1834.*

4. The **Indian Museum** of Lake County is located in the Kilcaley Building, Lake Erie College, 391 W. Washington St. Admission is free.

■ FAIRPORT

Fairport is 12 miles NE of Kirtland on State 535 where the Grand River empties into Lake Erie. It became **Fairport Harbor** sometime after the port was improved and a **lighthouse** built in 1825 on the NW corner of Second and High Streets. The lighthouse was

Fairport Harbor, OH, where the Grand River, left, empties into Lake Erie. (1989)

rebuilt in 1871 and is currently a maritime museum. The lighthouse was a welcome sight to the Latter-day Saints as they arrived in a new area as the Lord had commanded.

Lighthouse at Fairport Harbor, OH. (1989)

The proximity of Fairport to Church headquarters in **Kirtland** facilitated faster transportation for Saints migrating from **New York** and for missionaries heading for the eastern states. **Oliver Cowdery** wrote, "Fairport is an excellent Harbor, and affords a safe moorage for shipping" (M&A 1:3).

Three groups of Saints traveling from **New York** to **Ohio** came through Fairport Harbor on their way to **Kirtland**. The two groups of **Fayette Saints,** numbering about 110, were led by **Lucy Mack Smith** and **Thomas B. Marsh**. They arrived at Fairport Harbor between May 8 and 12, 1831 (HJS 195–208). The **Colesville Saints,** about 60 in number, were led by **Newel Knight**. They arrived in Fairport on May 14, 1831, after a stormy three-day crossing of Lake Erie. They settled in Thompson, 16 miles NE of Kirtland (CHC 1:250–51).

The **Twelve Apostles** set out on a **mission to the eastern states** via Fairport on May 4, 1835 (HC 2:222). Elder **Orson Pratt** recalled the experience:

> At half past 2 o'clock [A.M.] we (the Twelve) and two others left **Kirtland** for Fairport, where we arrived a little after sunrise, and went immediately on board of a steam boat which left the port a few minutes after we got on board. Thus the Lord in his mercy provided a boat for us at the very moment we arrived which was according to our prayers. We had a speedy and prosperous voyage (OPJ 60).

Mary Duty Smith, the nearly 93-year-old mother of **Joseph Smith Sr.**, arrived at Fairport Harbor a year later on May 16, 1836, with another group of **New York Saints.** She stopped that night in a hotel there (HC 2:442). **Joseph** and **Hyrum Smith** brought their aged grandmother from Fairport to Kirtland the next day, and the **Smith family** enjoyed a great reunion. **Mary Smith** died just days later on May 27, 1836, firm in the faith she had fully embraced and thankful that her life had been extended so that she could see her posterity again (HC 2:443).

In June 1837, **Heber C. Kimball** and **Orson Hyde** departed from Fairport as the first LDS missionaries to **Great Britain** (HC 2:492–93; TWP 37–38).

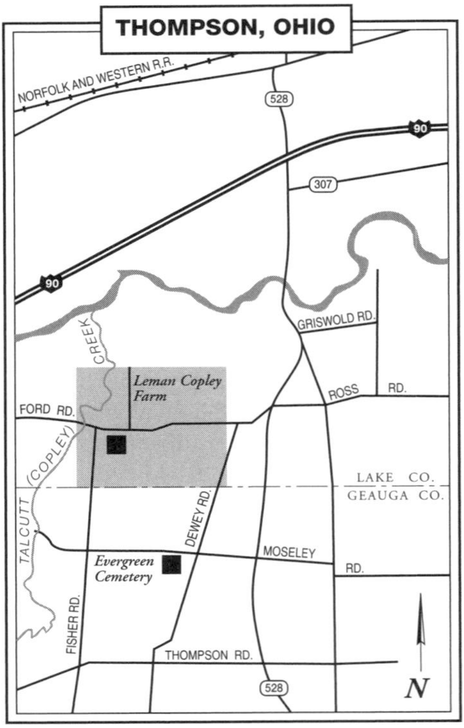

■ THOMPSON/MADISON—Leman Copley Farm and the Colesville Saints

Thompson is 16 miles NE of **Kirtland** and about seven miles south of I-90 on State 528. In 1831, **Leman Copley**, a former **Shaker** and recent **LDS** convert, owned 759 acres of land that is now part of Madison but was then part of Thompson. The stream located 1.8 miles SE of State 528 on Ford Road ran through this property and is still known by some old-time residents as **Copley Creek.** Today it is called Talcutt Creek. The center of Leman Copley's farm lies 1.7 miles west of State 528 on Ford Road. As you view the open farmland SE of the intersection of Ford and Fisher Roads, you can easily contemplate the **Colesville Saints** planting crops here. The land has most recently been used for farming and recreational purposes.

The **law of consecration,** first put into practice at the Copley Farm in May 1831, was implemented according to a revelation (D&C 51; HC 1:180). At first, Leman consecrated his property to the Lord, and the Saints received portions of it as their stewardships. But a month later he changed his mind and refused to allow the Saints to stay because of a problem at North Union (see Shaker Heights, pages 63–64). The Lord had said in a revelation, "I consecrate unto them this land for a **little season,** until I, the Lord, shall provide for them otherwise" (D&C 51:16).

When Leman broke his covenant, the Lord gave the **Prophet Joseph Smith** a revelation directing the homeless Saints to move to **Jackson County, MO**, which they did on June 28, 1831 (D&C 54). Before they left, **Jared Carter's** youngest child was healed in Thompson after being blessed by the Prophet (JH June 8, 1831). As directed by **revelation** (D&C 49), Leman filled an unsuccessful mission to the Shakers in North Union (**Shaker Heights**) with **Parley P. Pratt** and **Sidney Rigdon,** which resulted in his defection from the Church in 1831. He was rebaptized in 1836 but remained in **Ohio** when the Saints went west to **Missouri.**

The unmarked **graves** of **Leman Copley** (1780–1862), his wife, **Salley,** (1779–1861), and a three-month-old grandchild who died in 1861 are located in the **Evergreen Cemetery** in Thompson. The cemetery is on the south side of Moseley Road, about 0.6 miles west of the intersection of Dewey and Moseley Roads, just west of State 528. The cemetery entrance is on the west, and the unmarked graves are about 100 feet into the cemetery from the first headstone on the west, and about halfway into the cemetery from Moseley Road.

■ Unionville

The small community of **Unionville** is about 20 miles east of Kirtland on U.S. 84 and County Line Road, which divides Lake and

Old tavern in Unionville, OH. (1989)

Ashtabula Counties. A historic **old tavern** still operates in Unionville as a popular restaurant and antique shop. Formerly, the tavern was a **stagecoach stop** on the road between **Kirtland** and **New York**. Today the tavern looks essentially as it did when the Latter-day Saints lived in the area in the 1830s.

Levi Hancock wrote of his stay at the tavern in his journal (LHJ 28). Other missionaries and Church leaders undoubtedly stayed at the tavern as well, including **Joseph** and **Emma Smith**, who probably stopped here as they traveled on the stagecoach from New York to Kirtland in Jan. 1831.

■ Harpersfield

Harpersfield, two to three miles south of Unionville, was the home of the families of **Reynolds** and **William Cahoon** and **John Corrill**. **Reynolds Cahoon** was on the **Kirtland Temple Committee** (D&C 94:14–15), and John Corrill was appointed to take charge of the Kirtland Temple (HC 2:371). **John** became second counselor to **Bishop Edward Partridge** before apostatizing from the Church in **Far West, MO,** in 1838 (BiE 1:241–42).

■ Ashtabula

Ashtabula, a major 1830s harbor on Lake Erie, is located on the shores of Lake Erie about 35 miles NE of **Kirtland** on U.S. 20, the major road from Buffalo, **NY,** to Kirtland, and three miles north of I-90. It was the major transportation center for both water and overland traffic in the Western Reserve.

Joseph Smith served two short **missions to Canada.** Each time he booked passage on one of the many boats that filled the harbor at Ashtabula. **Sidney Rigdon** and **Freeman Nickerson** accompanied him on his 1833 mission. They spent the night here on Oct. 5,

1833, at Lamb's Tavern (HC 1:416). Joseph wrote of a short stay here during his second mission in 1837:

> We . . . enjoyed ourselves very much in walking on the beach and bathing in the beautiful, clear water of the lake. At four P.M. we took a deck passage on board the steamer for Buffalo. At night we all lay down to rest on the upper deck of the boat, and for pillows some took their boots, others their valises, and had a comfortable night's repose" (HC 2:502–503).

■ ROME

Rome is 27 miles east of Kirtland at the crossroads of U.S. 6 and State 45. Some of the early members of the Church were living here when they heard the gospel from the missionaries.

John Reed, the blacksmith on the **Kirtland Temple**, and his wife, **Rebecca Bearse Reed,** owned mills in this area. **Levi Hancock**, who later became a president of the First Quorum of the Seventy, settled here in 1827 (HC 2:203). He built many of the original structures in Rome, where he owned 14 acres. Levi was single when **Parley P. Pratt** and other missionaries passed through this area in 1830. Levi was converted at Kirtland and moved there. **Salmon Gee**, one of the first seven presidents of the Seventy (1837–38), lived in Rome, New Lyme, and Dorset in Ashtabula County (BiE 1:92–93).

South and Southeast of Kirtland

● BURTON—Amish Settlement

The **Amish settlement** of Burton is located 15 miles in a direct line SE of Kirtland and four miles west of Middlefield on state highway 87. It is 10 miles north of Hiram.

Orson Hyde, who later was an Apostle, attended the **Burton Academy** for two quarters. He studied grammar, geography, arithmetic, and rhetoric. The academy stood opposite the east side of the square (on the site of the home now at 14605 East Park Street). A **tavern** stood opposite the west side of the square. Members of the Church traveling through Burton stopped at the tavern to eat.

Just south of the village square, you can visit a restored

early-19th-century **Western Reserve Community** with four homes and eight other buildings complete with 19th-century furnishings.

Burton is in the heart of Ohio's large maple syrup-producing area. Most early Saints who owned land also made their own syrup and sugar. Workers in a log cabin in the Burton Village Square explain the process of making maple syrup, candy, and sugar. During the early spring when the sap is flowing from the maple trees, workers make syrup in the cabin. In addition, a country store in Burton features displays from the surrounding **Amish country,** including a wagon and a horse that visitors can pose with for photographs.

- **MIDDLEFIELD—Amish Settlement**

Middlefield is the center of one of the largest Amish communities in the United States. It is 19 miles in a direct line SE of Kirtland at the intersection of state highways 608 and 87. Other Amish communities in the area include Burton and West Farmington. Although these small settlements have relatively little to do with Latter-day Saint history, a visit reveals how the Saints may have lived in the area in the 1830s.

The **Amish** are a division of the Mennonite wing of the Anabaptist movement, which started in Europe in the mid-16th century as a result of the **Protestant Reformation. Jacob Ammann** founded the Anabaptist movement on the basis that there had been an apostasy from primitive Christianity. A converted priest, **Menno Simons**, founded the Mennonite movement in Holland. Persecution drove the Mennonites to America.

The Amish Mennonites reject infant baptism, accept the New Testament as the only rule of faith, and oppose taking oaths and serving in the military. They live lives of simplicity, neatness, and cleanliness (ARM 87–92).

Generally, the Amish people focus on their large families and the home. They continue to use horses and buggies or bicycles for transportation. They normally do not have electricity or phones, with the exception of dairy farmers who have electricity in their barns, and businessmen who may have a phone.

Congregations of 80 members meet together every second Sunday in one of the homes. The Amish spend the other Sundays at home with family. A lay minister who is appointed for life is the ecclesiastical leader; there is no central church organization. Every night, the typically large Amish families have what the Latter-day Saints might call family home evening. Twice a year the Amish pay their tithing, all of which goes to help the poor among them. They avoid debt and believe in self-sufficiency. They have no insurance, no house payments, and no utilities. About half the Amish are farmers.

Visitors to Middlefield may want to visit the Amish Swiss Cheese Factory, where there is a small museum and film presentation. It is located 1.2 miles north of the town on State 608. This community of Amish also manufactures washing machines and makes clothing. The Amish sell goods in their homes and in business houses.

■ West Farmington—Michael Chandler Grave

West Farmington is six miles directly SE of Middlefield on State 88, and one mile west of State 534.

Michael Chandler was a farmer in West Farmington who obtained 11 Egyptian mummies and some scrolls that had been discovered in Egypt by **Antonio Lebolo.** Chandler sold four of the mummies and some scrolls to the Latter-day Saints in Kirtland in 1835. Publication of the book of Abraham resulted from Joseph Smith's interest in the scrolls (HC 2:235–36, 348–51).

Michael Chandler's gravestone at West Farmington, OH.

Chandler's grave is located in the SE corner of the Hillside Cemetery, which is in West Farmington on the north side of State 88 at a point just west of State 534 (.1 mile east of First Street). The grave is marked by a nine-foot-wide stone base with a column and an urn on top. The monument has a plaque in recognition of the book of Abraham and its source (HC 2:235–36).

■ Nelson—Ezra Booth "Silenced"

Nelson is located in **Portage County,** 27 miles in a direct line SE from Kirtland and five miles east of Hiram on State 305.

Two early leaders—**John Whitmer**, a **Book of Mormon** witness, and **Lyman Wight**, an Apostle—established a branch of the Church in Nelson in the spring of 1831. Meetings were probably held in the home of **Charles Hulet,** a resident of Nelson and early convert to the Church.

A **conference** of the Church was held in Nelson on Sept. 6, 1831, with **Joseph Smith** presiding. In the meetings, "it was voted that **Ezra Booth** be silenced from preaching as an Elder in this Church" (FWR 12). Ezra was one of the 28 missionaries who went to **Missouri** to dedicate the land of Zion in 1831. Afterward, he defected from the Church. While in Nelson, Ezra wrote a **series of letters** against the Church. Published in the ***Ohio Star*** at Ravenna in Sept. 1831, the letters contributed to the bitter feelings of a mob that **tarred and feathered** Joseph Smith in Mar. 1832 (HC 1:261–65).

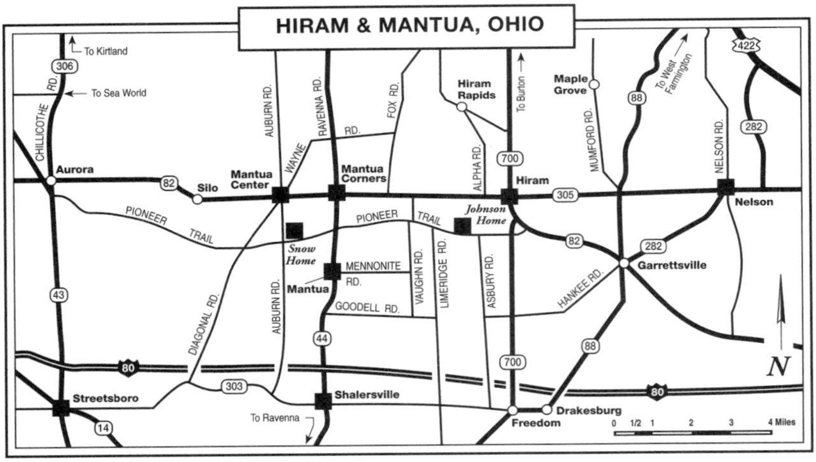

■ HIRAM—John Johnson Home

Hiram is about 25 miles in a direct line (and 35 miles via the roads—a one-hour drive) SE of Kirtland at the intersection of State highways 82 and 700. The most direct route from Kirtland is to go south on State 306 to State 82 at Aurora, then go east to Hiram. Hiram, the home of Hiram College, was one of the earliest settlements in

John Johnson home. (1989)

Aerial view, looking WNW, of John Johnson farm and home (center) in Hiram, OH. (1978)

Portage County (1798) and the most elevated point of the Western Reserve.

The 1829, **John Johnson farm home** is located at 6203 Pioneer Trail Road. From the center of Hiram (where State 700 and 82 cross), drive south on State 700 for 1.2 miles, then drive west on Pioneer Trail Road for 1.3 miles to the Johnson farm and house on the north side of the road.

The **John** and **Alice Johnson** family was prominent in the Church during the 1830s. Two sons, **Luke** and **Lyman**, were members of the restored Church's original **Quorum of the Twelve Apostles**. A daughter, **Marinda,** married **Orson Hyde**, another member of the Twelve. The Johnson home was also the home of **Joseph** and **Emma Smith** and their adopted twins (one of whom died in Mar. 1832) from Sept. 1831 to Sept. 1832. John and Alice Johnson invited the Smiths to

CHAPTER III.

CHAPTER IV.

CHAPTER V.

Joseph Smith's 1828 Bible, with Isaiah 3–5 showing an example of the method Joseph used in marking the scriptures as he worked from Nov. 1831 to Mar. 1832 on his translation of the Bible at the John Johnson home in Hiram, OH. Original in the RLDS Archives. (Courtesy of RLDSLA)

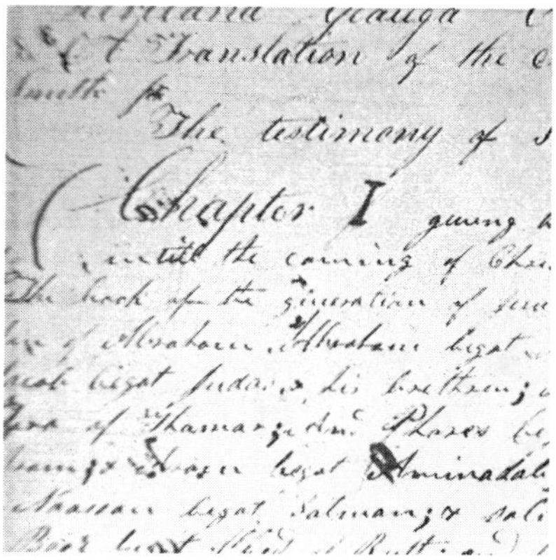

Translation of the

The testimony of

Chapter I

Handwritten copy by scribe John Whitmer of the Joseph Smith Translation of the Bible (Matthew 1), dated Apr. 4, 1831, in Kirtland, OH. Original in the RLDS Archives. (Courtesy of RLDSLA)

Joseph Smith and Sidney Rigdon receiving a vision of the three degrees of glory (D&C 76), while in Hiram, OH, Feb. 16, 1832. (Courtesy of LDSCA)

move from Kirtland to their quiet Hiram home after Joseph healed Alice of "chronic rheumatism" in her shoulder (PJE 162–63). **Sidney Rigdon** also moved to Hiram, where he and the Prophet worked on the **Joseph Smith Translation** of the Bible (HC 1:215).

The time Joseph spent in Hiram was a season of great **spiritual outpourings.** While there, Joseph received at least **16 revelations:** D&C 1, 65, 67, 68, 69, 71, 73, 74, 76, 77, 78, 79, 80, 81, 99, 133. Many of the revelations dealt specifically with the commandment to translate the Bible. Among these revelations are some of the most sublime instructions from the Lord in the Doctrine and Covenants. While Joseph and Sidney were translating the Bible on Feb. 16, 1832, and while in the presence of 12 men, they received a marvelous **vision of the three degrees of glory** (D&C 76). The Prophet characterized this revelation as "a transcript from the records of the eternal world" (HC 1:252; JI 27 [1892]: 303–04). While receiving this revelation,

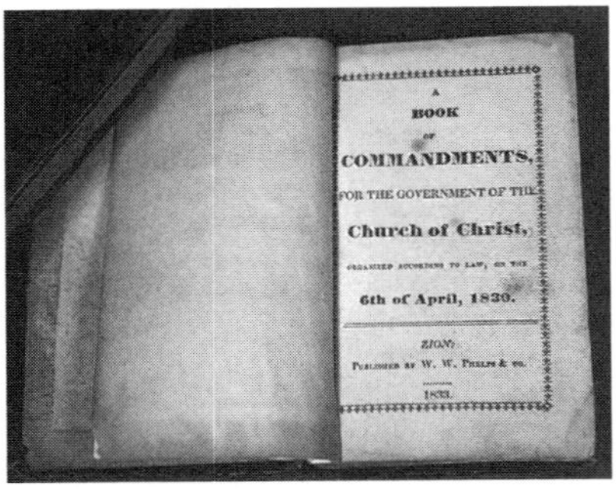

The Book of Commandments, approved in Hiram, OH, Nov. 1, 1831, was published in 1833 in Independence, MO. (Courtesy of Wilford C. Wood)

A mob trying to poison the Prophet Joseph Smith at Hiram, OH, Mar. 24, 1832. (Illustration by Vernon Murdock, 1973; courtesy of Vernon Murdock)

Joseph and Sidney also received a vision of **God the Father** and **Jesus Christ** (D&C 76:22–23).

Because the Johnson home was the **Church headquarters** for one year, many significant historical events occurred here. The forthcoming **publication of the Book of Commandments** was approved in a conference here Nov. 1, 1831 (HC 1:221–26). The book was in the process of publication in 1833 at Independence, MO, when a mob destroyed the press and all but about 100 copies. These **65 revelations** from the Book of Commandments were later included in the 1835 Kirtland edition (first edition) of the **Doctrine and Covenants**.

While the Prophet was in Hiram, a number of people opposed

Tarring and feathering of the Prophet Joseph Smith by a mob at Hiram, OH, Mar. 24, 1832. (Painting by C. C. A. Christensen; courtesy of MOABYU)

his work, including **Ezra Booth** and **Symonds Ryder**—both former ministers who converted to the Church but turned apostate. On Mar. 24, 1832, they helped **organize a mob** of about 50 men that took Joseph from the Johnson home, where he and Emma were tending their twins, who were sick with measles (CHC 1:280–82; HC 1:261–64). The mob carried Joseph out of the house, **tarred and feathered him,** and tried to poison him. The mob also took **Sidney Rigdon** from his home and dragged him across the street. He suffered a serious concussion, which left him delirious for some time, while being dragged by the feet across the frozen ground. He was also tarred and feathered (HC 1:265; PJE 161–74; JD 11:5).

The Prophet was "scarified and defaced" after a long night of having the tar scraped and peeled off his body (HC 1:264). The next day, though tired, bruised, and badly scratched, he "preached to the congregation as usual, and in the afternoon of the same day baptized three individuals" (HC 1:264). Five days later, on Mar. 29, 10-month-old **Joseph (Murdock) Smith**, one of Joseph and Emma's adopted twins, died as a result of the exposure he suffered during the night of mobbing.

Joseph left the Johnson home Apr. 1, 1832, and went to **Missouri** to visit the Saints. Following his Missouri trip, he returned to Hiram, where he resided until Sept. 12, 1832.

A modern (1986–87) LDS chapel is located on the farm, and the farmland is a part of the Church Welfare Services system.

■ Mantua Corners, Mantua Center, and Mantua—Birthplace of Lorenzo Snow

Mantua Corners is four miles due west of Hiram, OH, at the intersection of State 305 and 44. It is 23 miles SSE of Kirtland. The neighboring community of **Mantua Center** is two miles straight west of Mantua Corners on State 305. **Mantua** is two miles south of Mantua Corners on State 44.

People from these adjoining communities made up **Sidney Rigdon's** congregation in 1826 when he was a Reformed Baptist minister in Mantua Center. In 2000 the Mantua Center Christian Church claimed to be the oldest continuous congregation of Disciples of Christ (Campbellites) in Ohio, tracing its origins to Sidney Rigdon. The building itself was built in the 1840s, after Sidney had left the Reformed Baptists.

When **Sidney Rigdon** joined the LDS Church in 1830, many

Home of Oliver and Rosetta Snow, parents of Eliza R. Snow and Lorenzo Snow, Mantua, OH. The Snow home was the small house on the right side of the photo, not the larger home on the left, to which it is attached.

members of his Mantua-area congregation also joined, including the family of **Oliver** and **Rosetta Leonora Pettibone Snow**. Rosetta and her daughter **Leonora** joined the Church first. Another daughter, **Eliza R. Snow,** was baptized Apr. 5, 1835 (BYUS 11, no. 4 [1971]: 128). Her brother, **Lorenzo Snow**, was born in Mantua on Apr. 30, 1814. He was baptized in 1836 and in 1898 became the fifth president of the Church, serving until 1901 (BiE 1:26–30).

Lorenzo Snow was born in Mantua, OH, Apr. 30, 1814. He became the fifth president of the LDS Church.

When **Joseph Smith** visited the **Snow** family at their Mantua home, **Eliza** was very impressed by the Prophet. She wrote, "In the winter of 1830 and 31, **Joseph Smith** called at my father's, and as he sat warming himself, I scrutinized his face as closely as I could without attracting his attention, and decided that his was an honest face (BYUS 11, no. 4 [1971]: 127).

The **Oliver Snow home** where this event took place, and where Eliza, Leonora, and Lorenzo Snow grew up, is 1.2 miles south of State 82. It is the first home north of Pioneer Trail Road on the NE corner of Auburn Road and Pioneer Trail Road. The rear portion of the house is believed to be original. The home is a private residence not open to the public. Just east of the Snow home is an old pioneer cemetery.

Streetsboro

Streetsboro is 22 miles SE of Kirtland, 12 miles SW of Hiram, and two miles south of I-80, at the intersection of State 43 and 303. **Joseph Smith** and **Sidney Rigdon** preached in Streetsboro after being commanded in Dec. 1830 to "proclaim" the gospel in the area surrounding Hiram to combat the falsehoods being spread by apostate **Ezra Booth** (D&C 71).

Zion's Camp stayed in Streetsboro on the first night of its journey. Joseph Smith wrote about it: "This day we went as far as the town of Streetsborough [Streetsboro]. . . . We stayed in **Mr. Ford's Barn,** where Uncle **John Smith** and **Brigham Young** had been preaching three months before" (HC 2:63).

Shalersville

Shalersville is 27 miles SSE of Kirtland and six miles SW of Hiram, at the intersection of state highways 44 and 303, about .7 mile south of I-80.

Early missionaries found willing converts in Shalersville, and a branch was established there in 1831. Shalersville was one of the places where **Joseph Smith** and **Sidney Rigdon** preached during their mission in Dec. 1831 and Jan. 1832. They had been sent by revelation (D&C 71:1–2; HC 1:241) to preach the truth in response to the **scandalous letters** by apostate **Ezra Booth**, which were then being published in the ***Ohio Star*** in nearby **Ravenna.** Joseph and Sidney were successful (HC 1:241), but they still had enemies in Shalersville. The mob that **tarred and feathered Joseph and Sidney** on Mar. 24, 1832, was "a company formed of citizens from Shalersville, Garrettsville, and Hiram" (PJE 167).

Lorenzo Snow taught the gospel in the local Shalersville school during the winter of 1839–40 (LLS 30). **Brigham Young** and **Franklin Richards,** two of many missionaries sent out with information concerning **Joseph Smith's candidacy** for president of the United States, addressed the people of Shalersville on June 6, 1844. Along the way they distributed copies of the Prophet's political platform published under the title "Joseph Smith's Views on the Powers and Policy of Government" (HBY 168).

■ RAVENNA

Ravenna is 11 direct miles SW of Hiram, OH, six miles south of I-80, and five miles south of Shalersville on State 44. It is at the intersection of State 44 and 59.

Lorenzo Snow, fifth president of the Church (1898–1901), enrolled in the high school in Ravenna, where he spent one year. He also had one term under a professor of Hebrew (EnM 3:1367).

Ezra Booth wrote nine anti-Mormon letters that were published in the ***Ohio Star*** in Ravenna beginning in Sept. 1831. He had been converted when Alice Johnson's arm was healed by **Joseph Smith**, and he was one of the 28 missionaries called to **Missouri** to dedicate that land. He became the first apostate to publish anti-Mormon literature. "By their coloring, falsity, and vain calculations to overthrow the work of the Lord," the Prophet said, Booth's letters "exposed [Booth's] weakness, wickedness and folly, and left him a monument of his own shame, for the world to wonder at" (HC 1:217).

Joseph Smith and **Sidney Rigdon** preached here from Dec. 4, 1831, to about Jan. 10, 1832, and allayed the excited feelings resulting from Ezra Booth's letters (HC 1:215–17, 241). In answer to the commandment to "confound your enemies; call upon them to meet you both in public and in private" (D&C 71:7), Sidney Rigdon challenged Booth to a public debate to be held in **Ravenna** on Christmas day 1831. When Booth failed to appear, Sidney took the opportunity to testify to the assembled crowd that the letters were a "bundle of falsehoods" (HR 96–97).

● HALE FARM

The **Hale farm** and **village** are located 35 miles SW of Kirtland and one mile east of exit 138 on I-77 in the Cuyahoga Valley National Recreation Area. The farm is a living history museum that depicts Ohio's rural life in the mid-1800s. Visitors can watch craftsmen at their trades of carpentry, smithing, glassblowing, pottery, spinning, and weaving.

Many of the buildings at the farm date to the 1830s when the Saints were centered in **Ohio**. The supposed safe of the **Kirtland**

Safety Society is housed here. The farm is open all summer, and there is an admission fee.

HUDSON

Hudson is located 28 miles south of Kirtland at the intersection of state highways 303 and 91, and immediately south of I-80. The **Western Reserve Academy**—often called the "Yale of the West"—was established in Hudson in 1826. It was the first school of higher learning in the Western Reserve of **Ohio**.

Professor **Joshua Seixas** was teaching at the academy when **Joseph Smith** asked him to come to **Kirtland** and teach **Hebrew**. The Prophet sent **Orson Hyde** and **William E. McLellin** to hire **Seixas**, who early in 1836 taught the brethren in the **Kirtland Temple**. Joseph said, "My soul delights in reading the word of the Lord in the original, and I am determined to pursue the study of the languages, until I shall become master of them, if I am permitted to live long enough" (HC 2:396).

The reputation of the academy and of Professor Seixas persuaded **Lorenzo Snow** to come to Kirtland to study Hebrew with the leaders of the Church, during which time he became converted. A visitor to Hudson today can see many of the original academy buildings that were there when the Saints were in Ohio (HC 2:356, 368, 385–86). Today the academy buildings house a private high school.

BAINBRIDGE (GEAUGA COUNTY)

Bainbridge is 16 miles south of Kirtland on State 306 at a point one mile north of I-422. **Sidney Rigdon** was assigned as a **Reformed Baptist** minister in Bainbridge in 1826. He came here from Pittsburgh and preached about one year before moving to Mentor and establishing several congregations in NE **Ohio.** Sidney was influential in preparing many people to accept the restoration of the fulness of the gospel, including many members of his Bainbridge congregation. In Bainbridge, while looking forward to a "universal reformation" of Christianity, he taught "faith in God, repentance of sins, baptism by immersion in water for the remission of sins, and holiness of life—a godly walk and conversation" (HC 1:121).

Kirtland Camp passed through Bainbridge on July 7, 1838, on its way to **Far West, MO** (HC 3:101).

CHARDON

Chardon is 11 miles ESE of Kirtland at the intersection of U.S. 6 and State 44. It was settled beginning in 1812 and named after **Peter Chardon Brooks,** who owned the area as early as 1808. Chardon was the county seat of **Geauga County** when the Church was centered in **Kirtland**.

Joseph Smith had at least two good reasons to visit Chardon. His sisters **Catherine** and **Sophronia** lived there, and Joseph faced several trials held at the county courthouse. Records show that the Prophet was involved in more than 20 legal proceedings.

Geauga County Courthouse, Chardon, OH, which is representative of the old Geauga County Courthouse, where the Prophet Joseph Smith attended several trials while the Church was centered in Kirtland.

On Mar. 31, 1834, Joseph Smith recorded in his diary, "This day came to Sharden [Chardon] to tend the Court against Doctor P. Hurlbut" (HC 2:49; PWJS 31), an apostate who gathered affidavits against the Prophet that were used by **Eber D. Howe** in the first published anti-Mormon book, *Mormonism Unvailed* (1834). After Hurlbut's four-day trial for threatening Joseph's life, the court ruled that Joseph "had ground[s] to fear that . . . Hurlbut would wound, beat or kill him, or destroy his property." Hurlbut was fined and sentenced to pay court costs (PWJS 31–32, 647n90; HC 2:46–49).

More frequently, Joseph was in court here as a defendant or as a witness for his friends. The Prophet was charged with all kinds of vexatious lawsuits, including the false charge of the attempted murder of **Grandison Newell** in June 1837, of which he was acquitted.

Joseph went to Chardon with his brother **Samuel** on Oct. 26, 1835, to answer charges that Samuel had not enrolled in the militia as stipulated under the Militia Act of 1792. Samuel legally claimed exemption as a minister of the gospel, but an inadequate lawyer and a prejudiced court fined him $20, forcing him to sell his cow to make payment (PWJS 65).

West and Southwest of Kirtland

■ MAYFIELD

Mayfield is located eight miles SW of Kirtland along the east side of Route 91, east of I-271, and south of U.S. 6.

In a Mr. Jackson's home at Mayfield on Sunday, Nov. 7, 1830, **Parley P. Pratt** gave a sermon on Christ's ministry and the **Book of Mormon**. He was followed by **Oliver Cowdery,** who testified that he was an eyewitness of the coming forth of the Book of Mormon. **Sidney Rigdon**, apparently speaking before he had been baptized, expressed doubt that he would preach again as a minister (LHJ 24–25). At the conclusion of the meeting, 30 people were baptized in a pool in a nearby river, and a thriving branch of the Church was established shortly thereafter (JJM 8; HR 42).

Under the direction of **Lyman Wight,** the branch made an unsuccessful attempt to have all things in common in the fall of 1830. **Levi Hancock**, who later became one of the presidents of the Seventy, was present while the elders preached. He asked for baptism shortly thereafter (LHJ 24–25).

A local attorney named **Varnum J. Card** told his friend, deputy sheriff **John Barr,** "'Mr. Barr, if you had not been there, I certainly should have gone into the water.' . . . The impulse was irresistible" (BYUS 11, no. 3 [1971]: 491–92).

Visitors can park at Rogers Field Road and enjoy viewing the site of the baptisms, which is just south of the new bridge on State 174. This site is in the Metropark (**North Chagrin Reservation**), a nice area for viewing wildlife and enjoying a picnic. Squire's Castle, which has beautiful picnic areas, is about one mile north on River Road.

■ ORANGE

Old Orange is 15 miles SW of Kirtland and about one mile NE of the present community of Orange. State highways 87 (Pinetree

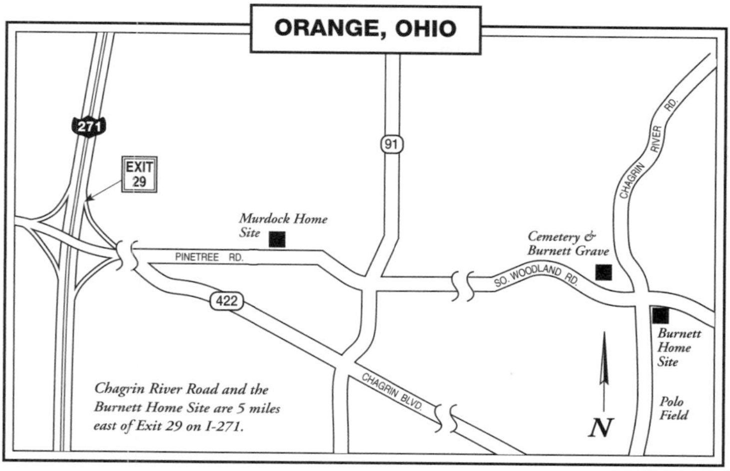

Road) and 91 intersect in the middle of Old Orange. Many joined the Church in this area. At least 65 members of the Church lived here by Nov. 1830, and one of the first four branches of the Church was organized in Orange/Warrensville (JJM 9; BiE 2:363; HR 42).

Orange was the home of **John Murdock**, one of the early pillars of the Church. His wife, **Julia Murdock**, apparently died at **Warrensville** on May 1, 1831, after giving birth to twins. Nine days later **Joseph** and **Emma Smith** adopted the twins, naming them **Joseph** and **Julia Smith** (HC 1:260; JJM 4). **John Murdock's home** no longer stands but was located two miles west of the **home** of **Serenus Burnett** (father of **Stephen Burnett)** on State 87 at about 32199 Pinetree Road.

Joseph Smith presided over a general conference Oct. 25–26, 1831, at the Burnett home on the SE corner of Chagrin River Road and State 87 (FWR 19–26). The original Burnett home stood on the site of the **clubhouse** overlooking the expansive Metropolitan Polo Field. "Much business was done" at the conference (HC 1:219), including the ordinations of 15 men to the **office of high priest** (FWR 25). This was the second group of high priests to be ordained. The first group was ordained at a conference in **Kirtland** that began June 3, 1831 (HC 1:175–76).

Twenty-four high priests—including those newly ordained at this conference—made a covenant to **consecrate** themselves to the Lord. **Joseph Smith** said "he had nothing to consecrate to the Lord of the things of the earth, yet he felt to consecrate himself and family" (FWR 22; HC 1:219–20, n. 1).

At the conference, the Prophet discussed **sealing people up to eternal life** (FWR 19–24; D&C 68:12). **Hyrum Smith** asked Joseph to relate the events of the coming forth of the **Book of Mormon** to all the elders, but **Joseph** said "it was not intended to tell the world all the particulars of the coming forth of the **Book of Mormon**; and also said that it was not expedient for him to relate these things" (HC 1:220; D&C 5:7). However, all **eleven witnesses** of the Book of Mormon, present at the conference, testified of its truthfulness (MS 26:835).

Serenus Burnet grave marker, Orange, OH. (1989)

Serenus Burnett's grave is located in a cemetery a few hundred yards west and a little north of the intersection near his home. Perhaps Julia Murdock, John's wife, was buried there also when she died after bearing twins.

■ WARRENSVILLE

Warrensville is 19 miles SW of Kirtland near the corner of U.S. 422 (Chagrin Boulevard) and Green Road. It is across I-271 and west of Orange. One of the first branches of the Church in Ohio was established here. **John Murdock**, who lived in nearby Orange, presided over this branch, which was one of the fastest growing in the Church. After his baptism in Nov. 1830, he wrote in his journal, "The **New York** brethren [missionaries to the **Lamanites**] held [a] meeting in **Warrensville**, four miles west of my house, . . . my wife, Brother Covey, and 3 others were baptized" (JJM 8).

Caleb Baldwin, cellmate of the **Prophet Joseph Smith** in Liberty Jail, also lived here. It was apparently in Caleb's home on Letchworth Road near the corner of Chagrin Boulevard and Green Road that **Julia Murdock** died just hours after giving birth to twins that were later adopted by **Joseph** and **Emma Smith**. **John** had left **Julia** and three children with the Baldwins while he served a mission.

Lyman Wight and **Frederick G. Williams** and their families also lived in **Warrensville**, having moved from there by 1830.

North Union Shaker settlement, now known as Shaker Heights, a suburb of Cleveland, OH. (Courtesy of LDSCA)

Shaker Heights (North Union)

Shaker Heights is 18 miles SW of Kirtland on the NE corner of Shaker Boulevard and Lee Road, west of I-271 along State 87. Today **Shaker Heights** is a suburb of **Cleveland**. From 1821–29 the area was known as the **North Union Colony of Shakers.**

The title "Shakers," like "Mormons," is a nickname. Shakers were known for clapping and dancing in regular beat to the music as a part of their worship services. The correct name of the organization is **United Society of Believers in Christ's Second Appearing.** Members of this society believed in modern revelation and "lived under a system of common ownership and use of property. Men and women slept in different dormitories, ate in a common dining room, worked on assigned tasks, and embraced the principle of celibacy" (HR 65).

Shakers performing a sacred dance, North Union (Shaker Heights), OH.

A gate marking the entrance to the Shaker meetinghouse site where Latter-day Saint missionaries visited in May 1831.

The **missionaries to the Lamanites** stayed at the colony for two nights in the fall of 1830. **Shaker** leader **Ashbel Kitchell** wrote in his journal that **Oliver Cowdery** visited his house, testified that he had seen an angel, and left seven copies of the **Book of Mormon** in hopes of converting the hospitable Shakers (BYUS 19, no. 4 [1979]: 95).

In accordance with a March 1831 revelation (D&C 49), **Sidney Rigdon**, **Parley P. Pratt**, and former Shaker **Leman Copley** served a brief mission among the Shakers in the spring of 1831. While there, Sidney read to them the revelation, which unequivocally denounced the basic doctrine of the Shakers. The Shakers did not accept the revelation.

After the Shakers rejected the gospel, **Leman Copley** lost his faith and broke his promise to the **Colesville** Saints who were living on his land. He was excommunicated in the summer of 1831 and rebaptized in 1836 (HC 2:433), but he remained in **Ohio** when the Saints left in 1838.

A gate and an old well set on a large grassy area located on the NE corner of Shaker Boulevard and Lee Road mark the location of the **meetinghouse** the missionaries visited. **Shaker** sites in the area include gate posts, a dam, a grove, a pond, and a museum.

■ CLEVELAND

Central **Cleveland**, situated on Lake Erie at the mouth of the Cuyahoga River, is about 20 miles SW of Kirtland on I-90. Although settlement began in **Cleveland** earlier than in **Kirtland**, the two villages were about the same size in 1830. Cleveland is frequently mentioned in the early journals as a stopping place along the road that ran SW from Kirtland.

In Aug. 1834, a plague of cholera broke out in Cleveland. Dr. **Frederick G. Williams**, a counselor in the **First Presidency** who practiced medicine, was sent to Cleveland by **Joseph Smith** to assist the afflicted (HC 2:146). The Prophet often traveled to Cleveland on business, and he probably visited newspapers, banks, and stores to buy merchandise. A bookbinder in Cleveland bound the first edition of the **Doctrine and Covenants** that was printed in Kirtland in 1835. **Cleveland** was also home to anti-Mormon sentiment and mob action. One early missionary reported, "We were abused and mistreated. Tar and feathers were prepared for our backs but the Lord delivered us" (BLAS 27).

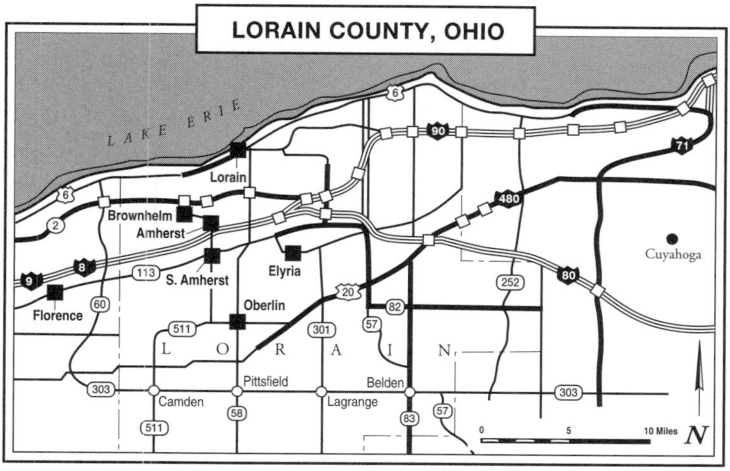

■ **LORAIN COUNTY—LORAIN, ELYRIA, FLORENCE, AND BROWNHELM**

Bridge over Vermilion River, near "old" Brownhelm, OH.

Lorain County was an important missionary area to the Latter-day Saints of the early 1830s. Significant events took place at many small communities (see map).

Lorain is located on the shores of Lake Erie on U.S. 6, about 30 miles west of the center of **Cleveland**. It is near the mouth of the Black River, where **Parley P. Pratt** and his wife, **Thankful Halsey,** arrived in **Ohio** after their marriage in 1827. They were on their way to their home in nearby **Amherst**.

Elyria, county seat of **Lorain County**, is located about seven miles south of **Lorain** on the south side of I-90. **Orson Hyde** was a Campbellite minister in **Elyria**, and he taught school and was a minister in **Florence**, located on State 113 about 15 miles west of **Elyria** (BYUS 11, no. 4 [1971]: 490).

Brownhelm is located about six miles SW of **Lorain,** on the north side of I-90. When he escaped from officer Elias Peabody and his bulldog, **Parley P. Pratt** crossed the bridge over the Vermilion

River at what is now Mill Hollow-Bacon Woods Memorial Park on Vermilion Road near "old" Brownhelm. Parley met the other **missionaries to the Lamanites** six miles west of the bridge (APPP 51).

Levi Hancock preached the gospel here in the spring of 1831 with great success. He baptized and confirmed 71 people (LHJ 30) and organized two branches of the Church in the area.

AMHERST (SOUTH AMHERST)

Amherst is in **Lorain County**, 50 miles SW of Kirtland on State 113, 30 miles SW of the center of **Cleveland,** and one mile south of the **Amherst** exit on I-90. The Amherst Town Square (now **South Amherst**) is near the intersection of State 113 and County 16.

The Amherst area was home to **Parley P. Pratt** and a fertile field for missionaries in the 1830s. At a conference here Jan. 25, 1832, "much harmony prevailed" and "considerable business was done to advance the kingdom, and promulgate the Gospel to the inhabitants of the surrounding country" (HC 1:242–43).

At the request of the elders at the conference, a revelation (D&C 75) was given invoking them to do missionary work. **William E. McLellin** was chastened for the murmurings of his heart, but the Lord forgave him and called him and **Luke Johnson** to go to the south countries to proclaim the gospel. Other

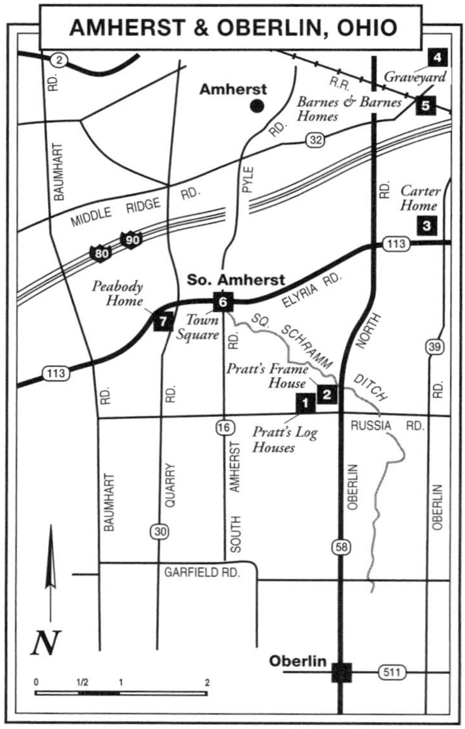

Parley P. Pratt had a home in the Amherst area of Ohio. (Courtesy of LDSCA)

missionaries were called, given instructions, and assigned to their fields of labor (D&C 75; HC 1:243–45).

At this same conference, the **Prophet Joseph Smith** was **sustained** as "**President of the office of the High Priesthood,**" which carries with it the office of **president of the whole Church** (D&C 107:91; HC 1:243). Sites of interest in the **Amherst** area include:

■ **1. Parley P. Pratt's Log Cabin Site.** The original **log cabin site** is .3 mile west of the intersection of State 58 and Russia Road. In 1826, **Parley P. Pratt** left **New York** and went to **Ohio** to spend his life "in the solitudes of the great West, among the natives of the forest [Indians]" (APPP 27). He built a small log cabin and lived alone during the winter of 1826–27, spending much of his time reading books, especially the Bible.

Parley P. Pratt's 1826–27 log cabin site. The brook is in the weeds on the left.

In the spring of 1827, 27-year-old Parley cleared land and commenced to build a new house. He then decided to return to Canaan, NY, and court his sweetheart, Thankful Halsey. After the couple's marriage Sept. 9, 1827, he returned with Thankful to the Amherst area. When **Parley** built a **small frame house** in 1828, Thankful used the log house as a **schoolhouse,** where she taught about 20 students (APPP 28–31).

■ **2. Parley P. Pratt's Small Frame House of 1828.** In the spring of 1828, **Parley** and **Thankful Pratt** were living in a **small frame house** that was located on State 58, a few hundred feet north of the NW corner of the intersection of State 58 and Russia Road. At this time in the area, **Sidney Rigdon** began preaching a **Reformed Baptist** doctrine, which Parley began following (APPP 31–32).

In Aug. 1830, Parley and Thankful left their small frame house, never to see it again. Parley's purpose in going east was "to devote [his] time in enlightening [his] fellow men" on the truths he had learned from the scriptures (APPP 33, 35). On the way, he stopped at **Newark, NY,** where he felt prompted to get off the Erie Canal riverboat. The stop led to his reading a copy of the newly published **Book of Mormon**, which in turn led to his baptism into the Church.

In Oct. 1830, Parley was called by revelation (D&C 32) to accompany **Oliver Cowdery**, **Peter Whitmer Jr.**, and **Ziba Peterson** on a **mission to the Lamanites** in the West. As the missionaries journeyed toward **Missouri**, they decided to take the recently restored gospel to Parley P. Pratt's friend, **Sidney Rigdon**, a minister who was then preaching in **Mentor, Ohio**. As a result of their missionary labors in Ohio, Sidney, along with more than 100 of his followers, joined the Church. By the spring of 1831, approximately 200 Latter-day Saint converts lived in northeast Ohio.

■ **3. Simeon Carter Home.** The **home** of **Simeon Carter** still stands as a private residence east of State 58 on State 113 (45640 Telegraph Road). **Oliver Cowdery**, **Parley P. Pratt**, **Ziba Peterson**, **Peter Whitmer Jr.**, and **Frederick G. Williams**, missionaries to the **Lamanites**, stayed in this home for a night as they passed through the **Amherst** area of **Ohio** in the fall of 1830 (APPP 48). While explaining the **Book of Mormon** to non-Mormon **Simeon Carter**, **Parley P. Pratt** was arrested on a "frivolous charge" (APPP 48). Parley left the Book of Mormon with Simeon and went with a magistrate two miles to face trial. The judge was abusive as he tantalized Parley and then sent him to a public house, the prison being some miles distant. The next morning, Parley made a miraculous escape (APPP 48–51). (See Amherst Town Square, Site No. 6, for an account of the escape.)

Simeon Carter read the Book of Mormon, was converted, and joined the Church. Because of the preaching of Parley and Simeon, a branch of about 60 members was established here (APPP 51).

■ **4. Graves of Ezekial and Fanny Barnes. Ezekial** and **Fanny Barnes** are buried in a graveyard at the corner of Middle Ridge Road No. 32 and Oberlin Road next to what was an old church. They were the parents of **Amanda Barnes Smith**, whose husband, **Warren Smith,** and son **Sardius Smith**, age 10, were slain in the **Haun's Mill Massacre** in **Caldwell County, MO,** on Oct. 30, 1839. Another son, Alma, was seriously wounded but was miraculously healed (HC 3:185, 323–25). Ezekial and Fanny probably never joined the Church.

Gravestone of Ezekial and Fanny Barnes, Amherst, OH. (1989)

■ **5. Barnes Family Homes.** The **home sites** of **Ezekial Barnes** and **Royal Barnes** are located on the south side of Middle Ridge Road and east of State 58. Ezekial's home was on the north side of the railroad tracks, and Royal Barnes's home was on the south side of the tracks.

■ **6. Amherst Town Square (South Amherst). Amherst Town Square** is located near the intersection of State 113 and County 16. It is on the SW corner of State 113 and Pyle-South Amherst Road near the fire station.

After Elias Peabody, the officer who arrested Parley P. Pratt, took him to breakfast, the two walked into the town square. Here Parley challenged the officer to a race. Peabody admitted he was not good at racing but indicated his big dog, Stu-boy, would "take

Amherst Town Square.

Parley P. Pratt with the bulldog Stu-boy chasing him at Amherst, OH. (Illustration by Vernon Murdock, 1973; courtesy of Vernon Murdock)

any man down at my bidding." Parley thanked the officer for his courtesy but explained that as a missionary he had no time to spare. Parley described the humorous race that followed:

> I then started on my journey, while he stood amazed and not able to step one foot before the other. Seeing this, I halted, turned to him and again invited him to a race. He still stood amazed. I then renewed my exertions, and soon increased my speed to something like that of a deer. He did not awake from his astonishment sufficiently to start in pursuit till I had gained, perhaps, two hundred yards. I had already leaped a fence, and was making my way through a field to the forest on the right of the road. He now came hallooing after me, and shouting to his dog to seize me. The dog, being one of the largest I ever saw, came close on my footsteps with all his fury; the officer behind still in pursuit, clapping his hands and hallooing, "stu-boy, stu-boy—take him—watch—lay hold of him, I say—down with him," and pointing his finger in the direction I was running. The dog was fast overtaking me, and in the act of leaping upon me, when, quick as lightning, the thought struck me, to assist the officer, in sending the dog with all fury to the forest a little distance before me. I pointed my finger in that direction,

clapped my hands, and shouted in imitation of the officer. The dog hastened past me with redoubled speed towards the forest; being urged by the officer and myself, and both of us running in the same direction.

Gaining the forest, I soon lost sight of the officer and dog, and have not seen them since (APPP 50–51).

■ **7. Elias Peabody Home.** The **home site** of **Elias Peabody** and his bulldog, **Stu-boy,** is 48238 Telegraph Road. The missionaries to the **Lamanites** were the first missionaries in the **Amherst** area but not the last. A number of prominent missionaries labored here, including **Thomas B. Marsh, Reynolds Cahoon, Levi Hancock,** and **Gideon, Jared,** and **Simeon Carter.**

■ Oberlin

Oberlin is 50 miles SW of Kirtland on state highways 511 and 58, between I-80 and U.S. 20, just south of **Amherst**. The community and the widely respected **Oberlin College** were established by **Presbyterian** ministers who wanted to found a Christian school where men and women would have an equal opportunity for learning. The town was named after **John F. Oberlin**, a German pastor.

The ministers drew up the "Oberlin Covenant" in Apr. 1833 for all who were willing to live in the communal order. They were to dedicate their lives to God. The community owned the land, but commune members could have as much land as they could care for. They ate plain and wholesome foods, and they used no tobacco, tea, coffee, or alcohol. They dressed modestly and took care of their widows.

The infamous **Spaulding Manuscript** is located in the college library archives. It is a fictional, romantic narrative about a group of Roman explorers blown off course while sailing to England in the fourth century A.D. Purporting to be the journal of one of the group's

Oberlin College library, Oberlin, OH. (1980)

members, it tells of the explorers' eventual arrival in North America.

Because the manuscript tells of the dealings of the Romans with the American Indians, apostate **Philastus Hurlbut** claimed that **Joseph Smith** had used it as the "original source document for the **Book of Mormon**" (EnM 3:1402). Some people accepted this theory after the publication of ***Mormonism Unvailed*** in 1839. The original Spaulding Manuscript was rediscovered in 1884 by L. L. Rice and given to Oberlin College president **James H. Fairchild.**

In 1885, both the **LDS** and the **RLDS** Churches published the manuscript to disprove the theory that it was the source document for the Book of Mormon. Additionally, Fairchild, Rice and others carefully compared the manuscript with the Book of Mormon and formally stated that there was no legitimacy to Hurlbut's claim (NWG 3:376; SMPM 20–21).

It was also at **Oberlin College** that **Lorenzo Snow** studied (HC 4:162). He was not deeply religious at the time, and while at Oberlin he became dissatisfied with the theology he was taught. "If there is nothing better than is to be found here in Oberlin College," he said, "good bye to all religions" (BLS 5). Lorenzo's experience at Oberlin prepared him to accept the invitation of his sister **Eliza** to come to **Kirtland** and study under **Hebrew** scholar **Joshua Seixas**. While in Kirtland, Lorenzo met several times with the **Prophet Joseph Smith** and soon joined the Church (BLS 6).

■ Tiffin

Tiffin is 40 miles SE of Toledo and 68 miles north of Columbus at state highways 231 and 53.

After **Oliver Cowdery** was excommunicated from the Church in 1838, he and his family moved to Tiffin in 1840 and lived there until 1847. Their stay in Tiffin is significant because **Oliver Cowdery**—a man in a position to expose **Joseph Smith**, had the Prophet been a fraud—remained true to his testimony even though he was out of harmony with the Church.

Oliver Cowdery lived at Tiffin, OH, 1840–47. (Courtesy of LDSCA)

Oliver and **Elizabeth Cowdery** were active in the **Methodist Protestant Church,** Oliver serving as the church secretary in 1843. The church they attended at 44 South Monroe Street is now a private residence.

Oliver **practiced law** in Tiffin, and according to local tradition his law office was in the old courthouse that stood on the same site as the current courthouse. Apparently he also had an office at 104–106 E. Market Street. Oliver was also **active in politics.** When publication of a newspaper began in Tiffin in preparation for the presidential election of 1840, "Oliver Cowdery was to have been editor, but was dropped on the discovery that he was one of the seven founders of Mormonism" (IBMW 40). Such discrimination forced Oliver to make a decision about his **testimony of the Book of Mormon**. He concluded that he would be true to his testimony, which he often bore in public and in private.

Despite career setbacks caused by his association with the restored Church, Oliver Cowdery was highly esteemed. One of Oliver's law students, **William Lang,** went on to become a prominent Tiffin attorney. He wrote, "Mr. Cowdery was an able lawyer. . . . His manners were easy and gentlemanly; he was polite, dignified, yet courteous." Lang added, "With all his kind and friendly disposition, there was a certain degree of sadness that seemed to pervade his whole being." He concluded that Oliver "was modest and reserved, never spoke ill of any one, never complained" (IBMW 41).

William Harvey Gibson, a Civil War general whose statue stands in front of the Seneca County Courthouse, was "Tiffin's most famous citizen." He called Oliver Cowdery an "able lawyer and [an] agreeable, irreproachable gentleman" (IBMW 42).

Oliver Cowdery corresponded with **Brigham Young** from Tiffin, offering his advice on political matters and his services as an agent to President James Polk. Oliver left Tiffin in 1847 and was rebaptized Nov. 12, 1848, at Mosquito Creek, Iowa. On Oct. 21, shortly before his baptism, he spoke at a special conference:

> I wrote, with my own pen, the entire **Book of Mormon** (save a few pages) as it fell from the lips of the **Prophet Joseph**, as he translated it by the gift and power of **God**, by the means of the Urim and Thumim, or, as it is called by the book, Holy Interpreters. I beheld with my eyes, and handled with my hands, the gold plates from which it was transcribed. I also saw

> with my eyes and handled with my hands the Holy Interpreters. That book is true. **Sidney Rigdon** did not write it. **Mr. Spaulding** did not write it. I wrote it myself as it fell from the lips of the Prophet. It contains the everlasting gospel, and came forth to the children of men in fulfillment of the revelations of **John**, where he says he saw an angel come with the everlasting gospel to preach to every nation, kindred, tongue and people (*Rev.* xiv). It contains principles of salvation; and if you, my hearers, will walk by its light and obey its precepts, you will be saved with an everlasting salvation in the **kingdom of God** on high (CHC 1:139–40).

From that time until his death Mar. 3, 1850, **Oliver Cowdery** lived in **Richmond, MO,** with his relatives the Whitmers because of poor health (IBMW 45–46). His grave is somewhere in the small pioneer cemetery in **Richmond**, where a large monument has been erected in remembrance of the Three Witnesses of the **Book of Mormon**.

■ Little Sandusky

Little Sandusky is 45 miles north of Columbus, immediately west of I-23 on State 294. The missionaries to the **Lamanites** met the **Wyandot Indians** in this area and preached the gospel to them. **Parley P. Pratt** recorded that the missionaries were "well received" by the Indians, among whom they stayed for several days. He added that the Indians "rejoiced" in hearing of their ancestors from the **Book of Mormon**. As the missionaries continued their journey, the Indians asked them to stay in contact and tell them of their success among other tribes in the West (APPP 51; HC 1:183).

■ New Portage

New Portage was located about 42 miles SW of Kirtland in the SW corner of greater Akron. It is immediately south of I-76, which is on the SW edge of Akron. In the 1830s, New Portage consisted of the area now known as Barberton. Many of the foremost missionaries of the Church preached here, and by 1831 a branch had been established. At times the New Portage Branch was one of the largest in the Church, and as such it received much attention from Church leaders.

Joseph Smith attended at least **seven conferences** of the Church here. During the winter of 1834–35, after participating in **Zion's Camp**, **Parley P. Pratt** moved to New Portage (APPP 117). In 1835, the Saints here began migrating to **Clay County**, **MO.** By 1837, the New Portage Branch had dwindled to only 20 active members (EJ 1 [Oct. 1837]: 15).

At the Feb. 9, 1834, conference, **Joseph Smith** admonished the members in New Portage to "erect only a temporary or cheap place for meeting" so they could consecrate their resources to help build the **Kirtland Temple** (HC 2:25).

New Portage was also designated as the **gathering** and **starting** place of Joseph Smith's division of **Zion's Camp**. On May 1, 1834, volunteers began to gather here, and by May 7 an army of about 130 men was formally organized into companies and began to march toward **Missouri** the following day (HC 2:61, 64). **Kirtland Camp** also passed through here July 11, 1838 (HC 3:104). New Portage was a stopover for many Church members traveling west.

In 1838, during a period of apostasy at Kirtland, Church leaders were forced to abandon Church headquarters in Ohio and flee to Missouri. **Joseph Smith** and **Sidney Rigdon** left **Kirtland** on horseback Jan. 12, 1838, to escape mob violence. They reached New Portage the next morning and remained there until their families arrived from Kirtland 36 hours later. From New Portage, they traveled to **Far West**, **MO** (HC 3:1–3, 8–9). During the next few days and months, New Portage was a place of refuge for the Smith family. **Joseph Smith Sr.** moved here for safety soon after the Prophet's flight. He escaped from Kirtland after being arrested because he performed a marriage without obtaining a license. **Father Smith** was aided in his flight by his son **Hyrum**, **John Boynton,** and **Luke Johnson.** Another son, **Don Carlos Smith**, and his family lived in New Portage in 1838. In May, **Lucy Mack Smith** and several other family members left New Portage for **Missouri** with a company of Saints (HR 345–46).

■ CINCINNATI

Cincinnati was a principal city of Ohio during the 1830s. **Elias Higbee,** Church recorder from 1838 to 1843, came here in about 1817 with his new bride, Sarah Wood. He received the gospel in 1832.

The missionaries to the Lamanites, **Elders Oliver Cowdery,**

Peter Whitmer Jr., Ziba Peterson, and **Parley P. Pratt,** spent several days preaching in Cincinatti with little success. They were on their way from Kirtland to Missouri (APPP 51). In late June 1831, **Joseph Smith** came to Cincinnati on his way to Missouri, visiting with Walter Scott of the Campbellite faith while here (HC 1:88).

William W. Phelps purchased a press and type here to use in publishing the Church's first periodical, *The Evening and the Morning Star,* which was published in Independence, MO, beginning in June 1832 (HC 1:266).

In 1833, **Lyman Wight** delivered a series of lectures in the local courthouse, then baptized nearly 100 persons who made up the first branch of the Church in Cincinnati. The Elias Higbee family was among the first baptized.

In 1840, another branch of the Church was established by **Elders Orson Hyde** and **John E. Page,** and the **third edition** of the **Book of Mormon** was printed here by Robinson and Smith and stereotyped by Shepard and Stearns in 1840 (T&S 9:9). Elder Hyde left from here for **Jerusalem** to **dedicate the Holy Land** for the return of the Jews, while Elder Page remained behind.

Lyman Wight, Heber C. Kimball, and **Brigham Young** held a **conference** with the elders in Cincinnati on May 27, 1844, while Joseph Smith was running for the presidency of the United States. **Amasa Lyman,** a member of the Quorum of the Twelve, was here when he received news of the Prophet's martyrdom (BiE 1:99).

Zion's Camp, Ohio

1834

Kirtland Camp, Ohio

1838

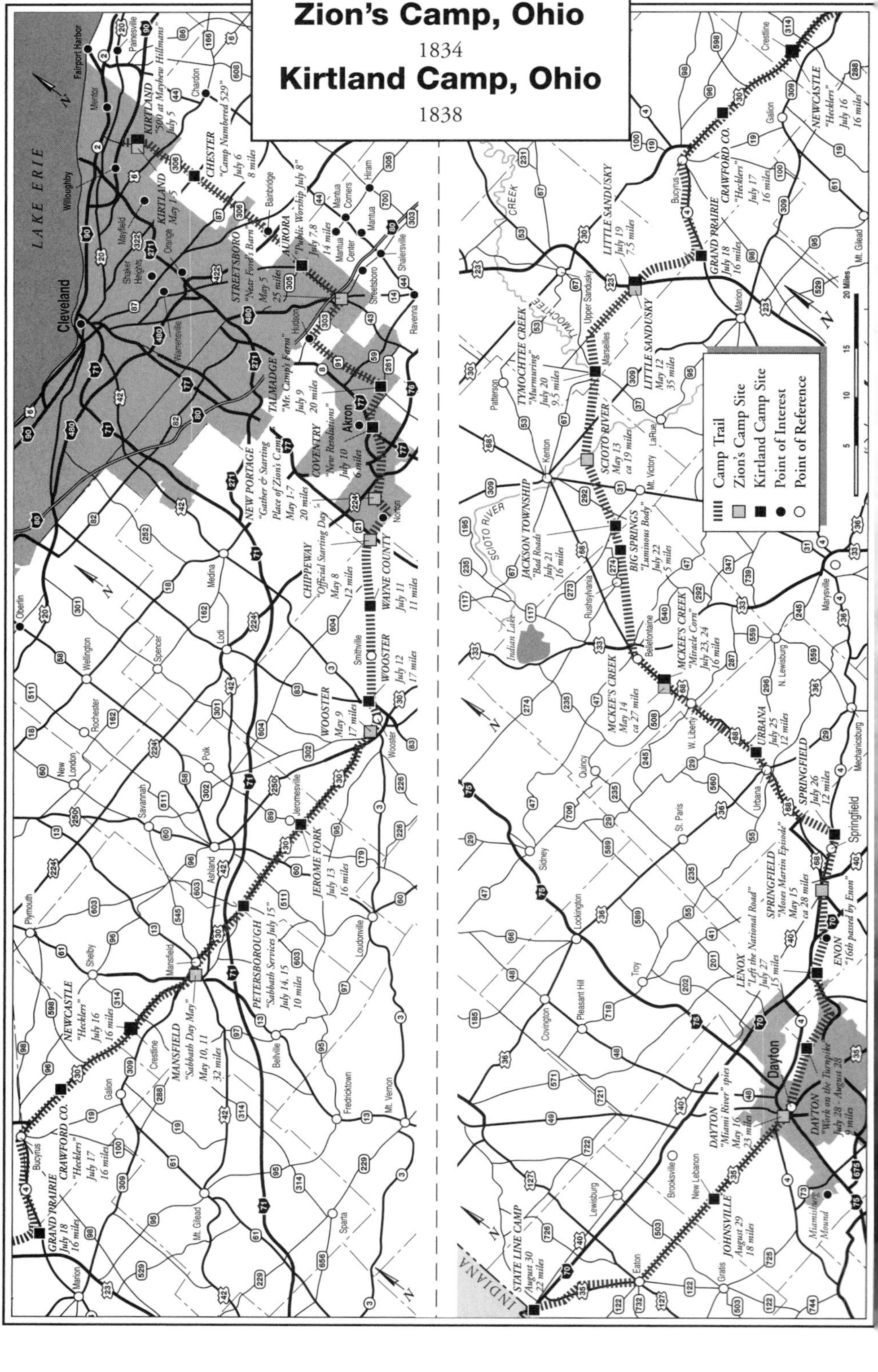

Zion's Camp and Kirtland Camp in Ohio and Indiana—1834 and 1838

LaMar C. Berrett and Keith W. Perkins

Joseph Smith's Division of Zion's Camp in Ohio—1834

During the spring and summer of 1834, **Joseph Smith** and **Hyrum Smith** led about 200 men to **Missouri** to reinstate the Saints onto their **Jackson County** lands, from which they had been driven by Missouri mobs in 1833.

> Peace officers, militia leaders, ministers, and merchants joined the mobs. They broke into homes, whipped men and threatened women, destroyed the Mormon press, and tarred and feathered Latter-day Saint leaders. The Saints fled in all directions, most of them crossing the **Missouri River** into **Clay County** (BYUS 1, no. 4 [1960]: 11).

When Joseph received word of the abuse the Saints had received in **Jackson County**, he counseled the **Missouri** Saints to pursue justice through legal channels. He received a revelation that said, "It is my will that they should continue to importune for redress, and redemption, by the hands of those who are placed as rulers and are in authority over you—according to the laws and constitution of the people" (D&C 101:76–77).

When appeals to Missouri leaders, including Governor Daniel Dunklin, failed to bring relief, the Lord revealed to Joseph that he should "go and gather together the residue of my servants, and take all the strength of mine house . . . and go ye straightway unto the land of my vineyard [**Jackson County**], and redeem my vineyard; for it is mine; I have bought it with money" (D&C 101:55–56).

The result was **Zion's Camp**, a militia unit made up of about 150 men from the East under the command of the Prophet, and about 45 men from the Pontiac, Michigan, area under the direction of **Hyrum Smith**. Members of Zion's Camp assembled to take material aid to their Missouri brothers and sisters, and to regain their stolen possessions in Jackson County—by force if necessary.

As the small army proceeded on its divinely mandated march, camp members followed a strict regimen that was centered on their faith in God:

> Every night before retiring to rest, at the sound of the trumpet, we bowed before the Lord in the several tents, and presented our thank-offerings with prayer and supplication; and at the sound of the morning trumpet, about four o'clock, every man was again on his knees before the Lord, imploring His blessing for the day (HC 2:64–65).

Except for traveling a few miles of the National Road (U.S. 40), which was under construction in 1834, **Zion's Camp** followed old roads and trails through **Ohio**. A summary of dates, campsites, and activities of Zion's Camp on its march through Ohio follows:

Camp	**Date (1834)**	**Miles (approximate)**
■ **Kirtland**	**May 1–5**	**25**

More than 20 brethren of Zion's Camp left Kirtland May 1, 1834, to go to New Portage, where the camp's organization was to take place. More than 100 additional members of Zion's Camp left Kirtland May 5 and arrived in New Portage May 6 after spending the night of the 5th in Streetsboro (HC 2:63).

■ **Streetsboro**	**May 5**	**0**

Zion's Camp stayed in Streetsboro on the first night of its journey. "This day we went as far as the town of Streetsborough [Streetsboro] . . . ," wrote the Prophet Joseph Smith. "We stayed in

Mr. Ford's barn, where Uncle **John Smith** and **Brigham Young** had been preaching three months before" (HC 2:63).

■ New Portage (Barberton) May 1–7 46

The Zion's Camp campground was about 46 miles SW of Kirtland in the area immediately south of I-76, on the SW edge of Akron. It was the **gathering** and **starting place** of Zion's Camp. By May 7, about 150 men were formally organized here into companies of 12 and, with 20 baggage wagons, were ready to march approximately 280 miles across Ohio on their way to **Missouri**. The Prophet instructed the officers that when the trumpet blew night and morning, every man was to kneel and pray (HC 2:64–65; T&S 6:1074–75).

■ Chippewa Creek May 8 12

The camp left New Portage going SW toward the National Road (U.S. 40), which I-70 essentially follows. Zion's Camp would first come to the National Road at Springfield, Ohio, but not follow it until reaching **Richmond, Indiana**. The camp would travel on it for about 100 miles to a point 30 miles SW of Indianapolis.

On May 8, camp members traveled 12 miles to Chippewa, where they camped on the banks of the Chippewa Creek in a beautiful grove of trees. The camp was about 3½ miles SW of Easton on State 585 (HC 2:65).

■ Wooster May 9 17

This camp was located in the SW corner of Wooster on Killbuck Creek on State 302, one mile west of Wooster on State 302. It is about 30 miles SW of the heart of Akron. The brethren completed the organization of the camp into companies of 12 this day (HC 2:65).

■ Mansfield (Richfield Township) May 10, 11 32

This camp was probably located about two miles west of the Mansfield city center. It had been following what became the Lincoln Highway (U.S. 30 of today), and the camp was near U.S.

30. The camp stayed here for the Sabbath on May 11. **Sylvester Smith** preached, and the sacrament was administered (HC 2:65).

■ **LITTLE SANDUSKY** **MAY 12** **35**

This camp was about 13 miles SW of Bucyrus and about where U.S. 23 crosses over State 294. Zion's Camp passed through Bucyrus during the day (HC 2:65).

■ **SCIOTO RIVER** **MAY 13** **19**

The campground was on the banks of the Scioto River, five miles NE of LaRue, close to Hepburn, and 24 miles NE of Bellefontaine. The camp was hampered by bad roads. "In many instances," ropes had to be fastened to wagons to pull them from sloughs and mud holes (HC 2:65).

■ **MCKEE'S CREEK** **MAY 14** **27**

Zion's Camp spent the night of May 14 by McKee's Creek, about three miles south of the center of **Bellefontaine,** the center of which is at the intersection of State 47 and 68. Here **Sylvester Smith** first showed "refractory feelings." He was evidently upset because the camp was "short of bread" (HC 2:65–66).

■ **SPRINGFIELD** **MAY 15** **28**

Zion's Camp camped on the west bank of the Mad River, three miles west of the Springfield city center, about where southbound U.S. 68 branches off I-70. It is 45 miles west of the center of Columbus, Ohio.

Eighteen-year-old **Jedediah M. Grant** got lost while hunting away from the camp, but he found the camp after having a vision of its location (ZCB 51–52). During the night, 20-year-old **Moses Martin** fell asleep on sentry duty. **Joseph Smith** "took his sword, and left him asleep" (HC 2:66).

■ **ENON** **MAY 16** **7**

On the morning of May 16, **Joseph's division of Zion's Camp** had a **unique experience** at Enon, located 15 miles NE of the

Enon Mound at Enon, OH. (1989)

center of Dayton and two–three blocks south of I-70 (Enon Road exit).

At about 9 A.M., the camp passed "a piece of thick woods of recent growth," where **Joseph Smith** said he "felt much depressed in spirit and lonesome, and that there had been a great deal of bloodshed in that place." He went on to explain that "whenever a man of God is in a place where many have been killed, he will feel lonesome and unpleasant, and his spirits will sink" (HC 2:66). After the camp traveled about 40 rods farther, it came upon a **mound** that camp members thought contained human bones. This mound was undoubtedly the **Enon Mound.** It is 40 feet tall and 574 feet in circumference, its base covering more than one acre. It is the second largest conical mound in Ohio and is estimated to have been built by Indians between 1200 B.C. and 800 A.D.

■ DAYTON (MIAMI RIVER) MAY 16 23

Zion's Camp camped on the west bank of the Miami River near I-75, about 1.5 miles west of Dayton's city center. After the unusual experience at Enon earlier this day, the camp passed through **Dayton,** where local residents met them with great curiosity. "Some of the inhabitants inquired of the company where they were from, when Captain [**Brigham**] **Young** replied: 'From every place but this, and we will soon be from this.' 'Where are you going?'" the curious would then ask. "To the West," was the usual answer (HC 2:67).

Wilford Woodruff remembered that **spies** followed the camp to find out the "object of their mission." Camp members kept their numbers, leaders, and destination a secret. In the evening a court-martial was held for **Moses Martin** because he fell asleep on sentry duty. He was acquitted but was warned (HC 2:67–68). On the west side of Dayton, the camp forded the Miami River and camped (T&S 6:1075).

Dayton is where **William W. Phelps** lived while he was out of the Church from 1839 to 1841. In 1841, he repented and wrote a letter to **Joseph Smith,** asking for forgiveness. The Prophet replied, "Believing . . . your repentance genuine, I shall be happy once again to give you the right hand of fellowship, and rejoice over the returning prodigal. . . . 'Come on, dear brother, since the war is past, For friends at first, are friends again at last'" (HC 4:163–64). Thereafter, William remained faithful in **Nauvoo** and Utah.

The Wright-Patterson Air Force Base, located just east of Dayton at Fairborn on State 444, houses an excellent Air Force museum. Admission is free.

Joseph Smith's Division of Zion's Camp in Indiana—1834

CAMP	**DATE (1834)**	**MILES (APPROXIMATE)**
■ **RICHMOND (OHIO-INDIANA BORDER)**	**MAY 17–18**	**34**

This campground was on the National Road (U.S. 40) just over the border into **Indiana** and four miles east of the center of **Richmond** (near present-day I-70). On May 17, Zion's Camp members suffered from sore feet after traveling 34 miles. "Our feet were very sore and blistered, our stockings wet with blood," wrote **Heber C. Kimball** (LHCK 42). It was evident that the difficult conditions affected some members of the camp. **Joseph Smith** found that **Sylvester Smith** had a "rebellious spirit," as did some other camp members (HC 2:68–69; ZCB 62–63; LHJ 53).

At this campground **Joseph prophesied** that Zion's Camp would "meet with misfortunes, difficulties and hindrances, and said 'and you will know it before you leave this place.'" When they awoke the next morning, they found that nearly every horse in camp was sick. After the brethren humbled themselves through faith and prayers, all their horses were restored to health except Sylvester Smith's, which died (HC 2:68–69). That evening, **George A. Smith** obtained buttermilk from a nearby farmer and shared it with the brethren (JGAS 115). The next day, the Sabbath, a sacrament meeting was held in the same camp (HC 2:69).

■ **LEWISVILLE (FRANKLIN TOWNSHIP) — MAY 19 — 31**

This camp was on the west side of Flatrock River, ½ mile west of Lewisville on the National Road (U.S. 40). Starting at **Richmond**, Zion's Camp followed the National Road for the first time, generally staying on it in Indiana until leaving it at a point 30 miles SW of the center of Indianapolis.

■ **SUGAR CREEK (PHILADELPHIA) — MAY 20 — 25**

Zion's Camp camped four miles west of the center of **Greenfield** on Sugar Creek and U.S. 40. During this day's travels, the camp battled muddy roads. **Moses Martin** "saw the Prophet wade in mud over the tops of his bootlegs and helped draw the wagons out" (ZCB 68). In the evening, three strangers who were spies visited the camp. Camp members answered their questions in vague terms (HC 2:69).

■ **INDIANAPOLIS — MAY 21 — 25**

The brethren set up camp near the western boundary of Indianapolis, near present-day **Bridgeport** on U.S. 40. I-65, I-70, and I-74 converge on Indianapolis, the largest city in **Indiana.**

As camp members approached Indianapolis, they received word that they were suspected of being an armed and dangerous force and would not be allowed to pass through the city. Joseph told the brethren "in the name of the Lord [that] we should not be disturbed and that we would pass through Indianapolis without the people knowing it" (HC 2:70). Camp members scattered throughout the city and passed through unmolested (HC 2:70; ZCB 69).

■ **BELLEVILLE** **MAY 22** **11**

The camp was on "a small stream of water in a grove near Belleville" (HC 2:70), which is 20 miles SW of the center of Indianapolis on U.S. 40, and about ½ mile SW of Belleville.

■ **GREENCASTLE** **MAY 23** **24**
(PROBABLY ON BIG WALNUT CREEK)

Greencastle is 40 miles west of Indianapolis at the intersection of U.S. 231 and State 240. Zion's Camp stayed four miles west of Greencastle (probably on Big Walnut Creek). The camp had left the National Road 10 miles SW of Belleville and went nearly directly west through Greencastle, Mansfield, and Clinton before camping near Blanford. The change in geography from flat plains to rolling hills and marshy bottoms made for a "hard drive" this day (HC 2:70).

■ **BLANFORD** **MAY 24–25** **35**

The Zion's Camp campground this day was in **Illinois**, ½ mile SW of Blanford, Indiana, just west of the Illinois-Indiana border. The camp reached the Wabash River around noon. The river was not fordable, so ferryboats had to be rented in nearby Clinton, Indiana.

While some members waited their turn to cross the river, **Joseph Smith** instructed them in proper prayer. He counseled them that "when we kneel to pray we should be in a graceful position," a position that would not seem irreverent to "any spectator" (ZCB 81).

Kirtland Camp in Ohio—1838

On Mar. 6, 1838, leaders of the Seventies who had met to formulate a plan to help the poor to leave Kirtland met in the **Kirtland Temple** and expressed a desire to join the Saints who had already settled in northwestern **Missouri**. After much discussion, the Spirit of the Lord manifested that the Saints should travel together as a body known as **Kirtland Camp**.

Camp members continued to meet together often in preparation for their July 6 departure. A **constitution** was drafted that outlined the rules and laws for the organization and government of the camp. **Daniel S. Miles** and **Levi Hancock** were already in the West, so **Elias Smith** and **Benjamin S. Wilber** were called as councilors. **Elias** and **Samuel D. Tyler** kept daily journals. Monies for the camp were to be controlled by the councilors, and the Word of Wisdom was to be strictly obeyed, along with all the commandments.

Obstacles posed by extreme poverty, apostates, and the organization of such a large body of people led **Oliver Granger** to predict that **Kirtland Camp** would be "the greatest thing ever accomplished since the organization of the Church or even since the exodus of Israel from Egypt" (HC 3:96).

On July 5, 1838, the camp commenced organizing on a piece of land behind a house formerly occupied by **Mayhew Hillman,** about 100 rods (.3 of a mile) south of the **Kirtland Temple,** where the **Kirtland High School** stands. The group left Kirtland about noon on July 6 with 529 members representing 105 families. During the entire 650-mile exodus, camp numbers varied between 500 and 600 people. They stopped in Springville, where they worked on the Springville-Dayton Turnpike for a month, and did not arrive in **Far West**, **MO,** until Oct 2. They arrived at their final destination, Adam-Ondi-Ahman, on Oct 4. Less than half the camp settled in Adam-Ondi-Ahman; the rest settled at other locations in Caldwell and Daviess Counties (HC 3:87–148). Maps show the route and campsites of Kirtland Camp, and a summary of dates, campsites, and activities of the camp on its march through Ohio follows:

Camp	**Date (1838)**	**Miles (approximate)**
■ **Kirtland**	**July 5**	**0**

Kirtland Camp met south of the temple, where 400–500 people stayed in tents for the night. Cloud cover kept the Saints from the "scorching rays of the sun" until evening, when the horizon was opened to their view, and "everything seemed to indicate that the

God of heaven has His all-searching eye upon the camp of the Saints, and had prepared the day for the express purpose of organizing the camp" (HC 3:99).

■ **CHESTER (NOW CHESTERLAND)** **JULY 6** **8**

Kirtland Camp left Kirtland at noon on July 6 and traveled eight miles to Chester, located south of Kirtland at the crossroads of state highways 306 and 322. Upon arriving in Chester, the camp numbered 529 members(HC 3:100).

■ **AURORA** **JULY 7–8** **14**

This campground was 21 miles south of Kirtland at the intersection of state highways 43 and 82. Several children became "dangerously" sick during the day (HC 3:101). July 8 was the first Sunday for Kirtland Camp, so members held a **public worship,** a practice they continued throughout their journey. In the evening, camp members met together and **renewed their covenant** to "observe the laws of the camp and the commandments of the Lord" (HC 3:101).

■ **TALMADGE (TALLMADGE)** **JULY 9** **20**

The camp was 20 miles SSW of Aurora, near State 91, and immediately north of I-76. This area is now a part of Greater Akron. Kirtland Camp traveled through Aurora, Streetsboro, Hudson, and Stowe Corners, and then stayed on Mr. Camp's farm in Talmadge (HC 3:102).

■ **COVENTRY** **JULY 10** **6**

The camp was one mile SE of the center of Akron about where I-77 is now located. After traveling through Talmadge and Middleburg, camp members camped at Coventry. Here they adopted a new set of **resolutions** concerning the organization of the camp (HC 3:102–103). The next morning, a six-month-old son of Brother and Sister Wilbur was buried on Israel Allen's farm (HC 3:104).

■ **WAYNE COUNTY** **JULY 11** **11**

The camp passed through New Portage (Barberton), camping about four miles from the town on the farm of Mr. Bockman of Chippewa Township, Wayne County (HC 3:104).

■ **WOOSTER** **JULY 12** **17**

The camp this day was two miles NE of the center of Wooster. The center of Wooster is 27 miles SW of the heart of Akron and one mile NW of the intersection of State 83 and U.S. 30.

After passing through Doylestown, Milton, Greene, and Wayne Townships, the camp stopped for the night. Brother Hammond's wagon broke down for the third time, and he was advised to go to New Portage to get another one. **Nathan Baldwin** and **Henry Harriman** both fell behind because of broken wagon wheels (HC 104–05).

■ **JEROME FORK IN MOHICAN TOWNSHIP** **JULY 13** **16**

The July 13 campground was 13 miles west of the center of Wooster, where U.S. 30 crosses the Jerome Fork stream. The camp traveled through Wooster in **Wayne County,** took the road to Mansfield, passed through Jefferson and Reedsborough, and camped on **William Crothers' farm**. Local settlers taunted camp members concerning their belief in the "fallacy" of "Jo Smith's" prophecies (HC 3:105–06).

■ **PETERSBOROUGH** **JULY 14–15** **10**

The campground was 23 miles west of Wooster on U.S. 30 and about a half-mile north of Mifflin, near where U.S. 30 crosses State 603. The camp went through Jeromeville and Hayesville and then camped on a hill near the eastern border of Petersborough Township on Mr. Solomon Braden's farm.

During the day, Brother Perry's wagon overturned, but no one was seriously hurt. John Vanleuven Jr.'s daughter "came very near being killed" when she was run over by a wagon. Sabbath public worship services were held July 15, and many town citizens attended and treated the Latter-day Saints with respect (HC 3:107).

■ **NEWCASTLE (CRESTLINE)** **JULY 16** **16**

The campground was 38 miles west of Wooster on State 30, and nine miles west of Mansfield. The camp traveled 16 miles along what is now U.S. 30 to **Frederick Castle's farm** at Newcastle. The sheriff and deputy in Madison Township arrested and imprisoned Josiah Butterfield, Jonathan Dunham, and Jonathan Hale for charges related to the downfall of the **Kirtland Safety Society**. The camp received persecution but remained unharmed. "We were *honored* by the discharge of artillery," a journal keeper wrote after hecklers fired their guns in the air (HC 3:108).

■ **CRAWFORD COUNTY** **JULY 17** **16**

The Crawford County campsite was 18 miles west of Mansfield on State 30 at its intersection with State 602, which is six miles east of Bucyrus on State 30. Those who had been arrested July 16 were "discharged by the court" and caught up to the main body of the camp that evening (HC 3:109).

■ **GRAND PRAIRIE** **JULY 18** **16**

The campsite was in the town of Grand Prairie, 10 miles SW of Bucyrus, just south of the Marion and Crawford County line, near the Scioto River on State 4. For the first time since leaving Kirtland 12 days earlier, Kirtland Camp camped without having to pay. The brethren were verbally assaulted along the way, but one local man came to the camp's defense (HC 3:109–10).

■ **LITTLE SANDUSKY** **JULY 19** **7.5**

Kirtland Camp traveled through the prairie and camped 1½ miles from the village of **Little Sandusky** (now on State 294). For the first time, the brethren camped with their wagons in a straight line, a practice that "presented a beautiful picture to a distant beholder" and reminded camp members of the ancient Israelites on their flight from Egypt (HC 3:110).

■ **TYMOCHTEE CREEK** **JULY 20** **9.5**

The morning after camping at Little Sandusky, the entire camp received a reprimand from the Kirtland Camp Council (consisting of the seven presidents of the Seventy) for murmuring and dereliction of duty. Afterward, the camp traveled west six miles and then SW 3½ miles to the campground on Tymochtee Creek, pitching tents "in the highway near a schoolhouse" (HC 3:111). This campground was near Marseilles at the intersection of state highways 37 and 67. It rained during the day and most of the night (HC 3:110–12).

■ **JACKSON TOWNSHIP** **JULY 21** **16**

This camp was on State 273, eight miles south of Kenton and four miles west of Mt. Victory. Kirtland Camp continued southwesterly from Tymochtee Creek nine miles to the Scioto River, stopping for lunch at Judge Wheeler's. This is where **Zion's Camp** spent the night of May 13, 1834 (HC 2:65). Kirtland Camp camped in **Jackson Township,** seven miles from Scioto. The weather was cool and pleasant, but "extremely bad" roads made "some places almost impassible." An axle on **Newel K. Knight's** wagon broke, but he was able to mend it (HC 3:112).

■ **BIG SPRINGS** **JULY 22** **5**
(IN LOGAN COUNTY)

This camp appears to have been near Big Springs on State 294, about four to five miles NE of Rushsylvania. The brethren moved five miles on the Sabbath to find forage for their animals. After going through the town of Rush Creek, they camped on the farm of a Mr. Partial, the town's innkeeper. During their move, egg-throwing settlers harassed them.

For the first time on the journey, camp members partook of the sacrament. They did not have the sacrament on the first two Sabbaths of their journey because they were thronged by visitors at their Sabbath meetings.

"Sometime in the night a **luminous body** about the size of a cannon ball came down from over the encampment near the ground then whirled round some forty or fifty times and moved off in a horizontal direction, soon passing out of sight" (HC 3:113).

■ **McKee's Creek** **July 23–24** **16**

Kirtland Camp's campground was three to four miles south of the center of Bellefontaine, now the site of U.S. 68, on the banks of McKee's Creek. The camp traveled through Rushsylvania, where members heard rumors that there were plans to arrest some of them for their dealings with the **Kirtland Safety Society**. No one in the camp was arrested, however, and the camp passed through Bellefontaine and camped at McKee's Creek, a branch of the Miami River.

A wagon ran over the leg of **Martin Peck's** son. Though painful, the injury was not serious, and the lad was blessed that his leg would heal. A miracle occurred at this site when the 620-member camp was amply fed for three days on 7½ bushels of corn (HC 3:113–14).

The brethren remained at the McKee's Creek campground July 24 to wash their clothes and refresh their teams. The brethren earned $20 chopping wood and making shoes (HC 3:114).

■ **Urbana** **July 25** **12**

This campground was two miles north of the Urbana city center on U.S. 68, near the residence and on the farm of **Governor Joseph Vance** of Ohio. The camp council reprimanded several camp members for their lack of Christian conduct, and complaints were settled (HC 3:114–15).

■ **Springfield** **July 26** **12**

This camp was four miles NE of Springfield in the area now known as Northridge. The camp traveled south through Urbana and then through Moneyfield in Clark County, finally camping for the night 4½ miles off the road at Springfield on the farm of Mr. A. Breneman, about where state highways 334 and 4 meet today. **Zera Pulsipher** spoke to a gathering of camp members to help unite the camp in spirit (HC 3:115).

■ **Lenox** **July 27** **15**

This campground was 13 miles NE of the center of **Dayton**, about one mile south of I-70 and one mile east of I-675. On this day, Kirtland Camp went through Springfield, a beautiful city of

3,000 people. A little west of Springfield, they "left the National road and took the road to Dayton." They spent the night near Lenox in Mad River Township (HC 3:115–16).

■ **DAYTON (FAIRBORN) JULY 28–AUG. 28 9**

This Kirtland Camp campsite was located about ½ mile south of the Mad River and 5½ miles NE of the center of Dayton. It is about three miles SW of the **Dayton Airport** and 251 miles from Kirtland (HC 3:116). Members of the Kirtland Camp stayed here for a month while working.

While at this campground, the Kirtland Camp Saints met **Elder John E. Page** and his company from St. Lawrence County, NY. They were also traveling to **Missouri** but were working in the Dayton area (HC 3:117–18).

On Sunday, July 29, Kirtland Camp held a public sacrament meeting during which members bore testimony of the truthfulness of the revelations given by the Lord through the **Prophet Joseph Smith** (HC 3:116–17).

On July 30, several gentlemen solicited the Saints to stay in Dayton to work on the Springfield-to-Dayton Turnpike. On July 31, the Saints contracted to make ½ mile of turnpike. They moved their campsite a quarter mile to the NE, still about ½ mile from the Mad River, and into a beautiful grove of trees on the edge of the prairie. There they prepared to commence work (HC 3:118–20). Camp members were admonished to work hard. On the Sabbath, religious services were held and many strangers joined the Saints in their meetings.

On Aug. 8, a child of Hiram N. Byington died. On Aug. 10, an 18-month-old daughter of **Thomas Carico** died, and on Aug. 11, **Sarah Emily,** two-year-old daughter of **Dominicus Carter**, died. Some were asked to leave the camp when they would not abide by the camp's constitution. On Aug. 21, two boys were born in the camp—sons of **Frederick M. Vanleuven** and **Gardner Snow** (HC 3:124–30).

The camp finally began moving after a month of working on the National Road to raise money—about $1,200—for the journey to Missouri (HR 363). Camp members were grateful for the additional funds and were eager to resume their journey.

After completing work on the turnpike and on other odd jobs, Kirtland Camp members spent a few days preparing to continue their journey to Missouri. Finally, on Aug. 29, 1838, they left Dayton and headed west (HC 3:131–32).

■ **JOHNSVILLE** **AUG. 29** **18**

The Johnsville campsite was 12 miles due west of downtown Dayton, located on present-day U.S. 35 in the western side of the community of New Lebanon.

■ **STATE LINE CAMP** **AUG. 30** **22**

This Kirtland Camp campground, the last one in Ohio, was located on what is now I-70 just before it crosses the **Ohio-Indiana line,** which is a few rods from the campground. The site is two miles SW of New Paris on U.S. 40 (National Road). A young daughter of Otis Shumway died at Eaton and was buried at State Line Camp in the nearby woods (HC 3:133).

Kirtland Camp in Indiana—1838

CAMP	DATE (1838)	MILES (APPROXIMATE)

■ **GERMANTOWN** **AUG. 31** **16**

Kirtland Camp passed over the **Ohio-Indiana border** and through the city of **Richmond**. Between Richmond and the border, the camp began traveling on the National Road. Members went from there to a campground near Germantown (East Germantown), where they camped 12 miles west of Richmond on what is now U.S. 40 (HC 3:133–34).

■ **KNIGHTSTOWN** **SEPT. 1** **23**

This campground was one mile west of Knightstown on U.S. 40 and 35 miles west of the center of Richmond (HC 3:134).

■ **BUCK CREEK** **SEPT. 2** **21.5**

This camp was on the eastern edge of present-day Indianapolis, where U.S. 40 enters the city limits. At midday the camp stopped at a Mr. Caldwell's, "about nine miles" west of Knight's Town. The son of **Elijah P. Merriam** died while the camp was here. His body was carried to Buck Creek, where he was buried the next morning (HC 3:134–35).

■ **Indianapolis** **Sept. 3** **17**

This campground was located where I-465 crosses over U.S. 40 on the west side of Indianapolis. Early on the morning of Sept. 3, **Bathsheba Willey** died. Both she and the Merriam boy, who had died the day before, were laid to rest in the NE corner of Ruther's Orchard, Jones Township, Hancock County, about ¼ of a mile east of Buck Creek. This same day, a stagecoach ran into Lucius N. Scovil's wagon and broke the front wheel (HC 3:135).

■ **Stilesville** **Sept. 4** **23**

The Stilesville campsite was about 28 miles WSW of the center of Indianapolis on U.S. 40, which Kirtland Camp followed across Indiana (HC 3:135–36).

■ **Clay County** **Sept. 5** **20**

The Kirtland Camp campground was just inside the east boundary of **Clay County** on what is now U.S. 40. During the night of Sept. 4, **Thomas Nickerson's** son died. He was buried this day at noon when the camp stopped on the farm of Noal Fouts, west of Putnamville (HC 3:136).

■ **Terre Haute** **Sept. 6** **20**

Kirtland Camp camped on what is now U.S. 40, about two miles east of the Wabash River, near the center of the city of Terre Haute. During the night of Sept. 6, a daughter of Otis Shumway died, and in the morning a son of J. A. Clark died. Both were buried in the graveyard in Terre Haute (HC 3:136).

■ **Illinois Border** **Sept. 7** **9**

This campground was located ¾ of a mile east of the **Indiana-Illinois border** on what is now U.S. 150. Kirtland Camp ferried over the Wabash River at both ferries in Terre Haute and then left the National Road and traveled north toward Paris, IL, on the North Arm Prairie Road (U.S. 150). The camp traveled about nine miles before camping (HC 3:136).

Illinois

Donald Q. Cannon

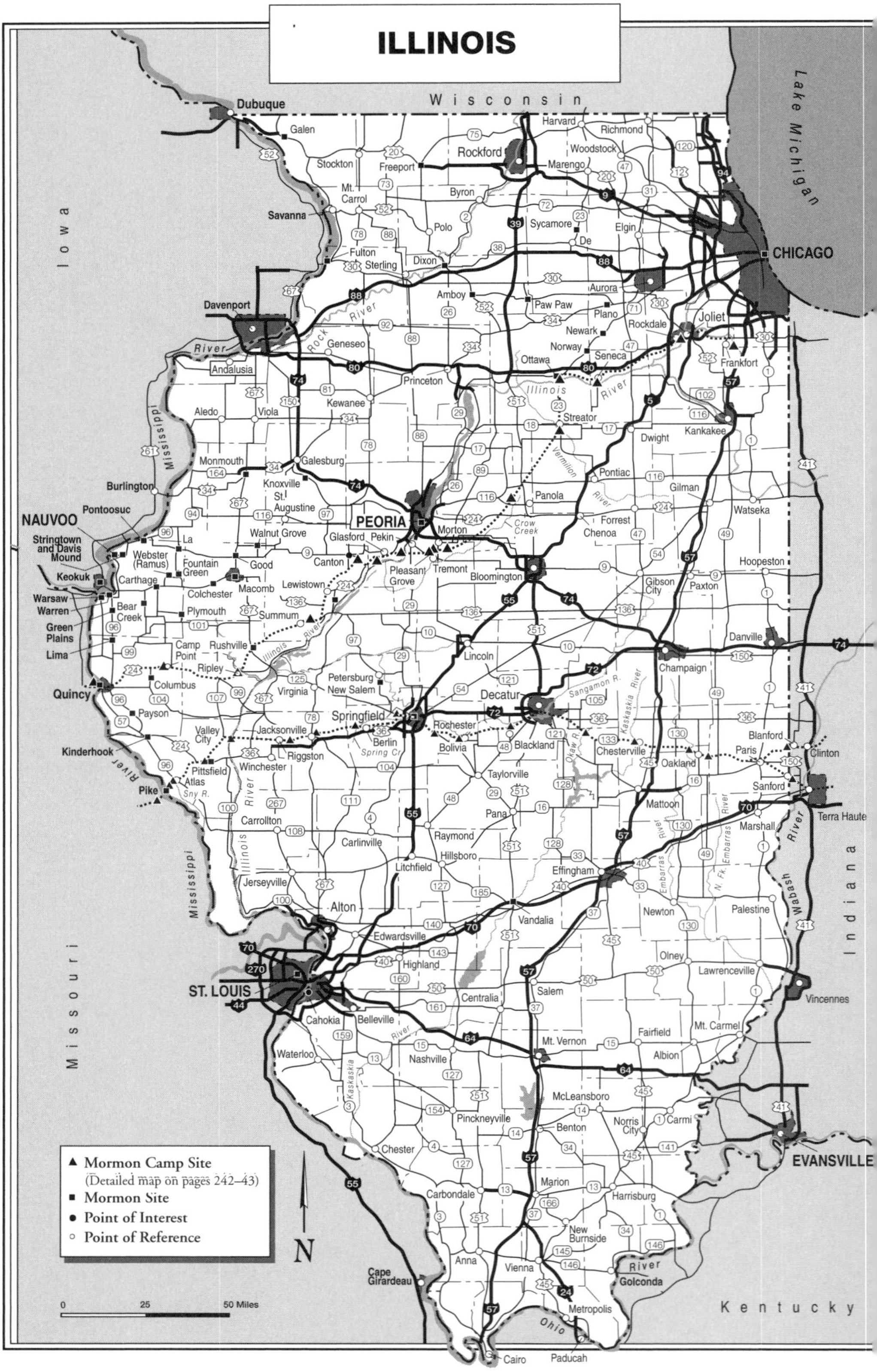
ILLINOIS
Wisconsin
Iowa
Missouri
Indiana
Kentucky
Lake Michigan
Dubuque
Galen
Stockton
Freeport
Rockford
Harvard
Richmond
Woodstock
Marengo
Mt. Carroll
Savanna
Byron
Polo
Sycamore
De
Elgin
CHICAGO
Fulton
Sterling
Dixon
Amboy
Paw Paw
Aurora
Plano
Newark
Rockdale
Joliet
Norway
Seneca
Ottawa
Frankfort
Davenport
Geneseo
Rock River
River
Andalusia
Princeton
Kewanee
Aledo
Viola
Illinois River
Streator
Kankakee
Dwight
Mississippi
Monmouth
Galesburg
Burlington
Knoxville
St. Augustine
Pontiac
Vermilion
Gilman
Watseka
NAUVOO
Pontoosuc
Stringtown and Davis Mound
Webster (Ramus)
La
Fountain Green
Walnut Grove
Glasford
Pekin
PEORIA
Morton
Panola
Forrest
Chenoa
Crow Creek
Keokuk
Carthage
Good
Canton
Pleasant Grove
Tremont
Bloomington
Gibson City
Paxton
Hoopeston
Warsaw
Warren
Colchester
Macomb
Lewistown
Green Plains
Bear Creek
Plymouth
Summum
Lima
Camp Point
Rushville
Lincoln
Danville
Champaign
Ripley
Columbus
Quincy
Petersburg
New Salem
Virginia
Decatur
Sangamon R.
Kaskaskia River
Payson
Springfield
Rochester
Valley City
Jacksonville
Berlin
Bolivia
Blackland
Chesterville
Oakland
Blanford
Paris
Clinton
Kinderhook
Winchester
Riggston
Spring Cr.
Okaw R.
Taylorville
Pittsfield
Atlas
Sny R.
Pike
Sanford
Terre Haute
Pana
Mattoon
Carrollton
Raymond
Marshall
Carlinville
Hillsboro
Litchfield
Effingham
Embarras River
N. Fk. Embarras
Jerseyville
Alton
Vandalia
Newton
Palestine
Wabash River
Edwardsville
Highland
Olney
Lawrenceville
ST. LOUIS
Salem
Centralia
Vincennes
Cahokia
Belleville
Fairfield
Mt. Carmel
Mt. Vernon
Albion
Waterloo
Nashville
Kaskaskia
McLeansboro
Pinckneyville
Norris City
Carmi
Benton
Chester
EVANSVILLE
Marion
Carbondale
Harrisburg
New Burnside
Anna
Vienna
Cape Girardeau
Golconda
Metropolis
Ohio
Cairo
Paducah
▲ Mormon Camp Site (Detailed map on pages 242–43)
■ Mormon Site
● Point of Interest
○ Point of Reference
N
0
25
50 Miles

Introduction to Illinois

Illinois, nicknamed "The Prairie State," derives its name from the Illini Indians. The first Europeans in Illinois were the French explorers **Marquette** and **Joliet**, arriving in 1673. Peoria was where the earliest French colonists engaged in the fur trade. France ceded Illinois to Britain in 1763, following the French and Indian War.

The Northwest Territory, formed in 1787, included Illinois. Settlers from Maryland, Virginia, Kentucky, and Tennessee moved in and occupied lands formerly held by the French. In 1809, Illinois became a separate territory, and in 1818 it became a state, although it had only 40,000 settlers. Most of the early settlers had come from the South. The state did not have as many migrants from the North as from the South until 1832.

Most of the early settlers earned their living as farmers, first in the woodlands and then on the prairies, whose richness and fertility astonished them. As prosperity increased, frontier towns paved the way for growing cities, including Chicago, which became a major agricultural market and business center. By the twentieth century, most Illinoisans lived in cities rather than on farms. By 1965, only 5 percent of the total population lived in rural areas.

Latter-day Saints in Illinois

Latter-day Saint missionaries had preached in Illinois as early as 1832, having baptized **Charles C. Rich** in April of that year. By the time the Saints were driven from Missouri, a small number of Latter-day Saints were scattered throughout Illinois.

Mormon refugees from Missouri settled in the Quincy area in 1839 and were generally well received by the old settlers. The Saints purchased land in Iowa and at Commerce, IL, where they began to establish their major settlement. Eventually, the name Commerce was changed to Nauvoo, a Hebrew word meaning "the beautiful place." On a spectacular horseshoe bend along the Mississippi, the

Saints built a city that eventually rivaled Chicago in size. Converts from the United States, Great Britain, and elsewhere streamed into Nauvoo and the surrounding area. By 1845, Nauvoo had a population of about 11,100, with approximately another 3,000 in surrounding communities.

In addition to their major settlement at Nauvoo, Latter-day Saints established settlements in other parts of Hancock County, elsewhere in Illinois, and in Iowa.

For a variety of political, social, economic, and religious reasons, the Saints were persecuted and finally driven from Illinois in 1846, relocating in present-day Utah in 1847.

A socialistic company of French Icarians moved to Nauvoo after the Saints left. Some of their buildings remain today.

Nauvoo, "The City of Joseph"

When the Saints were driven from Missouri in the spring of 1839, they settled in an area near Quincy, IL, at a place called Commerce. They settled on the "flats" at first, but later many settled on the "bluffs," 70 feet higher. On May 1, 1839, **Joseph Smith,** along with other members of a Church committee, purchased two farms: (1) a farm of about 135 acres owned by **Hugh White,** which cost $5,000; (2) a farm owned by **Dr. Isaac Galland,** who, when he learned of the persecutions of the Saints, offered to sell them 47 acres for $9,000 (BYUS 19, no. 3 [1979]: 261–84). He also traded some land in Nauvoo for land in Missouri. The area was described as having, at the time of purchase, "one stone house, three frame houses, and two block houses, which constituted the whole city of Commerce." The land was mostly covered with trees and bushes. Part of it was "so wet that it was with the utmost difficulty a footman could get through" (HC 3:375). It was considered a very unhealthy place to live, but Joseph Smith believed the Saints could build it up.

On May 10, 1839, Joseph Smith arrived from Quincy and set up residence in a small log house on the White farm, located on the bank of the Mississippi River about a mile south of the village of Commerce. The cabin had served as the first Indian agency in Illinois. **Sidney Rigdon** and **George W. Robinson** settled on the Galland farm. **Brigham Young** arrived here from Quincy on May 18,

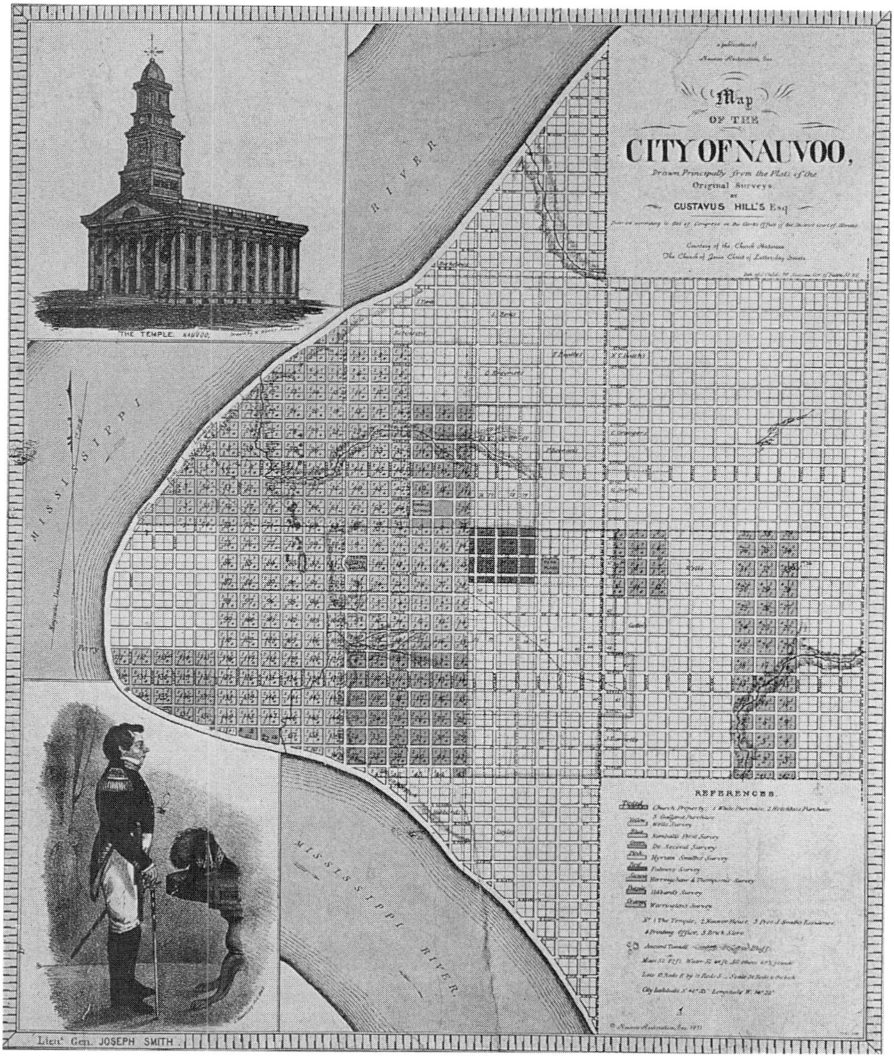

Map of Nauvoo, IL, drawn by Gustavus Hills, Esq., 1840s. The map is a projection of what could have been had Nauvoo become fully developed. (Courtesy of LDSCA)

a few days after the Prophet arrived. The first home built by the Saints was raised by **Theodore Turley** in June 1839, located 25–30 rods NE of the Prophet's home on the NE corner of lot 4, block 147, of the White farm. Most of the houses in Nauvoo (1,200, or 65 percent) were built of logs. About 400, or 20 percent, were frame, and about 250, or 15 percent, were brick.

As the Saints arrived in Commerce in the spring and summer of 1839, many of them suffered greatly from malaria. On July 22,

Nauvoo, IL, from the air, looking north. (1978)

1839, Joseph Smith, assisted by other elders of the Church, miraculously healed **Elijah Fordham, Henry G. Sherwood, Benjamin Brown, Joseph B. Noble,** and many others.

The third and fourth purchases of land at Nauvoo were made Aug. 12, 1839. They included the Hotchkiss purchase of about 400 acres, which included the paper town (planned but never built) of Commerce, for about $114,000, and the William White purchase of 80 acres for about $3,500.

The Church's first general conference held in Commerce took place Oct. 6–8, 1839. On the first day, a stake of Zion was organized with **William Marks** called as its president. Three wards were also organized. Joseph Smith presided over the conference and agreed that this was "a good place" for the gathering of the Saints.

Nauvoo, looking north from the Iowa side of the Mississippi River. (Engraving by Herrman J. Meyer, circa 1845; courtesy of LDSCA)

Daguerreotype of Nauvoo, looking NE from the vicinity of the corner of Parley and Hyde Streets. Charles W. Carter made this copy from the original, which was probably made by Lucian R. Foster. (Courtesy of LDSCA)

The *Times and Seasons* newspaper was first published in Nauvoo in Nov. 1839 by **Don Carlos Smith** and **Ebenezer Robinson.** At the time, this publication was the only paper published in Hancock County.

In Dec. 1839, the high council of Nauvoo "voted to print ten thousand copies of the hymn-books, and an edition of the Book of Mormon, under the inspection of the First Presidency of Nauvoo, so soon as means can be obtained" (HC 4:49).

The U.S. Post Office officially recognized Commerce as Nauvoo on Apr. 21, 1840 (HC 4:121). After the martyrdom of the Prophet Joseph Smith, Nauvoo became known as "The City of Joseph" (HC 7:386).

Like a phoenix rising from the ashes, Old Nauvoo has been restored in western Illinois by the Latter-day Saints. Just as they drained the swamps and built a thriving city of 12,000 in the 1840s, they have restored many of the historic federal-style buildings of Old Nauvoo. Most of the restoration has been accomplished by The Church of Jesus Christ of Latter-day Saints, with some restoration done by the Reorganized Church of Jesus Christ of Latter Day Saints, now known as the Community of Christ. This work began when land and buildings were purchased by **Wilford C. Wood, James LeRoy Kimball,** and others under the auspices of Nauvoo Restoration, Inc.

Most of the homes and shops restored by the Latter-day Saints and Community of Christ are open to the public and have tour guides available. In addition to the homes and buildings which have been restored, there are other places of interest including historic sites where other buildings now stand, rock quarries, parks, and cemeteries.

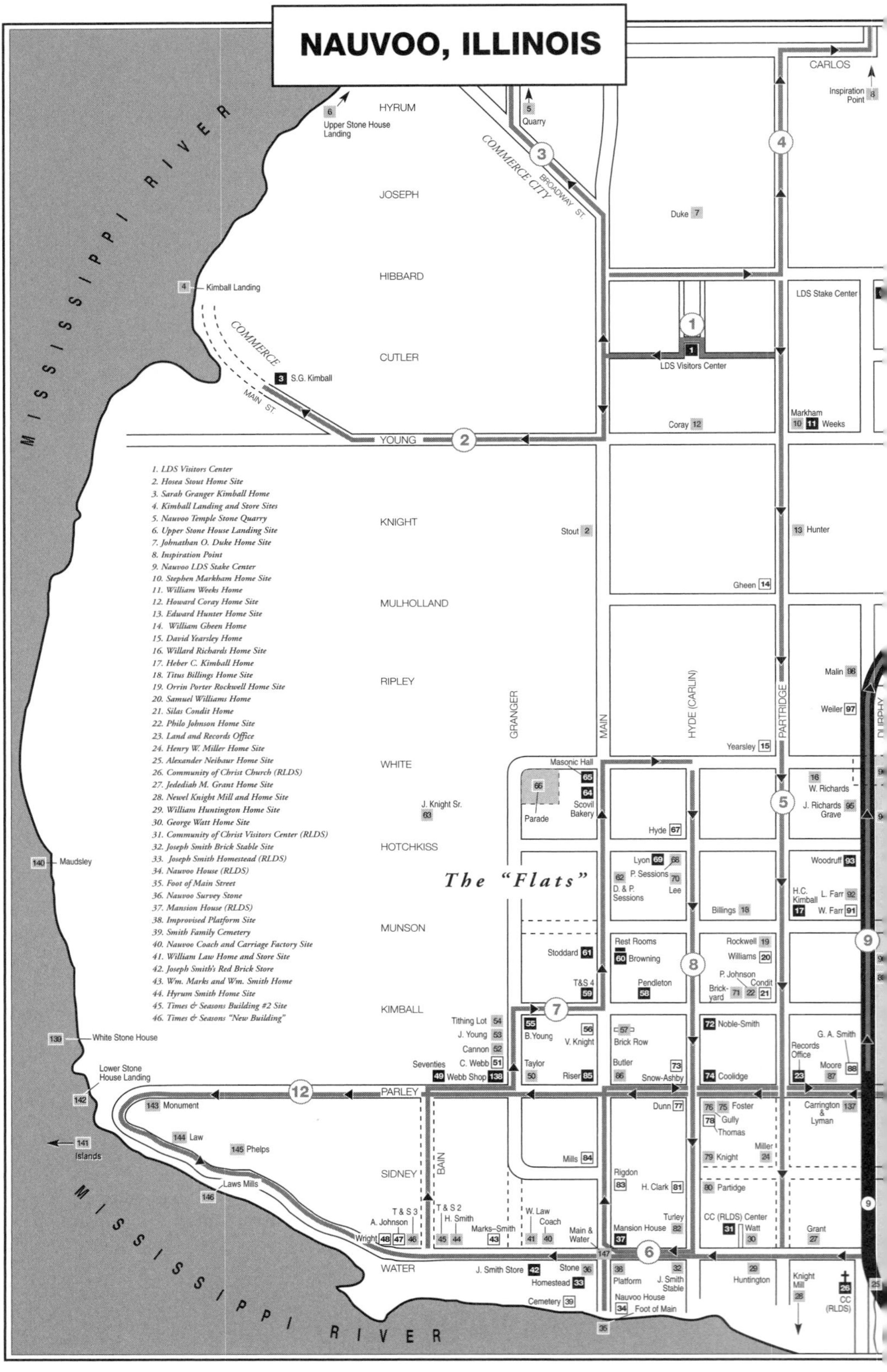
NAUVOO, ILLINOIS
1. LDS Visitors Center
2. Hosea Stout Home Site
3. Sarah Granger Kimball Home
4. Kimball Landing and Store Sites
5. Nauvoo Temple Stone Quarry
6. Upper Stone House Landing Site
7. Johnathan O. Duke Home Site
8. Inspiration Point
9. Nauvoo LDS Stake Center
10. Stephen Markham Home Site
11. William Weeks Home
12. Howard Coray Home Site
13. Edward Hunter Home Site
14. William Gheen Home
15. David Yearsley Home
16. Willard Richards Home Site
17. Heber C. Kimball Home
18. Titus Billings Home Site
19. Orrin Porter Rockwell Home Site
20. Samuel Williams Home
21. Silas Condit Home
22. Philo Johnson Home Site
23. Land and Records Office
24. Henry W. Miller Home Site
25. Alexander Neibaur Home Site
26. Community of Christ Church (RLDS)
27. Jedediah M. Grant Home Site
28. Newel Knight Mill and Home Site
29. William Huntington Home Site
30. George Watt Home Site
31. Community of Christ Visitors Center (RLDS)
32. Joseph Smith Brick Stable Site
33. Joseph Smith Homestead (RLDS)
34. Nauvoo House (RLDS)
35. Foot of Main Street
36. Nauvoo Survey Stone
37. Mansion House (RLDS)
38. Improvised Platform Site
39. Smith Family Cemetery
40. Nauvoo Coach and Carriage Factory Site
41. William Law Home and Store Site
42. Joseph Smith's Red Brick Store
43. Wm. Marks and Wm. Smith Home
44. Hyrum Smith Home Site
45. Times & Seasons Building #2 Site
46. Times & Seasons "New Building"
MISSISSIPPI RIVER
HYRUM
JOSEPH
HIBBARD
CUTLER
YOUNG
KNIGHT
MULHOLLAND
RIPLEY
WHITE
HOTCHKISS
MUNSON
KIMBALL
PARLEY
SIDNEY
WATER
CARLOS
COMMERCE CITY
BROADWAY ST.
COMMERCE
MAIN ST.
GRANGER
MAIN
HYDE (CARLIN)
PARTRIDGE
DURPHY
BAIN
The "Flats"
6 Upper Stone House Landing
5 Quarry
Inspiration Point 8
Duke 7
4 Kimball Landing
3 S.G. Kimball
1 LDS Visitors Center
LDS Stake Center
Coray 12
Markham 10 11 Weeks
Stout 2
13 Hunter
Gheen 14
Malin 96
Weiler 97
Yearsley 15
Masonic Hall 65
64 Scovil Bakery
66 Parade
J. Knight Sr. 63
16 W. Richards
J. Richards Grave 95
Hyde 67
Lyon 69 68
62 P. Sessions 70
D. & P. Sessions
Lee
Woodruff 93
H.C. Kimball 17
L. Farr 92
W. Farr 91
Billings 18
140 Maudsley
Rest Rooms
60 Browning
Stoddard 61
Rockwell 19
Williams 20
P. Johnson
Condit
Brick-yard 71 22 21
Pendleton 58
T&S 4 59
Tithing Lot 54
J. Young 53
Cannon 52
C. Webb 51
Seventies 49 Webb Shop 138
55 B.Young
56 V. Knight
Taylor 50
Riser 85
57 Brick Row
Butler 86
73 Snow-Ashby
72 Noble-Smith
74 Coolidge
G. A. Smith 88
Records Office 23
Moore 87
139 White Stone House
Lower Stone House Landing
142
143 Monument
141 Islands
144 Law
145 Phelps
Laws Mills
146
Dunn 77
76 75 Foster
78 Gully
Thomas
Carrington & Lyman 137
Mills 84
79 Knight
Miller 24
Rigdon 83
H. Clark 81
80 Partidge
T & S 3
A. Johnson
Wright 48 47 46
T & S 2
H. Smith
45 44
Marks–Smith 43
W. Law
Coach
41 40
Main & Water
147
Mansion House 37
Turley 82
CC (RLDS) Center 31
Watt 30
Grant 27
J. Smith Store 42
Stone 36
Homestead 33
Cemetery 39
38 Platform
32 J. Smith Stable
Nauvoo House 34
Foot of Main
35
29 Huntington
Knight Mill 28
26 CC (RLDS)
25

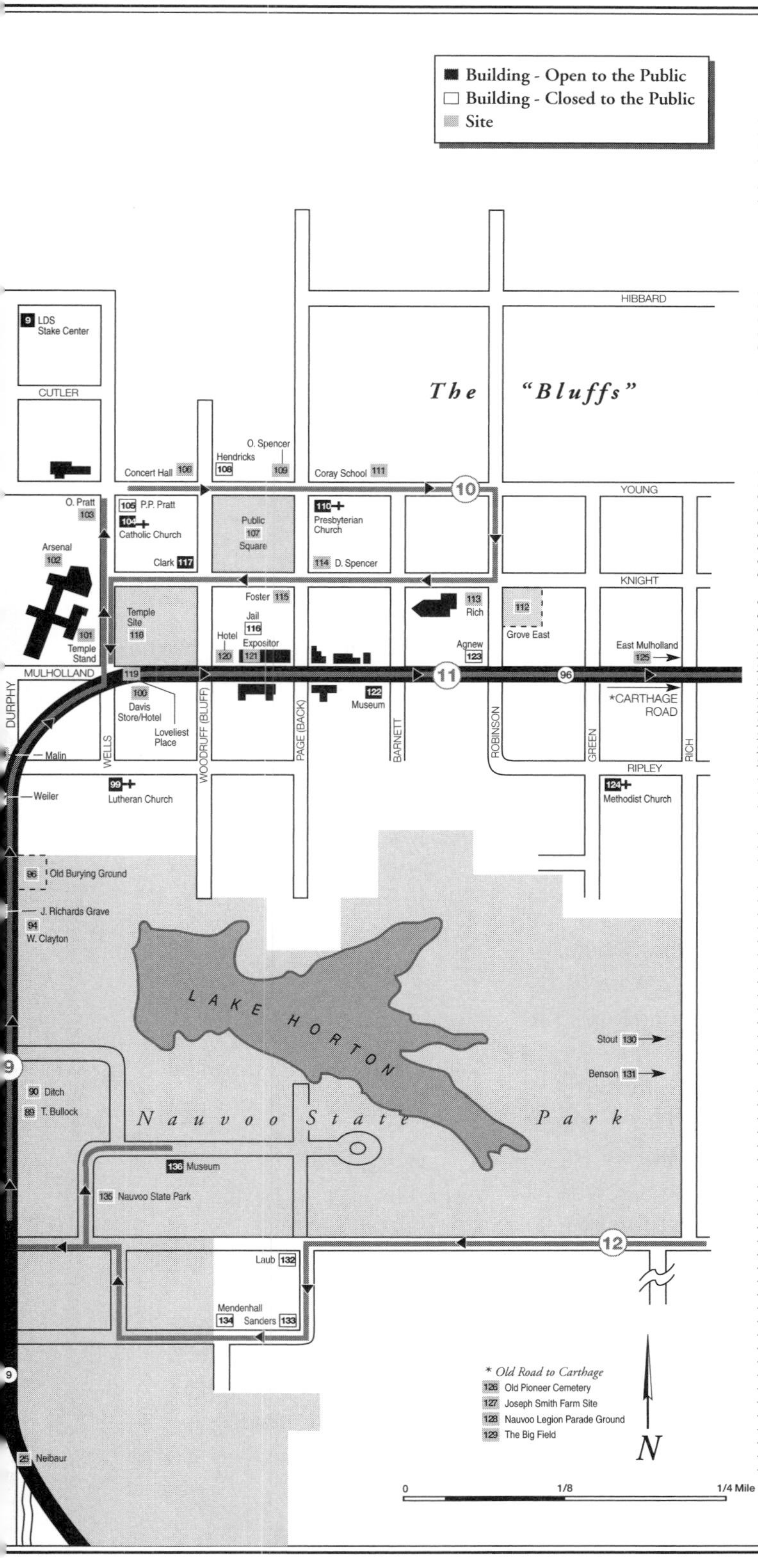

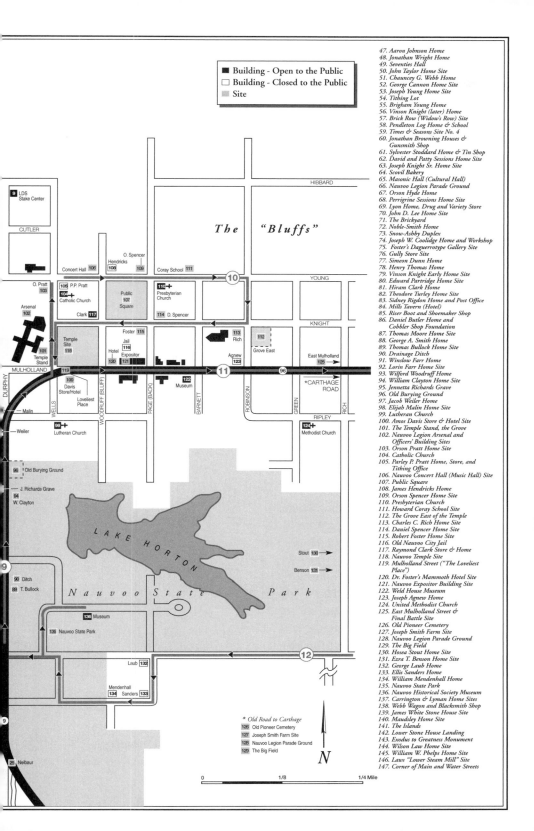

47. Aaron Johnson Home
48. Jonathan Wright Home
49. Seventies Hall
50. John Taylor Home Site
51. Chauncey G. Webb Home
52. George Cannon Home Site
53. Joseph Young Home Site
54. Tithing Lot
55. Brigham Young Home
56. Vinson Knight (later) Home
57. Brick Row (Widow's Row) Site
58. Pendleton Log Home & School
59. Times & Seasons Site No. 4
60. Jonathan Browning Houses & Gunsmith Shop
61. Sylvester Stoddard Home & Tin Shop
62. David and Patty Sessions Home Site
63. Joseph Knight Sr. Home Site
64. Scovil Bakery
65. Masonic Hall (Cultural Hall)
66. Nauvoo Legion Parade Ground
67. Orson Hyde Home
68. Perrigrine Sessions Home Site
69. Lyon Home, Drug and Variety Store
70. John D. Lee Home Site
71. The Brickyard
72. Noble-Smith Home
73. Snow-Ashby Duplex
74. Joseph W. Coolidge Home and Workshop
75. Foster's Daguerrotype Gallery Site
76. Gully Store Site
77. Simeon Dunn Home
78. Henry Thomas Home
79. Vinson Knight Early Home Site
80. Edward Partridge Home Site
81. Hiram Clark Home
82. Theodore Turley Home Site
83. Sidney Rigdon Home and Post Office
84. Mills Tavern (Hotel)
85. Riser Boot and Shoemaker Shop
86. Daniel Butler Home and Cobbler Shop Foundation
87. Thomas Moore Home Site
88. George A. Smith Home
89. Thomas Bullock Home Site
90. Drainage Ditch
91. Winslow Farr Home
92. Lorin Farr Home Site
93. Wilford Woodruff Home
94. William Clayton Home Site
95. Jennetta Richards Grave
96. Old Burying Ground
97. Jacob Weiler Home
98. Elijah Malin Home Site
99. Lutheran Church
100. Amos Davis Store & Hotel Site
101. The Temple Stand, the Grove
102. Nauvoo Legion Arsenal and Officers' Building Sites
103. Orson Pratt Home Site
104. Catholic Church
105. Parley P. Pratt Home, Store, and Tithing Office
106. Nauvoo Concert Hall (Music Hall) Site
107. Public Square
108. James Hendricks Home
109. Orson Spencer Home Site
110. Presbyterian Church
111. Howard Coray School Site
112. The Grove East of the Temple
113. Charles C. Rich Home Site
114. Daniel Spencer Home Site
115. Robert Foster Home Site
116. Old Nauvoo City Jail
117. Raymond Clark Store & Home
118. Nauvoo Temple Site
119. Mulholland Street ("The Loveliest Place")
120. Dr. Foster's Mammoth Hotel Site
121. Nauvoo Expositor Building Site
122. Weld House Museum
123. Joseph Agnew Home
124. United Methodist Church
125. East Mulholland Street & Final Battle Site
126. Old Pioneer Cemetery
127. Joseph Smith Farm Site
128. Nauvoo Legion Parade Ground
129. The Big Field
130. Hosea Stout Home Site
131. Ezra T. Benson Home Site
132. George Laub Home
133. Ellis Sanders Home
134. William Mendenhall Home
135. Nauvoo State Park
136. Nauvoo Historical Society Museum
137. Carrington & Lyman Home Sites
138. Webb Wagon and Blacksmith Shop
139. James White Stone House Site
140. Maudsley Home Site
141. The Islands
142. Lower Stone House Landing
143. Exodus to Greatness Monument
144. Wilson Law Home Site
145. William W. Phelps Home Site
146. Laws "Lower Steam Mill" Site
147. Corner of Main and Water Streets

NAUVOO

Numerical Key to Map

TOUR ONE: LDS VISITORS CENTER

1. LDS Visitors Center

TOUR TWO: COMMERCE AREA

2. Hosea Stout Home Site
3. Sarah Granger Kimball Home
4. Kimball Landing and Store Sites

TOUR THREE: COMMERCE CITY AREA

5. Nauvoo Temple Stone Quarry
6. Upper Stone House Landing Site
7. Jonathan Oldham Duke Home Site

TOUR FOUR: INSPIRATION POINT

8. Inspiration Point

TOUR FIVE: PARTRIDGE STREET

9. Nauvoo LDS Stake Center
10. Stephen Markham Home Site
11. William Weeks Home
12. Howard Coray Home Site
13. Edward Hunter Home Site
14. William Gheen Home
15. David Yearsley Home
16. Willard Richards Home Site
17. Heber C. Kimball Home
18. Titus Billings Home Site
19. Orrin Porter Rockwell Home Site
20. Samuel Williams Home
21. Silas Condit Home
22. Philo Johnson Home Site
23. Nauvoo Lands and Records Office
24. Henry W. Miller Home Site

TOUR SIX: WATER STREET

25. Alexander Neibaur Home Site
26. Community of Christ Church (RLDS)
27. Jedediah M. Grant Home Site
28. Newel Knight Mill and Home Site
29. William Huntington Home Site
30. George Watt Home Site
31. Community of Christ Joseph Smith Historic Visitors Center
32. Joseph Smith Brick Stable Site
33. Joseph Smith Homestead*
34. Nauvoo House*
35. Foot of Main Street
36. Nauvoo Survey Stone
37. Mansion House*
38. Improvised Platform Site
39. Smith Family Cemetery
40. Nauvoo Coach and Carriage Factory Site
41. William Law Home and Store Site
42. Joseph Smith's Red Brick Store*
43. William Marks and William Smith Home
44. Hyrum Smith Home Site
45. *Times & Seasons* Site No. 2
46. *Times & Seasons* Site No. 3

47. Aaron Johnson Home
48. Jonathan Wright Home

TOUR SEVEN: PARLEY, GRANGER, KIMBALL, AND MAIN STREETS

49. Seventies Hall
50. John Taylor Home Site
51. Chauncey G. Webb Home
52. George Cannon Home Site
53. Joseph Young Home Site
54. Tithing Lot
55. Brigham Young Home
56. Vinson Knight Home (later)
57. Brick Row (Widow's Row) Site
58. Pendleton Log Home and School
59. *Times & Seasons* Site No. 4 and John Taylor Home
60. Jonathan Browning Complex
61. Sylvester Stoddard Home and Tin Shop
62. David and Patty Sessions Home Site
63. Joseph Knight Sr. Home Site
64. Scovil Bakery
65. Masonic Hall (Cultural Hall)
66. Nauvoo Legion Parade Ground

TOUR EIGHT: HYDE, SOUTH MAIN, AND PARLEY STREETS

67. Orson Hyde Home
68. Perrigrine Sessions Home Site
69. Lyon Home, Drug and Variety Store
70. John D. Lee Home Site
71. The Brickyard
72. Noble-Smith Home
73. Snow-Ashby Duplex
74. Joseph W. Coolidge Home
75. Foster's Daguerreotype Gallery Site
76. Gully Store Site
77. Simeon Dunn Home
78. Henry Thomas Home
79. Vinson Knight Early Home Site
80. Edward Partridge Home Site
81. Hiram Clark Home
82. Theodore Turley Home Site
83. Sidney Rigdon Home and Post Office
84. Mills Tavern (Hotel)
85. Riser Boot and Shoemaker Shop
86. Daniel Butler Home
87. Thomas Moore Home Site

TOUR NINE: DURPHY AND WELLS STREETS

88. George A. Smith Home
89. Thomas Bullock Home Site
90. Drainage Ditch
91. Winslow Farr Home
92. Lorin Farr Home Site
93. Wilford Woodruff Home
94. William Clayton Home Site
95. Jennetta Richards Grave
96. Old Burying Ground
97. Jacob Weiler Home
98. Elijah Malin Home Site
99. Lutheran Church
100. Amos Davis Store and Hotel Site
101. The Temple Stand, the Grove
102. Nauvoo Legion Arsenal and Officers' Building Sites
103. Orson Pratt Home Site
104. Catholic Church
105. Parley P. Pratt Home, Store, and Tithing Office

TOUR TEN: YOUNG AND KNIGHT STREETS

106. Nauvoo Concert Hall Site
107. Public Square
108. James Hendricks Home
109. Orson Spencer Home Site
110. Presbyterian Church
111. Howard Coray School Site
112. The Grove East of the Temple
113. Charles C. Rich Home Site
114. Daniel Spencer Home Site
115. Robert Foster Home Site
116. Old Nauvoo City Jail
117. Raymond Clark Store and Home
118. Nauvoo Temple Site

TOUR ELEVEN: MULHOLLAND STREET AND OLD ROAD TO CARTHAGE

119. Mulholland Street ("The Loveliest Place")
120. Dr. Foster's Mammoth Hotel Site
121. *Nauvoo Expositor* Building Site
122. Weld House Museum
123. Joseph Agnew Home
124. United Methodist Church
125. East Mulholland Street and the Final Battle Site
126. Old Pioneer Cemetery
127. Joseph Smith Farm Site
128. Nauvoo Legion Parade Ground
129. The Big Field

TOUR TWELVE: PARLEY AND WATER STREETS

130. Hosea Stout Home Site
131. Ezra T. Benson Home Site
132. George Laub Home
133. Ellis Sanders Home
134. William Mendenhall Home
135. Nauvoo State Park
136. Nauvoo Historical Society Museum
137. Carrington and Lyman Home Sites
138. Webb Wagon and Blacksmith Shop
139. James White Stone House Site
140. Maudsley Home Site
141. The Islands
142. Lower Stone House Landing
143. Exodus to Greatness Monument and Pioneer Memorial
144. Wilson Law Home Site
145. William W. Phelps Home Site
146. Laws "Lower Steam Mill" Site
147. Corner of Main and Water Streets

NAUVOO

Alphabetical Key to Map

* **Community of Christ (RLDS)**

Touring Nauvoo

Nauvoo is located on a bend of the Mississippi River, on State 96. It is 50 miles north of Quincy, IL, and 25 miles south of Burlington, IA. To tour Nauvoo in a chronologically and geographically convenient way, visit the following twelve areas in the order listed: (1) LDS Visitors Center; (2) Commerce Area (early settlement); (3) Commerce City Area (proposed city); (4) Inspiration Point (viewing point); (5) Partridge Street (miscellaneous homes); (6) Water Street (Joseph Smith's homes); (7) Parley, Granger, Kimball, and Main Streets; (8) Hyde, South Main, and Parley Streets; (9) Durphy and Wells Streets; (10) Young and Knight Streets; (11) Mulholland Street and Old Road to Carthage (including the cemetery); (12) Parley and Water Streets (exodus and conclusion).

Sites of interest are identified by both map and narrative for easy finding. In addition, the narrative identifies people and describes significant historical events. Site identification and verification has been made possible through the careful research of James L. Kimball Jr., whose father, Dr. James LeRoy Kimball, was the prime leader in the restoration of Nauvoo. James Jr. has willingly shared records of Nauvoo that have made accuracy possible.

Tour One: LDS Visitors Center

The LDS Nauvoo Restoration **Visitors Center** is located one block east of Main Street between Young and Hibbard Streets (see Nauvoo map).

■ **1. LDS Visitors Center.** The LDS Visitors Center, which is constructed of handmade red bricks, was dedicated Sept. 4, 1971, by N. Eldon Tanner, first counselor in the First Presidency. Tour guides are available to show a movie on Nauvoo and explain the exhibits, and free maps are available. A research room where visitors can identify property holdings of the Saints who lived in Nauvoo has been moved from the visitors center to the land and records office a few blocks away.

Interest in preserving and restoring Nauvoo began at least as early as 1918, when Wilford C. Wood, who had just completed a mission for the Church to the northern states, vowed to secure properties of historical interest to the Church. Over a period of years, and at great personal expense and effort, he purchased seven out of the 10 parcels of property that made up the original temple block. He also purchased the Masonic Hall and the John Taylor home in the Printing Complex.

After Dr. James LeRoy Kimball restored his grandfather Heber C. Kimball's home in the 1950s, he spearheaded a movement to restore Nauvoo as it was in the 1840s. Nauvoo Restoration, Inc., was organized in July 1962, and through Dr. Kimball's great effort and leadership, Nauvoo was restored.

Monument Garden, Nauvoo, IL, dedicated to women. (1983)

The **Monument Garden**, dedicated to **women**, is located immediately south of the visitors center. Sculptors **Florence Hansen** and **Dennis Smith** sculpted the monuments, which depict the varied nature of **women's** vital role in society (ENS Sept. 1978, 72)

A pageant, **"City of Joseph,"** is held annually in August on the lawns just east of the center.

Tour Two: Commerce Area

From the visitors center, visit the oldest settled area of Nauvoo by traveling SW (see Nauvoo map). Old Commerce was a paper town owned by the Horace Hotchkiss Syndicate, a group of land speculators.

■ **2. Hosea Stout Home Site.** One of **Hosea Stout**'s early **home sites** is located on the "flats" at the SW corner of Main and Knight Streets, where a **marker** has been placed. His 1844–46 home site is located on the SE corner of Munson and Gordon Streets on the "bluffs" (DHS 1:115).

Hosea Stout was born in 1810 in Kentucky. He taught school in Illinois, married Surmantha Peck in Jan. 1838, in Caldwell County, MO, and was baptized by Charles C. Rich on Aug. 25, 1838. In Nauvoo, Hosea was the **chief of police** and a **colonel** in the **Nauvoo Legion.** In Utah, he became a lawyer, was president of the House in the territorial legislature, and ran a Pony Express station. He was one of the most faithful diarists of the early restored Church (DHS 1:xiii–xix).

■ **3. Sarah Granger Kimball Home.** The **Sarah Granger** and **Hiram S. Kimball** 1½-story frame home is located on Main Street of old Commerce, which runs SE to NW. The home is ½ block north of Young Street and 3½ blocks west of Nauvoo's Main Street.

Hiram S. Kimball, fifth cousin (once removed) of Heber C. Kimball, was a resident and landowner in Commerce as early as 1833. In 1840, he married Sarah Granger, who was baptized in 1833 when her family joined the Church. Hyrum was baptized in 1843 and endowed in 1846.

Hiram, a prosperous businessman, owned the Kimball Landing and store NW of his home and also had a lumberyard. The Kimball Landing was one of the most important points of departure for the Saints as they began their journey west.

Hiram insinuated evil against Joseph Smith in 1842, and on May 19, Joseph received a **revelation** addressed to Hiram. Joseph wrote it down and threw it across the room to him. The revelation verified that Hiram had

Sarah Granger Kimball home, Nauvoo, IL. (1985; courtesy of Jim Frederick)

indeed been "forming evil opinions against" Joseph (HC 5:12–13; 6:236–39, 549).

Hiram joined the Saints in the final battle of Nauvoo and moved to Utah Territory in 1850. He had the mail contract between Salt Lake City and Independence, MO, in 1856. In 1863 he was killed when a steamship boiler exploded while he was traveling to his mission field, the Sandwich Islands (BiE 2:372).

Sarah Granger Kimball was a leader among Mormon women. In the spring of 1842, she teamed up with her seamstress, Miss Cook, to give service to builders of the temple. Sarah furnished the materials, and Miss Cook sewed shirts for temple workmen. Other women were invited to participate. Meeting in Sarah's parlor, they decided to organize a ladies' society. Sarah asked Eliza R. Snow to write bylaws, which she did. Eliza then read them to the Prophet Joseph Smith (RSM 6:129). The result of this Mar. 11, 1842, meeting in Sarah's small frame home was the organization of the **Relief Society** in the Red Brick Store on Mar. 17, 1842 (BiE 2:372; ENS May 1982, 109–11; JMH 13:7).

■ **4. Kimball Landing and Store Sites.** The **Hiram Kimball wharves** and **steamboat landing** were located in the Hotchkiss Purchase near the foot of Old Commerce Main Street, two "Nauvoo blocks" NW of the Sarah Granger and Hiram S. Kimball Home (HC 6:248). It was one of the best landings in Nauvoo (HC 4:408).

Kimball seems to have had a different opinion about the city's right to tax boats that docked at the Kimball Landing. He told steamboat captains that they did not need to pay taxes to land at his landing. Joseph Smith, however, believed the city owned the beach and wharves and therefore had a right to tax their use. He gave Kimball "the word" on Mar. 5, 1844, and Kimball began charging taxes (HC 6:234, 238–39, 248).

Here **Captain Dan Jones** prepared boats for the Saints to cross the Mississippi River on their **exodus** west. The Nauvoo City police, under the supervision of **Hosea Stout,** were in charge of the river crossings. On Feb. 4, 1846, Charles Shumway and his family became the first Mormon pioneers to cross the Mississippi. The next day, Stout recorded in his journal that "[Jesse D.] Hunter and I then went to the river at Kimball's landing to see how Capt. Jones came on preparing the boats [ferries] for crossing the river. All was well and the boats was in a forward state for use" (DHS 1:112–13;

punctuation modernized). It seems that the Kimball Landing may have been the most used landing during the Saints' exodus.

The foundation of the **Hiram S. Kimball store** is located NW of the Sarah Granger and Hiram S. Kimball home and about 10 yards from the Mississippi riverbank.

Hiram S. Kimball store, Nauvoo, IL. (1975)

Tour Three: Commerce City Area

The Commerce area, which was little more than a paper city, is located NW of the LDS Visitors Center (see Nauvoo map).

■ **5. Nauvoo Temple Stone Quarry.** This limestone quarry is a more modern version of the few quarries the Saints operated in the 1840s. It furnished large quantities of limestone for use in homes and public buildings, especially in the Nauvoo Temple (T&S 3:775). The quarry is located between Main and Broadway Streets of Old Commerce, which forks off from Main Street and leads to the Colusa grain elevators on the bank of the Mississippi River. Limestone deposits are quite common along this section of the

One of the Nauvoo Temple stone quarries, Nauvoo, IL. (1972; courtesy of Jim Frederick)

river. At least four **lime kilns**—run by J. Boyce, W. Niswanger, J. Owens, P. Shirts, and H. Mathews—once existed near the quarry. The quarry was also the beginning of a projected canal, which would have run from north to south along Main Street and provided waterpower. Although some rock was removed from the quarry site, the canal project never materialized (BYUS 18, no. 2 [1978]: 246–54).

■ **6. Upper Stone House Landing Site.** This landing site, part of the Hotchkiss Purchase, is in Commerce, just left of the north end of Main Street in block 11, which was owned by Joseph Smith or the Church. It was about two miles from the Mansion House (RoOW 5; FOP 379–80). The Prophet said in 1841 that although the Hotchkiss Purchase in Nauvoo was the most "sickly," it had the best **steamboat landing** (HC 4:408).

In addition to a steamboat landing, the property included a **stone house,** designated as the "Upper Stone House" to distinguish it from the James White "Lower Stone House" near the Montrose Crossing, or steamboat landing. The stone house served as a **warehouse, hotel,** and **grocery store** (DHS 1:52). Edwin D. Wooley ran a store at the upper landing. **Missionaries** leaving Nauvoo for their mission fields gathered here and secured passage on steamships (HC 5:385).

Josiah Quincy docked here May 14, 1844, and slept near the dock for one night "in an old mill, which had been converted into an Irish shanty," which was probably the Upper Stone House (FOP 379). The next day, Quincy spent time with Joseph Smith and saw the sights of Nauvoo, including the Egyptian mummies housed in the Mansion House (HC 6:377; DoJS 479; ATM 136–37). Quincy was mayor of Boston from 1845 to 1848, and in 1883 he wrote *Figures of the Past,* which included a chapter titled "Joseph Smith at Nauvoo." In his analysis of Joseph Smith, he said:

> It is by no means improbable that some future text-book, for the use of generations yet unborn, will contain a question something like this: What historical American of the nineteenth century has exerted the most powerful influence upon the destinies of his countrymen? And it is by no means impossible that the answer to that interrogatory may be thus written: *Joseph Smith, the Mormon prophet.* And the reply, absurd as it

> doubtless seems to most men now living, may be an obvious commonplace to their descendants. History deals in surprises and paradoxes quite as startling as this. The man who established a religion in this age of free debate, who was and is today accepted by hundreds of thousands as a direct emissary from the Most High,—such a rare human being is not to be disposed of by pelting his memory with unsavory epithets. Fanatic, impostor, charlatan, he may have been; but these hard names furnish no solution to the problem he presents to us. Fanatics and impostors are living and dying every day, and their memory is buried with them; but the wonderful influence which this founder of a religion exerted and still exerts throws him into relief before us, not as a rogue to be criminated, but as a phenomenon to be explained (FOP 376–77).

Brigham Young rode to the upper landing on Mar. 26, 1845, and welcomed the 50 **British Saints** who came from Liverpool to New Orleans, then traveled up the Mississippi River on a steamboat under the direction of Amos Fielding (HC 7:388).

The old *Times and Seasons* two-story frame printing office (Site No. 2) was moved and placed on a rock foundation near the Upper Stone House Landing (DHS 1:52).

■ **7. Jonathan Oldham Duke Home Site. Jonathan Oldham Duke's house** was located on the SE corner of Joseph and Hyde Streets. Jonathan, born in 1807 and baptized in 1839, married Mary Elois Stone on Dec. 30, 1828 (JJOD 7). He was a faithful Latter-day Saint who crossed the plains, settled in Provo, UT, and served as a major in the Utah War in 1857.

Tour Four: Inspiration Point

Inspiration Point is located north and a little east of the LDS Visitors Center (see Nauvoo Map).

● **8. Inspiration Point.** To reach **Inspiration Point**, travel .7 mile north on Partridge Street from the LDS Visitors Center to a turnaround on a high point overlooking the Mississippi River. This site affords a panorama of the river and the Iowa shore.

Tour Five: Partridge Street

This segment of the tour of Nauvoo begins at the north end of Partridge Street and goes south for nearly 1¼ miles to Water Street. Partridge Street is named after **Edward Partridge,** the first bishop in the Church.

■ **9. Nauvoo LDS Stake Center.** The **Nauvoo LDS Stake Center** is on the SE corner of Hibbard and Durphy Streets. This building is the first LDS chapel built in Nauvoo specifically for regular Church services. It was dedicated May 24, 1969. The Saints used various meeting places outdoors and indoors during their seven-year stay in Nauvoo beginning in 1839. When the **original stake** was organized there during a conference Oct. 5–7, 1839, William Marks was sustained as the stake president.

On Feb. 18, 1979, **President Ezra Taft Benson,** then president of the Quorum of the Twelve, again created a stake in Nauvoo (the Church's 1,000th stake). Gene Lee Roy Mann was sustained as stake president (CN Feb. 24, 1979, 3–11).

■ **10. Stephen Markham Home Site. Stephen Markham's home** was located on the NE corner of Young and Partridge Streets. Stephen was born in 1800 and was baptized in 1837. His first wife was Hannah Vogelboon. He was a colonel in the Nauvoo Legion, served as a bodyguard to Joseph Smith, and warned the Prophet of his impending arrest at Dixon, IL. Stephen was in the **Carthage Jail** with Joseph Smith before the Martyrdom and was a faithful member of the original pioneer company in 1847. Eliza R. Snow wrote the lyrics to the popular hymn **"O My Father"** in the attic of Stephen Markham's home.

When Joseph Smith was hampered with lawsuits in 1844, Stephen Markham sold his newly built home for $1,200 and gave the proceeds to Joseph. Stephen then moved his family into a tent until he could build a cabin (BiE 3:676–77).

■ **11. William Weeks Home.** The **William Weeks** single-story brick **home** and **office** is located on the north side of Young Street between Durphy and Partridge Streets. A basement housed the original kitchen, where an original fireplace still exists. Copies of

William Weeks's original drawings of the Nauvoo Temple are on display.

William was born in 1813 and married Caroline Matilda Allen in 1839 at Quincy, IL. They had 10 children, seven of whom died at young ages.

William Weeks home, Nauvoo, IL. (1985)

William was the **general superintendent** and **architect** of the **Nauvoo Temple** construction, working under the supervision of Joseph Smith, who had seen the temple in vision (HC 5:353; 6:196–97). William did the architectural drawings, and in 1841 he did the initial carving on the wooden oxen that supported the wooden Nauvoo Temple baptismal font. A stone baptismal font replaced the wooden one in 1845. William showed the stonecutters how to carve the oxen and font, and he helped design the Nauvoo House, Nauvoo Legion Arsenal, and Masonic Hall.

Weeks went to the Salt Lake Valley in 1847, but very soon became disaffected with the Church. He died in Los Angeles in 1900 (BYUS 19, no. 3 [1979]: 337–60).

■ **12. Howard Coray Home Site.** The traditional **Howard Coray** single-story **log cabin** was located on the NE corner of Hyde and Young Streets on lot 3, block 70.

Howard was born in 1817 in New York state. He was baptized in 1840 and married Martha Knowlton on Feb. 6, 1841, at Nauvoo. He served as a clerk to Joseph Smith and helped compile and write the *History of the Church.*

In 1840, as the men returned to the Homestead after looking at Joseph Smith's horses across the road, 200-pound Joseph wrestled

Howard Coray home, Nauvoo, IL. (Courtesy of LDSCA)

130-pound Howard in the middle of Main Street. The match left Howard's leg broken three inches above the ankle joint. Joseph had his father give Howard a blessing, and the Prophet prophesied that Howard would soon find a wife and have many children. The prophecy was fulfilled (JHC 18–19). (See Site No. 33.) Howard's wife, **Martha Knowlton Coray,** served as scribe to Lucy Mack Smith while Lucy dictated her *History of Joseph Smith* (HC 7:519).

■ **13. EDWARD HUNTER HOME SITE. Edward Hunter's** two-story brick **home** was located in lot 2, block 82, on the SE corner of Partridge and Knight Streets. Edward, born in 1793, married Ann Stanley in 1830, was baptized in 1840, and moved to Nauvoo in 1842. He was a wealthy "iron-monger," selling iron, steel, rasps, nails, kettles, pans, ovens, and other items. In a single year, he donated $15,000 to the Church. He served as bishop of the Nauvoo Fifth Ward.

Edward Hunter home, Nauvoo, IL.

Joseph Smith hid in Edward Hunter's home when Missouri officers attempted to arrest the Prophet in the fall of 1842 (HC 5:146). Joseph also secluded himself in the home of John Smith, Newel K. Whitney, Edward Sayers, and Carlos Granger (HC 5:89–90, 107, 147).

The Prophet wrote part of his revelation on baptism for the dead (D&C 128) in the Hunter home in the presence of Edward Hunter and William Clayton (OMN 61). After the Prophet's death, Brigham Young, Heber C. Kimball, and Willard Richards worked on the *History of the Church* while in hiding in the upper room of the home (OPW 110).

Edward Hunter was a member of the Nauvoo City Council, met with Illinois governor Thomas Ford to seek protection for the Saints in June 1844, and helped bury Joseph and Hyrum Smith. Edward led a company of Saints to the Salt Lake Valley in the fall of 1847, where he served as bishop of the 13th Ward and then became the third **presiding bishop** after the death of **Newel K. Whitney** (BiE 1:227–32).

■ **14. William Gheen Home.** The two-story brick **home** of **William Gheen** is located in the lot just north of the corner lot, on the NW corner of Mulholland (named after James Mulholland, the Prophet's scribe) and Partridge Streets (immediately north of the number 14 square on the map).

William, born in 1798, married Ester Ann Pierre in 1823 and was baptized in 1840. His daughter, Anna, married Heber C. Kimball, making William and Ester the great-grandparents of Spencer W. Kimball, twelfth president of the Church. William Gheen died in 1845 in Nauvoo (OMN 64).

■ **15. David Yearsley Home.** The **David Yearsley home,** located on the NW corner of Partridge and White Streets, is the only three-story brick home in Nauvoo. David, born in 1808, married Mary Ann Hoopes in 1830 and was baptized in 1841 at Nauvoo. He operated two **stores** in Nauvoo (OMN 65–66).

David Yearsley home, Nauvoo, IL.

■ **16. Willard Richards Home Site.** The **Willard Richards' home site** is located on the south side of White Street, near the center of the block between Durphy and Partridge Streets (east side of lot 2, block 103). The eastern half of an existing house was built partly over the original basement walls, which are still visible (ThC 7:300).

Willard Richards was born in 1804 in Massachusetts and was baptized Dec. 31, 1836, by Brigham Young. He married **Jennetta Richards** in Preston, England, Sept. 24, 1838, and was an Apostle from 1840 until his death in 1854. He also served as a counselor to Brigham Young (1847–54) and as Church historian (1842–54).

Many chapters of the *History of the Church* were written in Elder Richards's home under Joseph Smith's direction (HC 7:389). Willard's nephew **Franklin D. Richards** helped his uncle write the chapters (ThC 7:300–301; BiE 1:53–56). For a time in 1845, the Apostles and other brethren met together every evening—sometimes more often—at Willard Richards' home to unite in faith (Wex Apr. 15, 1883, 170).

When Elder Richards's wife, Jennetta, died at age 28 on July 9, 1845, she was buried about 20 feet SW of the couple's house (InD 470–71). Her remains were moved twice to their current burial site on Durphy Street.

■ **17. Heber C. Kimball Home.** Located on the NE corner of Munson and Partridge Streets, the **Heber C. Kimball home** is one of the most elaborate two-story brick homes in Nauvoo. The 1½ stories on the east were built after the Church's Nauvoo period. An engraving on a stone above the balcony reads "HCK 1845," revealing the home's builder.

Heber C. Kimball home, Nauvoo, IL. (Courtesy of USHS)

Many of the rooms have been furnished with period furniture and musical instruments from the era. Most of the basic structure is the original home, with the exception of the porches and other frills. Heber lived in this home for only five months. Unable to find a buyer for it in 1846, he abandoned it to move west. Dr. J. LeRoy Kimball, great-grandson of Heber C. Kimball, purchased the home in 1956 and restored it, initiating Nauvoo Restoration, Inc., and efforts to restore Nauvoo as it was in 1845. Dr. Kimball led the efforts for many years.

Heber C. Kimball, born in 1801 in Vermont, married Vilate Murray in 1822 and was baptized in 1832 at Mendon, NY. He became one of the original Twelve Apostles in 1835 and served as a counselor to Brigham Young for 21 years (HC 1:296).

The **Mutual Improvement Association,** organized in Utah in 1869, had its roots in the Young Gentlemen and Young Ladies Relief Society, which held its first meeting in Heber C. Kimball's home. Elder Kimball gave instructions in this and subsequent meetings held elsewhere. The Prophet Joseph Smith expressed gratitude to Elder Kimball for having commenced this organization for the youth of the Church (HC 5:320–22).

Joseph Smith sealed William Clayton to Margaret Moon in the Heber C. Kimball home on Apr. 27, 1843.

■ **18. Titus Billings Home Site.** The **home** of **Titus Billings,** born in 1793, was on the west side of the lot on the NW corner of Partridge and Munson Streets. Titus was one of the first people to be baptized in Kirtland in Nov. 1830 and was **second counselor** to Bishop Edward Partridge, the first bishop in the Church (D&C 41:9). Titus was captain of the first 50 in Heber C. Kimball's pioneer company in 1848. He settled in Manti, then Provo. He died in 1866 (BiE 1:242).

■ **19. Orrin Porter Rockwell Home Site.** The **Porter Rockwell home site** is on the SW corner of Munson and Partridge Streets. Porter Rockwell, born in 1813 in Massachusetts, was baptized Apr. 6, 1830. He married Luana Beebe in 1832. He was a "rough and ready sort" and was a deputy marshal and guard to Joseph Smith and Brigham Young (OPR 3, 8). A **marker** dedicated to Rockwell is located at the home site.

■ **20. Samuel Williams Home.** The **Samuel Williams** two-story brick **home,** with a post-1840s addition, is on the west side of Partridge Street between Munson and Kimball Streets. Samuel was born in 1789, married Ruth Bishop in 1810, and was baptized in 1839. He presided over the elders quorum in Nauvoo in 1841 and worked as a stonecutter on the Nauvoo Temple (OMN 84–85).

■ **21. Silas Condit Home.** The **Silas Condit home** is on the NW corner of Partridge and Kimball Streets. Condit was born in New Jersey and was baptized in 1842 (OMN 86).

■ **22. Philo Johnson Home Site. Philo Johnson's home** was in the SW quarter of lot 4, block 119, or just east of the center of the block between Partridge and Hyde Streets, on the north side of Kimball Street, about where the current reconstructed brick kilns are located.

Philo Johnson was born in 1814 and baptized in 1839, the same year he married Maria Mills. He drove a team of oxen that pulled the wagon with an **odometer** mounted on it to measure the mileage of Brigham Young's 1847 party of pioneers. He also helped William Clayton put up mileage boards every 10 miles along the Mormon Trail. His name is carved on the walls of Cache Cave, a prominent pioneer landmark in Echo Canyon, UT. He settled in Payson, UT, where he was a prominent hat maker for 25 years (MoC 26).

■ **23. Nauvoo Lands and Records Office.** The **Nauvoo Lands and Records Office** is located in a brick home on the NE corner of Parley and Partridge Streets (originally owned by Newel K. Whitney). It contains the land record of Hancock County and some records of Lee County. Visitors may use this office to identify property and homes owned by early settlers of Nauvoo and vicinity. Genealogical records and biographical materials, such as diaries of early Church members who lived in the area, are also available.

■ **24. Henry W. Miller Home Site.** The **Henry W. Miller home** was located on the NW corner lot of Partridge and Sidney Streets. Miller, born in 1807, married Elmyra Pond in 1831 and was baptized in 1839.

The **Council of Fifty** was organized in the lodge room over Henry Miller's house on Mar. 11, 1844 (HC 6:260–61). This council was the municipal or civil governing department of the kingdom of God on earth. It sought refuge for the Saints, under the jurisdiction of the priesthood.

The council also sought to obtain redress for wrongs inflicted upon the Saints, and it sought the best manner of settling people in some distant and unoccupied territory (HC 7:213), assisting in planning for the exodus to the West. Its members were captains of hundreds, fifties, and even tens. At times, the council was called the "Council of the YTFIF," with the word *fifty* spelled backward. This was done to maintain the secret nature of the council (DHS 1:107).

Tour Six: Water Street

Water Street, so named because it was adjacent to the Mississippi River, was one of the most important streets of Nauvoo.

It had many businesses and some homes. This part of the tour begins on the east end of Water Street and goes west to Bain Street.

■ **25. Alexander Neibaur Home Site.** The **Alexander Neibaur home** was on the east side of Durphy Street between Water and Lumber Streets on the south half of lot 2, block 159, at the point where State 96 joins the south end of Durphy Street.

Alexander, born in 1808, married Ellen Breakell in 1833 and was baptized in 1838. He was a close friend and bodyguard of Joseph Smith. He was also a barber, wheelwright, and dentist. The *Times and Seasons* advertised Alexander as a "surgeon dentist" from Preston, England (T&S 2:502). In addition, he manufactured matches in his home, calling his company "The Nauvoo Match Factory."

Alexander Neibaur helped teach Joseph Smith and others to read Hebrew and German (HC 6:402, 426).

● **26. Community of Christ (formerly RLDS Church).** The **Community of Christ** (Reorganized Church of Jesus Christ of Latter Day Saints) chapel is located on the SW corner of Durphy and Water Streets. The RLDS Church was organized at Amboy, IL, during an Apr. 6, 1860, conference. Joseph Smith III was ordained as its prophet by Zenos Gurley, William Marks, Samuel Powers, and William Blair.

■ **27. Jedediah M. Grant Home Site.** The **Jedediah M. Grant home** was located on the east side of lot 3, block 145, which was on the north side of Water Street, near the center of the block between Durphy and Partridge Streets.

Jedediah was born in 1816, was baptized in 1833, and was a member of Zion's Camp at age 18. He is known as one of the great missionaries in North Carolina and Virginia, where he gave the "blank text" sermon, which he delivered extemporaneously. He crossed the plains in 1847, was elected first **mayor** of Salt Lake City in 1851, was called as an **Apostle** and **second counselor** to President Brigham Young in 1854, and led the Mormon Reformation of 1856–57 under the direction of President Young. He died Dec. 1, 1856 (BiE 1:56–62).

■ **28. Newel Knight Mill and Home Site. Newel Knight** was born in 1800 in Vermont, married Sally Coburn in 1825, and had an evil spirit cast out of him by Joseph Smith shortly after being baptized in 1830. Following his first wife's death in 1834, Newel married Lydia Goldthwait in 1835 and moved to Nauvoo in 1839. He died in Nebraska in 1847. He was a miller by trade and helped build several mills in the Nauvoo area at Joseph Smith's request. Because Newel needed funds for materials, he had many partners, including John Scott, in the milling business. Some of his mills were horse operated and some were water powered.

Newell's house and grist and sawmill, powered by water diverted from a dam, were located near the foot of Partridge Street in lot 2, block 162 (DHS 1:38; TAMF 143).

■ **29. William Huntington Home Site. William Huntington's home** was located on the west side of the SW corner lot at the corner of Partridge and Water Streets. William was born Mar. 28, 1784, in New Hampshire. He married Zina Baker in 1806, and they had nine children. He was baptized in 1835, and in 1840 he married Lydia Partridge, widow of Edward Partridge. He was the sexton of the Old Nauvoo Cemetery and sold "Ready-made and Made-to-Order Coffins." He presided over the Saints at Mount Pisgah, Iowa, and died there in 1846 (RPJS 262).

■ **30. George Watt Home Site.** On the west side of lot 4, block 146, located on the north side of Water Street, just right of the center of the block between Partridge and Hyde Streets, is the **home site of George Watt** (not to be confused with George D. Watt, the first baptized convert in England). George Watt, born in Scotland in 1816, was a member of the Nauvoo First Ward (MoC 25).

■ **31. Community of Christ Joseph Smith Historic Visitors Center.** The **Community of Christ Visitors Center** is located on the north side of Water Street between Partridge and Hyde Streets. It is a spacious modern building with a theater, gift shop, and museum. Center personnel guide visitors on **tours,** originating at the center, of the **Homestead** and **Mansion House.**

■ **32. Joseph Smith Brick Stable Site.** Foundations of **Joseph Smith's** two-story **brick stable** are still visible at the SW corner of Water and

Hyde Streets. A David Smith painting shows the stable NE of the Nauvoo House (OMN 149–50).

Joseph Smith said, "I have erected a large and commodious brick stable, and it is capable of accommodating seventy-five horses at one time, and storing the requisite amount of forage, and is unsurpassed by any similar establishment in the State" (HC 6:33).

■ **33. Joseph Smith Homestead (CC). Joseph's Smith's** first Nauvoo **block house** (square logs) home is located at the foot of Main Street on the west side of the street (the SW corner of Main and Water Streets). Part of this building—the 16-by-18-foot two-story log portion—was standing when the Saints arrived in 1839 (HC 3:349; OMN 156–58). It was probably used as the first Indian Agency in Illinois in 1803. Joseph Smith added the north room in 1840, and when Joseph Smith III moved into the home in 1858, he added the portion on the west side of the original log structure. The summer kitchen on the back is a reconstructed log cabin on the original site. The original log cabin was occupied by Joseph Smith Sr. The Prophet Joseph Smith hid from enemies in a secret place under the house's cellar stairs.

It was from the **Homestead** that the Prophet arose from his sick bed and administered to the sick in his own house and dooryard. He then walked along the Mississippi riverbank to the Lower Stone

Joseph Smith homestead, Nauvoo, IL. (1994)

House, healing the sick "on every side." He went to Montrose and did the same there. The day, July 22, 1839, is known as **"a day of God's power"** (HC 4:3–5; JWW 1:347–48).

In June 1840, while working as a scribe to Joseph, Howard Coray had a unique wrestling experience with Joseph Smith in the middle of Main Street just east of the Homestead. Howard recorded the following in his journal:

> In the following June, I met with an accident, which I shall mention: The Prophet and myself, after looking at his horses and admiring them that were just across the road from his house, we started thither, the Prophet at the same time put his arm over my shoulder. When we had reached about the middle of the road, he stopped and remarked; "Brother Coray, I wish you was a little larger, I would like to have some fun with you." I replied, perhaps you can as it is—not realizing what I was saying—Joseph a man of over 200 lbs weight, while I scarcely 130 lbs, made it not a little ridiculous for me to think of engaging with him in anything like a scuffle. However, as soon as I made this reply, he began to trip me; he took some kind of a lock on my right leg, from which I was unable to extricate it, and throwing me around, broke it some 3 inches above the ankle joint. He immediately carried me into the house, pulled off my boot, and found, at once, that my leg was decidedly broken; then got some splinters and bandaged it. A number of times that day did he come in to see me, endeavoring to console me as much as possible. The next day when he happened in to see me after a little conversation I said: Bro. Joseph, when Jacob wrestled with the Angel, and was lamed by Him, the Angel blest him; now I think I am also entitled to a blessing. To that he replied: "I am not the Patriarch, but my father is, and when you get up and around, I'll have him bless you." He said no more for a minute or so, meanwhile looking very earnestly at me; then said, "Bro. Coray, you will soon find a companion, one that will be suited to your condition, and whom you will be satisfied with. She will cling to you, like the cords of death; and you will have a good many children" (JHC 18–19; spelling modernized).

This prophecy was fulfilled.

Egyptian mummies were stored for a time in the upstairs of the Homestead, and sometimes sacred temple ordinances were performed there (DoJS Nov. 12, 1843, 426).

Sheriffs Harmon T. Wilson and Joseph H. Reynolds arrested Joseph Smith at Dixon, IL, June 23, 1843, hoping to take him to Missouri. A few days later, brethren who had come from Nauvoo to the Prophet's aid compelled the sheriffs to take Joseph to Nauvoo to stand trial. The Saints at Nauvoo greeted the Prophet on his return with cheering, cannon and musket fire, and music by the Nauvoo band (HC 5:459). Of this occasion, Angus M. Cannon recorded that Joseph "mounted the well-curb, at the east side of his old residence [Homestead]," and while swinging his hat he "proclaimed aloud with a voice that thrilled my entire being . . . 'I am thankful to the God of Israel who has delivered me out of the hands of the Missourians once more,' his words so affected many of the people that they wept tears of joy" (HC 5:459 and 433–84 for the full account of the arrest in Dixon).

■ **34. Nauvoo House (CC).** The **Nauvoo House** is located on the bank of the Mississippi River, on the east side of the foot of Main Street, across Main Street from the Homestead.

In a **revelation** to Joseph Smith on Jan. 19, 1841 (D&C 124:22–24, 56–83, 119–22; HC 4:274–86), George Miller, Lyman Wight, John Snider, and Peter Haws were named trustees of the proposed **Nauvoo House,** to be built to house immigrants and other Saints who were arriving in Nauvoo in large numbers.

Stock in the building sold for $50 a share to those who believed in the Book of Mormon and the revelations of Joseph Smith. Lucian Woodworth was the architect. The house was L shaped with a 120-foot riverfront and a 40-foot side running north and south. The first-story walls were rock, and the other two stories were to be brick.

On Oct. 2, 1841, the presidency of the Church laid the house's **SE cornerstone** (T&S 2:576), which contained the following items: small Bible, Book of Doctrine and Covenants, copies of the *Times and Seasons,* coins, and the **original manuscript** of the **Book of Mormon,** written mostly by Oliver Cowdery (AWF 15).

After the Martyrdom, the bodies of Joseph and Hyrum were secretly, and temporarily, buried in the basement of the unfinished

Nauvoo House $50 stock certificate. (Courtesy of Wilford C. Wood)

Nauvoo House cornerstone, Nauvoo, IL. (1958)

Painting of the Nauvoo House in Nauvoo, IL, by David Smith, youngest son of the Prophet Joseph Smith. The Nauvoo House was never finished, and David's painting shows the building as it looked when the Saints left Nauvoo in 1846. (Courtesy of Wilford C. Wood)

Unfinished Nauvoo House in Nauvoo, IL, showing the Emma and Lewis C. Bidamon house built in 1869 on the SW corner.

Outdoor toilet at the back of the Nauvoo House, Nauvoo, IL, with Mormon missionaries William Ellsworth (left) and Ray Davis (right). (Photo by C. H. Spencer, 1916; courtesy of Gale Bullock)

Emma, wife of the Prophet Joseph Smith and later the wife of Lewis C. Bidamon, died in her house on the SW corner of the unfinished Nauvoo House in 1879. (Courtesy of Wilford C. Wood)

Emma and Lewis C. Bidamon house on the SW corner of the unfinished Nauvoo House, Nauvoo, IL. (1985)

Nauvoo House (HC 6:628). They were subsequently moved to the family cemetery across the street. The Nauvoo House was never finished, but after the Martyrdom, Emma and her new husband, Lewis C. Bidamon (married Dec. 23, 1847, on the Prophet's birthday), tore down parts of the building and in 1869 built this home at the building's SW corner. Emma died here Apr. 30, 1879.

By the time Lewis Bidamon removed the SE cornerstone in 1882, most of the original Book of Mormon manuscript had been destroyed by dampness. Bidamon gave some of the manuscript and a coin to Franklin D. Richards. The LDS Church now has them (ThC 7:303–304). After approximately 1872, the house was used as a small hotel known as the Bidamon House or Riverside Mansion. Emma and Lewis lived here until their deaths in 1879 and 1891, respectively.

Foot of Main Street, Nauvoo, IL, looking south toward the Mississippi River. (Courtesy of LDSCA)

■ **35. Foot of Main Street.** The **Nauvoo House Landing,** or **wharf,** for steamboats was located at the foot of Main Street near the Nauvoo House. It was one of at least four docking places for riverboats at Nauvoo. The other landings were the Lower Stone House Landing ("Montrose Crossing"), Kimball Landing, and Upper Stone House Landing.

This was where the ***Maid of Iowa*** landed. Joseph Smith called it "her landing" (HC 5:481). The *Maid of Iowa* was a 60-ton, 115-foot stern-wheeler steamboat built by Levi Moffit and Welshman Dan Jones, who was the captain (BYUS 19, no. 3 [1979]: 321, 323). At this wharf the steamship took on or unloaded both freight and passengers.

On Apr. 12, 1843, the *Maid of Iowa* landed at the Nauvoo House Landing with its anxious passengers. The Prophet Joseph Smith, with tears in his eyes, was the first to board the steamboat and

Foot of Main Street in the winter, looking north from the frozen Mississippi River (circa 1945; courtesy of Wilford C. Wood). Note the wagon and horses on the ice. Joseph Smith's homestead is on the left side of Main Street, and the Nauvoo House-Bidamon House is on the right side of Main Street. A person might envision the riverboat Maid of Iowa *docked or Saints being baptized near the place where the men and horses are standing.*

welcome the 200 British converts being led by Parley P. Pratt and Levi Richards (HC 5:354). When Joseph met the captain, Dan Jones, he said, "God bless this little man" (BiE 3:658; HC 5:354). Dan was baptized within a month, and the Prophet purchased half-interest in the *Maid of Iowa.*

The *Maid of Iowa* was used for **preaching services** on Sunday, Apr. 14, 1844 (HC 6:333; DoJS 471), for **transporting English converts** to Nauvoo, and for carrying **missionaries** toward their fields of labor. It was also used to **intercept** the sheriffs who were trying to take the Prophet to Missouri, to **ferry** people to and from **Montrose**, and to take the Saints on **social excursions** featuring band music and other entertainment (HC 5:384–85, 418, 447, 510; BYUS 19, no. 3 [1979]: 321, 323).

The Mississippi River served as a **baptismal font** at the foot of Main. After preaching at the **temple stand** on Mar. 20, 1842, Joseph baptized 80 persons here, including L. D. Wasson, Emma Smith's nephew. He was the first of her kin to join the Church. Despite the taxing nature of Joseph's open-air preaching and the baptism of 80 persons, the Prophet led the group back to the temple stand, where he confirmed 50 of those he baptized (HC 4:557; T&S 3:751–53; HiR 491; MHBY 1846–47, 126). Several persons were baptized in the river east of Main Street on Sunday, Apr. 28, 1844.

The Saints in Nauvoo were **baptized for the dead** in the Mississippi River during the fall of 1840 (HC 4:206, 231, 426, 557; NCJ 67). During this period, the Saints were rebaptized for health reasons or to renew their covenants. Those who had been disfellowshipped or excommunicated were also rebaptized (JJT 82).

During the winter of 1842–43, the Saints used the Mississippi, frozen for months, for winter **recreation.** At the foot of Main, the Prophet played with his sons Joseph III, Alexander, and Frederick G. Other children joined them as they slid down the sloping end of Main Street, gaining enough momentum to send loaded sleighs onto the smooth ice (BYUS 18, no. 2 [1978]: 148; HC 5:265).

■ **36. Nauvoo Survey Stone.** The **Nauvoo survey stone** is at the SW corner of Main and Water Streets. Like the streets planned for the City of Zion in Independence, MO, in 1833, Nauvoo's streets were to run along the four main points of the compass.

City **blocks** contained four **lots** of one acre each. Originally there was to be only one home per lot, set back 25 feet from the street. But as people began crowding into the city, the one-house lots were subdivided into more lots.

Streets were to be 49½ feet wide, with the exception of Main Street, which was 82 feet wide so it could accommodate a two-mile canal that was planned to run from river to river to provide shipping, wharfs, water power, and general industry. The canal was never built. Another exception was Water Street, which was 64 feet wide to serve the business section of Nauvoo along the waterfront. The streets were also to have sidewalks 8 feet wide.

Although the famous Gustavus Hills Map shows all the land in the river bend and on the "bluffs" to be platted, the Saints were forced to leave Nauvoo before their plans could be realized (NCJ 35–40).

■ **37. Mansion House (CC).** This large, two-story frame house on the NE corner of Water and Main Streets was built as a residence for **Joseph Smith.** He moved into the Mansion House on Aug. 31, 1843 (HC 5:556). At one time it contained a large wing that was used as a hotel, but the wing was demolished in 1890. The total structure had 22 rooms. Here in the Mansion House dining room 10,000 people viewed the bodies of Joseph and Hyrum after the Martyrdom (HC 6:627–29; ThC 1:136; BYUS 19, no. 2 [1979]: 238). George Cannon made death masks of the slain leaders (ERA Nov. 1951, 792).[1]

It was also in the Mansion House that the RLDS Church displayed the remains of Joseph and Hyrum after they had been unearthed under the direction of Frederick M. Smith in 1928 (see

The Mansion House, Joseph Smith's home in Nauvoo, IL, 1843–44, was built in the shape of an L. (Circa 1880; courtesy of LDSCA)

[1] Other sources attribute the death masks to Philo Dibble (LHPD).

Site No. 39). Samuel O. Bennion, president of the Central States Mission, was present to verify that the skeletons belonged to Joseph and Hyrum.

When Ebenezer Robinson leased the hotel in Jan. 1844 for $1,000 a year, Joseph kept three rooms for his family (DoJS 442; HC 6:185). Only the home has been restored, although some archaeological digging has been done on the hotel portion.

Josiah Quincy, mayor of Boston, visited Joseph Smith here May 14, 1844, as did **Sac** and **Fox Indians** on May 23, 1844 (HC 6:402). **Porter Rockwell** arrived here Dec. 25, 1843, after being imprisoned nearly a year in Missouri (HC 6:134–35).

The **mummies** of Pearl of Great Price fame were shown to Quincy and Charles Adams in the Mansion House. Joseph invited each of them to give Lucy Mack Smith, who was living in the Mansion House (FOP 386), 25 cents for the privilege. In *Figures of the Past,* published in 1883, Quincy said the Prophet was a

The Mansion House, Nauvoo, IL, without the wing on the back part, which ran east and west. (Circa 1900; courtesy of LDSCA)

The Mansion House, Nauvoo, IL. (1958)

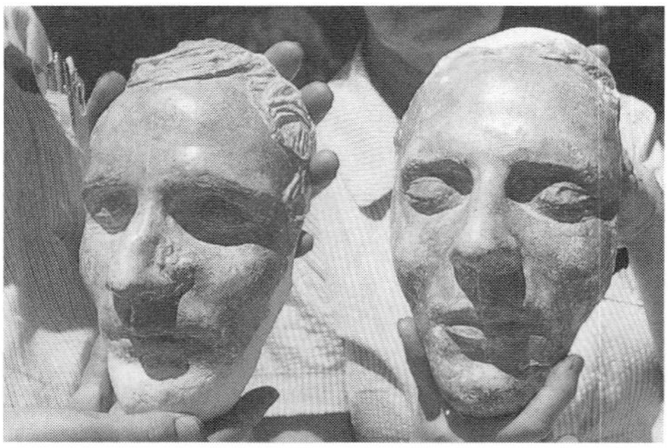

The death masks of Joseph Smith (right) and Hyrum Smith (left) were made in the Mansion House by George Cannon. Former owners Wilford C. Wood and his wife, Lillian, hold the masks (1964), which the Wood Foundation donated to the LDS Church Museum.

phenomenon to be explained for having exerted a "wonderful influence" (FOP 377).

■ **38. Improvised Platform Site.** On the SE corner of Main and Water Streets, directly opposite the south end of the Nauvoo Mansion, was an **improvised platform** on the "frame of a building" (HC 6:497).

Here the **Nauvoo Legion** was placed under **martial law** on June 18, 1844, as legion members assembled in the street around the improvised platform and Joseph Smith, in full uniform, gave his last **public discourse** to the legion (BYUS 18, no. 2 [1978]: 160). Edward Stevenson said of Joseph's discourse to the legion: "Joseph spoke with great power, so much so that many tears were shed by the multitude who were assembled around that memorable frame building. His speech occupied about one and one-fourth hours" (AES 108). Joseph Smith had been commissioned a lieutenant general by **Illinois governor Thomas Ford** (HC 7:277). After the Prophet's death, Brigham Young was commissioned a lieutenant general.

When Governor Ford and 50 troops came to Nauvoo from Carthage on June 27, 1844, the governor broke his promise to Joseph Smith that "he would take Joseph with him if he went to Nauvoo." At 5 P.M. Governor Ford ascended the improvised platform

Joseph mustering the Nauvoo Legion. (Painting by C. C. A. Christensen; courtesy of MOABYU)

Lt. Gen. Joseph Smith of the Nauvoo Legion. (Courtesy of LDSCA)

Flag of the First Battalion of the Second Regular Infantry, Nauvoo Legion.

Lt. Gen. Joseph Smith addressing the Nauvoo Legion from the improvised platform. (Oil painting by Robert Campbell, 1845; courtesy of LDSCA and the Museum of Church History and Art)

Lt. Gen. Joseph Smith delivering his last public address while standing on the improvised platform in Nauvoo, IL. (Painting by John Hafen, 1888; courtesy of LDSCA)

and addressed the citizens of Nauvoo in an attempt to make a military display and overawe the Saints. He insulted the Saints and upbraided them. He then visited the temple before leaving for Carthage. About the same hour he delivered his speech, the Prophet Joseph and Hyrum were martyred (HC 7:132; CHC 2:260, 275–79).

■ **39. Smith Family Cemetery.** Adjacent to and SW of the Homestead, at the foot of Main Street, is the **Smith Family Cemetery,** where many of Joseph Smith's family are buried, including the **Prophet Joseph Smith, Hyrum Smith, Joseph Smith Sr.** (d. Aug. 14, 1840), **Don Carlos Smith** (d. Aug. 7, 1841), **Samuel H. Smith** (d. July 30, 1844), **Lucy Mack Smith** (d. May 5, 1855), and **Emma Smith Bidamon** (d. Apr. 30, 1879).

After the Martyrdom, **Joseph** and **Hyrum** were given a mock burial in a vault just south of the Nauvoo Temple. Their real, and secret, burial site was in the dirt floor of the uncompleted **Nauvoo House.** They were buried secretly in order to preserve the bodies from desecration.

Under cover of darkness, the bodies of Joseph and Hyrum were later reburied 38 feet south and 20 feet west of the SW corner of the Homestead, under the floor of a small shed called a "bee house" or "spring house," which has subsequently been restored to identify its location.

After Emma's death in 1879, the exact location of Joseph and Hyrum's grave was lost. When the waters of Lake Cooper, formed in 1913 behind a dam at Keokuk on the Mississippi River, threatened to flood the area where the graves were thought to be, RLDS Church leaders decided to locate and remove the bodies to higher ground. A second reason for locating the graves was so that Joseph, Emma, and Hyrum could be honored with an appropriate monument over their graves. A third reason was to quiet rumors that the pioneers had taken the bodies of Joseph and Hyrum west and buried them on Temple Square.

W. O. Hands directed the search for the missing graves, and in 1928 he found them. Samuel O. Bennion, president of the Central States Mission, was on hand and verified to the LDS First Presidency that the bodies were properly identified.

On Jan. 20, 1928, the remains of Joseph, Emma, and Hyrum were arranged in silk-lined wooden boxes that were placed side-by-side, 17 feet north of where they were found, in the center of a solid slab of concrete 10 feet square and 3½ feet thick. The graves, now located 18 feet SW of the Homestead, were marked for the first time.

On Aug. 4, 1991, a newly renovated cemetery, including the remains of Joseph, Emma, and Hyrum, was dedicated by President Wallace B. Smith, great-grandson of Joseph Smith and president of the then-RLDS Church (NCJ 122; CN Aug. 10, 1991, 3, 6–7; JWHJ 11:17–33).

■ **40. Nauvoo Coach and Carriage Factory Site.** The **Nauvoo Coach and Carriage Factory** was on the north side of Water Street, just west of the center of the block between Main and Granger Streets, and across from Joseph Smith's Red Brick Store, on property owned by Almon W. Babbitt. The factory was controlled by the Nauvoo Coach and Carriage Association, with George W. Harris as president and Elijah Fordham and Richard Ballantyne as clerks.

More than 300 businesses operated in Nauvoo. Artists, auctioneers, bakers, blacksmiths, boot makers, entertainers, brick makers, builders, painters, undertakers, manufacturers, dentists, doctors, gunsmiths, hatmakers, lawyers, horticulturists, hotel owners, lumberjacks, merchants, grain millers, musicians, printers, realtors, teachers, watchmakers, surveyors, tailors, tanners, ironmongers, wheelwrights, and others made all or part of their living in business.

■ **41. William Law Home and Store Site.** The **home** and **store** of **William Law** was located on the NE corner of Water and Granger Streets. William Law was born in 1809 and baptized in 1836. He married Jane Silverthorn. He was **second counselor** to the Prophet Joseph Smith from 1841 to 1844 (D&C 124:126), succeeding Hyrum Smith. He was a wealthy and prominent man in Nauvoo, a captain in the Nauvoo Legion, and the owner of a store and steam-operated grain and sawmill.

William Law apostatized toward the end of 1843 and was excommunicated Apr. 18, 1844. He became a bitter enemy of Joseph and was one of the publishers of the ***Nauvoo Expositor.*** He was also one of the instigators of the martyrdom of the Prophet; **secret meetings** were held in his home to plot Joseph's death. Two boys, Robert Scott and Dennison Harris, attended the meetings as spies for the Prophet (ThC 5:251–60). William Law died in Wisconsin in 1892.

■ **42. Joseph Smith's Red Brick Store (Community of Christ).** Joseph Smith's general store, reconstructed 1978–79, is located on the south side of Water Street, near Granger Street, one block west of Main Street. Built in 1841 (HC 4:470, 476, 491), the store is 44 feet by 25 feet and made of red brick.

Early photo of the Joseph Smith's Red Brick Store, Nauvoo, IL. (Circa 1870; courtesy of USHS)

The **first floor** contained the **store** (with its original daybook preserved) and the office of **Bishop Newel K. Whitney,** which served as a **tithing office**. Bishop Whitney's desk is on display in the office. The second floor included a large council room, or assembly room, and the office of Joseph Smith, which served as Church headquarters and the city's social center. Several historically important events took place in this building, making it one of the most important and sacred buildings in Nauvoo.

In Joseph's **private office,** he kept his sacred writings, wrote his political platform with help from William W. Phelps, translated sacred writings (such as the book of Abraham), organized the Council of Fifty, received revelations, and wrote down D&C 132 on plural and eternal marriage, which he had received earlier (ThC 7:301; HC 5:1–2; RBS). When endowments were first given in the store, this room was used for initiatory ordinances (DLJN Feb. 7, 1877).

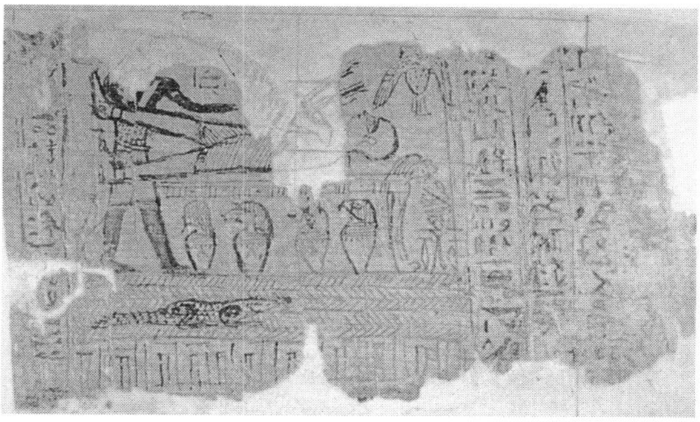

Facsimile No. 1 from the book of Abraham. The Prophet Joseph Smith used his private office in the Red Brick Store in Nauvoo, IL, as he translated the book of Abraham.

Elder David O. McKay and George D. Pyper, who became general superintendent of the Deseret Sunday School Union in 1934, are surrounded by the foundation of Joseph Smith's Red Brick Store, Nauvoo, IL. (Circa 1940; courtesy of Wilford C. Wood)

Joseph Smith's Red Brick Store in Nauvoo, IL, reconstructed 1978–79 by the RLDS Church under the direction of F. Mark McKiernan and others. (1985)

The larger **upstairs council room**, or "Lodge room" (HC 4:552)—Joseph's general business office—served as a Church office and a variety of other purposes:

(1) Various groups held **meetings** here, including the Masons (1842–44), school students, priesthood quorums, the Nauvoo Temple Committee, the Nauvoo House Committee, the Nauvoo Legion, city administrators, Church administration committees, and politicians (HC 5:1).

(2) The **Relief Society** was organized here Mar. 17, 1842, with **Emma Smith,** an "elect lady," as president (D&C 25:3; HC 4:552–53, 602–607).

Joseph Smith organized the Female Relief Society of Nauvoo on Mar. 17, 1842, in his Red Brick Store in Nauvoo, IL, with (left to right) Emma Smith as president, Sarah M. Cleveland as first counselor, and Elizabeth Ann Whitney as second counselor.

(3) The first **temple endowments** in this dispensation were given here May 4, 1842 (HC 5:1–2). Before Joseph's death, he gave endowments to more than 60 people. Temple ordinances were also given in the Homestead, the Mansion House, and the Brigham Young Home (DoJS Nov. 5, 1843, 425–26).

(4) The Prophet gave a **blessing** to his son Joseph Smith III here on Jan. 17, 1844 (RBS 31–32).

(5) **The Young Gentlemen and Young Ladies Relief Society,** forerunner of the Mutual Improvement Association, was formally organized here on Mar. 21, 1843, with William Walker as president (T&S 4:154–57).

(6) The Prophet instructed the Twelve Apostles here on Feb. 20, 1844, about the future **move of the Saints to the West.** Joseph said, "I instructed the 12 to send out a delegation and investigate the locations of California and Oregon and find a good location where we can remove after the Temple is completed and build a city in a day and have a government of our own in a healthy climate" (DoJS 447).

(7) Regular **prayer meetings,** where temple ordinances were administered, took place here (HC 6:107, 133).

(8) At a **state convention** here May 17, 1844, Joseph Smith and Sidney Rigdon were nominated as president and vice president of the United States, respectively (HC 6:88, 386–97).

(9) From 1841 to 1845, the **University of Nauvoo** held classes here, in the Masonic temple building, and in the Nauvoo Seminary building.

NOTE: While visitors may visit the Red Brick Store separately, the Community of Christ Church (RLDS) recommends that they start at the Community of Christ Visitors Center and visit each of the sites in the company of a tour guide.

■ **43. WILLIAM MARKS/WILLIAM SMITH HOME. William Marks's** two-story brick **home** is located on Water Street between Bain and Granger Streets. Born in 1792, William married Rosannah Robinson in 1813. They had 11 children. He was baptized Apr. 1835, served on the high council at Kirtland, OH, and was commanded to move to Far West, MO (D&C 117:1, 10).

William was appointed president of the stake at Commerce, IL, in Oct. 1839, and served faithfully for a time. After the death of Joseph Smith, he sympathized with Sidney Rigdon and would not

William Marks and William Smith home, Nauvoo, IL.

acknowledge the authority of the Twelve. He later became a counselor to James Strang, then associated with John E. Page, and finally joined with the promoters of the RLDS Church. Marks later served as counselor to Joseph Smith III until he died in 1872 at Plano, IL (RPJS 230–31; BiE 1:283–84).

William B. Smith, Joseph Smith's younger brother born in 1811, lived in this home in May 1845. He was ordained patriarch to the whole Church on May 24, 1845, and gave patriarchal blessings in this home in the summer of 1845 (T&S 6:905). He was dropped from this position Oct. 6, 1845, and six days later was excommunicated for the second time. He associated with James Strang and later with the RLDS Church. He died in Osterdock, Iowa, in 1893 (RPJS 276–77).

■ **44. HYRUM SMITH HOME SITE.** The **home of Hyrum Smith** was on the NE corner lot where Water and Bain Streets intersect (lot 3, block 149). The second site of the *Times and Seasons* office was right on the corner, and Hyrum's house was nearby.

Hyrum was born Feb. 9, 1800, and in 1826 married Jerusha Barden, by whom he had six children. He was baptized in June 1829 and married Mary Fielding in 1837. He was one of the Eight Witnesses, served as a counselor to Joseph Smith and as a patriarch to the Church, was called to take Oliver Cowdery's place as assistant president of the Church, and was martyred with his brother in June 1844 (BiE 1:52).

Hyrum erected a comfortable **office** opposite his home, and in 1841 gave patriarchal blessings while James Sloan recorded them.

Copies of blessings were available immediately after being pronounced (T&S 3:585). Joseph also used this office.

Here, on Aug. 12, 1843, the Nauvoo High Council heard the revelation indicating that plural marriage was to be a "new and everlasting" covenant to the Saints. This caused an immediate rift in the council, which was one of the forerunners of fatal opposition to Joseph (JSFM 335).

■ **45. *TIMES AND SEASONS* BUILDING SITE NO. 2 (1839–41).** The **second office** of the ***Times and Seasons*** newspaper was located on the NE corner of Bain and Water Streets, where foundations are visible. The Church published the *Times and Seasons* in Nauvoo from Nov. 1839 to Feb. 1846.

Foundation of the Times and Seasons *Building Site No. 2, Nauvoo, IL, 1839–41. (1994; courtesy of Jim Frederick)*

The size of the paper's printed matter was 4½ by 8 inches. It was published monthly, then semimonthly. The ***Wasp,*** which became the ***Nauvoo Neighbor,*** was also published by the Church. Publishers used the same type that had been used in Far West, MO, to print the ***Elders Journal.*** Editors included Ebenezer Robinson, Don Carlos Smith, Robert B. Thompson, Gustavus Hill, Joseph Smith, John Taylor, and Wilford Woodruff (HiR 751; T&S 1:1; HC 5:193).

Places of publication included (1) the cellar of an old warehouse, no longer in existence, on the bank of the Mississippi River (1839) (T&S 3:695); (2) a cheaply constructed 16-by-32-foot frame building on the NE corner of Water and Bain Streets (1839–41); (3) a new building, no longer in existence, built expressly for a printing establishment and located on the NW corner of Bain and Water Streets (1842–45) (HC 4:513; T&S 3:695); and (4) a brick building at the printing complex on the NW corner lot of Main and Kimball Streets (1845–46) (T&S 4:129; RTF Nov. 1975, 4–6; HC 4:513–14).

The *Times and Seasons* press published a **hymnbook,** with selections chosen by Emma Smith, in a building on this site in Mar. 1841 (T&S 2:355).

■ **46. *Times and Seasons* Site No. 3.** The third offices of the *Times and Seasons* were located on the NW corner of Bain and Water Streets. It was a new building built expressly for a printing establishment and was used from 1842 to 1845. In 1845 the office was moved to a brick building on the NW corner of Main and Kimball Streets. The *Nauvoo Neighbor* was published here from 1843 to 1845.

The **book of Abraham** was first published in this building, appearing in the Mar. 1, 1842, issues of the *Times and Seasons* (T&S 3:703–706). The **Wentworth Letter, Articles of Faith,** and some portions of the history of the Church were also published first in the *Times and Seasons,* appearing Mar. 1, 1842 (T&S 3:706–710).

The third and fourth editions (1840, 1842) of the **Book of Mormon** and four editions (1844–46) of the **Doctrine and Covenants** were also published in Nauvoo (AMB 209).

■ **47. Aaron Johnson Home. Aaron Johnson's** two-story brick **house,** with a unique white stone design over the door, is located ½ block west of the corner of Bain and Water Streets and faces south onto Water Street.

Aaron was born in 1806 in Connecticut. He married Polly Z. Kelsey in 1827 and moved to Nauvoo in 1839. He was a justice of

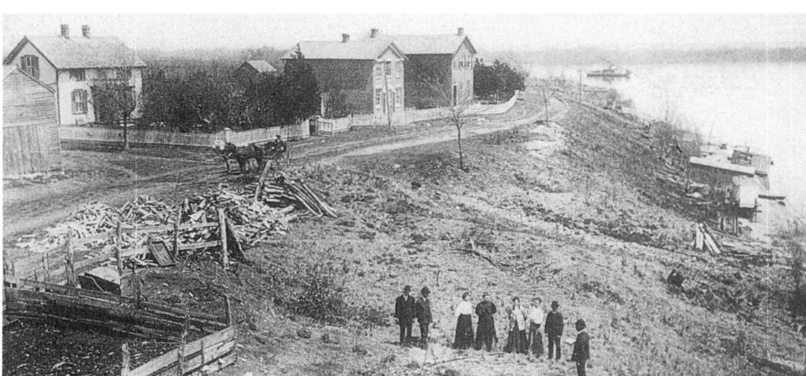

West end of Water Street in Nauvoo, IL, with Aaron Johnson's house in the center. Note the low water level of the Mississippi River, which is much higher now because the dam at Keokuk, Iowa, backs up the river, forming Lake Cooper around Nauvoo. (Courtesy of LDSCA)

Aaron Johnson home on Water Street, Nauvoo, IL. (1985)

the peace and a member of the Nauvoo High Council.

After attempts were made on the Prophet's life following the destruction of the *Nauvoo Expositor,* Joseph Smith decided to flee to the West, where he had prophesied the Saints would go. Late on the night of June 22, 1844, Joseph and Hyrum Smith, along with Willard Richards and Orrin Porter Rockwell, went to **Aaron Johnson's small dock** in front of his home. About 2 A.M., June 23, they borrowed Johnson's small leaky boat, which Orrin rowed across the Mississippi River. The boat was so leaky that they had to bail out water with their boots and shoes to keep from sinking. Once across the river, the men went to John Killian's home in Montrose.

Later that day, **Emma Smith** requested that Joseph return to Nauvoo, and some accused the Prophet of cowardice. Joseph replied, "If my life is of no value to my friends it is of none to myself." He returned to Nauvoo the same day and spent the night there. On June 24 he went to Carthage, where he and Hyrum were martyred June 27, 1844 (HC 6:547, 548–60).

■ **48. JONATHAN WRIGHT HOME. Jonathan Wright's** two-story brick **home** is located on Water Street about one-half block west of Bain Street, immediately west of Aaron Johnson's home.

Jonathan was born in 1805 and married Rebecca Wheeler in 1838. He was baptized May 29, 1843, in the Mississippi River at Nauvoo. He served on the Nauvoo City Council and as a marshal (OMN 140).

Tour Seven: Parley, Granger, Kimball, and Main Streets

From Water Street, turn north on Bain Street to Parley Street (named after Parley P. Pratt). Go east one block on Parley Street, north one block on Granger Street (named after Oliver Granger), east one block on Kimball Street (named after Heber C. Kimball), north three blocks on Main Street (the main business district in the 1840s), and east one block to Hyde Street (named after Orson Hyde), where this tour ends.

■ **49. SEVENTIES HALL.** This impressive reconstructed two-story brick building is located on the original site at the NE corner of Parley and Bain Streets. The main floor was a chapel built for 34 quorums of seventies and for the training of missionaries. The second floor had offices for the seventies, who directed much of the Church's missionary work, and a large hall used as a museum and city library. **John D. Lee** supervised construction of the Seventies Hall, built by volunteer labor. Brigham Young and other leaders dedicated the building for five consecutive days beginning Dec. 27, 1844 (NCJ 127; HC 7:330–45). The building now contains pottery and other artifacts uncovered in the restoration process.

Sidney Rigdon met here with the **Twelve, the Nauvoo High Council,** and **several high priests** on Aug. 7, 1844, and proposed that he be named guardian of the Church (WW 212).

■ **50. JOHN TAYLOR HOME SITE. John Taylor's home** was located in the acre lot on the NE corner of Granger and Parley Streets. He lived here until he moved to the printing complex home in 1845.

John Taylor was born in England in 1808 and was baptized in Canada in 1833, the same year he married Leonora Cannon. He served on the Nauvoo City Council, in the Nauvoo Legion, and as a regent for the University of Nauvoo. He was editor of the *Times and Seasons* from 1842 to 1846. He was a member of the Twelve and was with Joseph Smith in Carthage Jail at the time of the Martyrdom.

John Taylor home, Nauvoo, IL. (Courtesy of LDSCA)

He served as third president of the Church from 1880 to 1887 (BiE 1:14–19).

A marker honoring John Taylor is located on the north side of Parley Street between Main and Granger Streets.

■ **51. Chauncey G. Webb Home. Chauncey G. Webb's** brick **home** is located in the acre lot on the NW corner of Parley and Granger Streets, just north of the blacksmith shop (Site No. 138). Chauncey was born Oct. 24, 1812. He married Eliza J. Churchill in 1834, the same year he was baptized in Kirtland. Chauncey and his brothers ran the Webb Blacksmith Shop. He was the father of Ann Eliza Webb, who was married to Brigham Young for a short time (OMN 129; ELDSH 1374).

■ **52. George Cannon Home Site. George Cannon's home** was located on the south half of the north half of lot 4, block 127. It faced east onto Granger Street and was north of Parley Street just south of the center of the block.

The oldest son of George and Ann Quayle was **George Q. Cannon,** who was age 15 when he arrived in Nauvoo with his father and family. His mother had died at sea, and after his father died in Nauvoo, young George lived for a time with John Taylor.

George Q. Cannon served as **first counselor** to Church presidents John Taylor, Wilford Woodruff, and Lorenzo Snow (BiE 1:42–51).

■ **53. Joseph Young Home Site. Joseph Young's** large federal-style brick **home** was built on the acre lot on the SW corner of Kimball and Granger Streets. The house had a large widow's walk on the roof.

Joseph Young home, Nauvoo, IL. (Courtesy of LDSCA)

Joseph, Brigham Young's older brother, served as senior member of the First Council of the Seventy from 1837 to 1881 (BiE 1:187–88). He was born in 1797 and baptized in Apr. 1832. He married Jane Adeline Bicknell.

■ **54. Tithing Lot.** According to tradition, the **tithing lot** was located at the SW corner of Granger and Kimball Streets, where animals, food, and other goods "in kind" were collected, stored, and disbursed. There seems to be little evidence of this tradition, however. Brigham Young owned the property.

■ **55. Brigham Young Home.** This small two-story home, finished in May 1843 for a family of seven, is located on the SE corner of Kimball and Granger Streets. As originally built, it was 22 feet by 16 feet. The wings were added in 1844. This **home** of **Brigham Young,** the great American colonizer and successor to Joseph Smith, includes a room on the east, where important meetings of Church leaders were held. This room became the Church office after Joseph Smith's death and was where the exodus to the West was planned (BYAM 105). Brigham Young organized and led the Mormon pioneers to Utah, presiding over the Church from 1844 to 1877 (HC 7:592).

Brigham Young home, Nauvoo, IL. (Courtesy of LDSCA)

■ **56. Vinson Knight Home (Later).** The two-story brick **Vinson Knight home** is located on the south half of the lot at the SW corner of Kimball and Main Streets. Vinson was born in 1804 and has no known relationship to the Joseph Knight family. He married Martha McBride in 1826 and was baptized in 1834. He was appointed bishop over the lower Nauvoo ward in 1839. By revelation given in 1841, Vinson was commanded to purchase stock in the Nauvoo House and "to preside over the bishopric" (D&C 124:74–76, 141). After his death July 31, 1842, in Nauvoo (RPJS 265), Martha continued living in the house. Vinson's earlier home was built on the NE corner of Hyde and Sidney Streets (see Site No. 79).

Vinson Knight later home, Nauvoo, IL. (1985)

■ **57. Brick Row Site. Brick Row,** also called **Widow's Row** because it was a tenement owned by a widow who preferred widows as tenants, was located in the acre lot on the SE corner of Main and Kimball Streets. A 12-foot-wide alley ran east and west through the center of the lot. A long single-story brick building had 10 small, comfortable rooms that opened into the garden plot. The front apartment opened west onto Main Street (OMN 119–20).

Brick Row (Widow's Row), Nauvoo, IL. (Courtesy of LDSCA)

■ **58. Pendleton Log Home and School.** The **Calvin Pendleton log home** and **schoolroom** addition is a 14-by-20-foot cabin constructed in 1990 by Charles Allen. It is located on the north side of Kimball Street, just west of the center of the block between Main and Hyde Streets.

Pendleton was born in Maine in 1811, married Sally Ann Seavey in 1843, and taught school in his home (MoC 406). He was also a gunsmith and an herbal doctor skilled in setting broken bones.

This log cabin is typical of about 1,200 (60 percent) of all homes built in Nauvoo. About 20 percent of the homes were frame, and about 15 percent were brick.

Pendleton log home and school, Nauvoo, IL. (1991)

■ **59. *TIMES AND SEASONS* SITE NO. 4 (PRINTING OFFICE COMPLEX) AND JOHN TAYLOR HOME.** **Three brick buildings** make up the **printing office complex** on the NW corner of Main and Kimball Streets. **James Ivins,** born in 1797 and a convert to the Church, purchased this lot in 1842 and built three two-story brick buildings. The south one on the corner was used as a store, and the center one was his house.

Times and Seasons *printing office complex and John Taylor home. (Courtesy of RLDSLA)*

John Taylor, new editor of the ***Times and Seasons,*** moved into the **home** May 10, 1845. The exact use of the reconstructed **north building** is unknown, but when Elder Taylor procured the buildings in 1845, the complex housed a stereotype foundry, typesetting department, pressroom, bookbindery, book and stationery store, and post office (T&S 3:695; JJT 47–48).

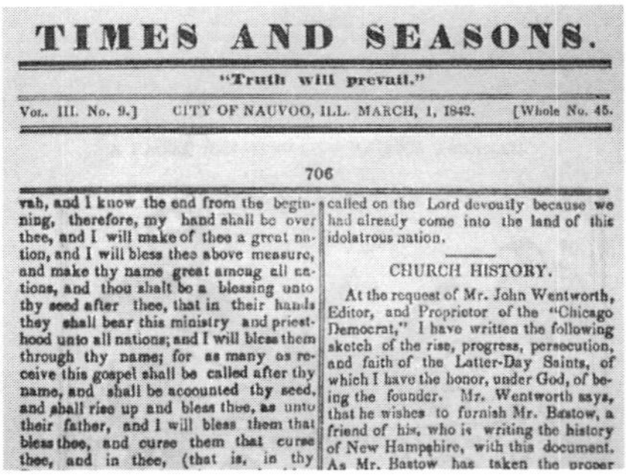

TIMES AND SEASONS.

"Truth will prevail."

VOL. III. No. 9.] CITY OF NAUVOO, ILL. MARCH, 1, 1842. [Whole No. 45.

706

vah, and I know the end from the beginning, therefore, my hand shall be over thee, and I will make of thee a great nation, and I will bless thee above measure, and make thy name great among all nations, and thou shalt be a blessing unto thy seed after thee, that in their hands they shall bear this ministry and priesthood unto all nations; and I will bless them through thy name; for as many as receive this gospel shall be called after thy name, and shall be accounted thy seed, and shall rise up and bless thee, as unto their father, and I will bless them that bless thee, and curse them that curse thee, and in thee, (that is, in thy

called on the Lord devoutly because we had already come into the land of this idolatrous nation.

CHURCH HISTORY.

At the request of Mr. John Wentworth, Editor, and Proprietor of the "Chicago Democrat," I have written the following sketch of the rise, progress, persecution, and faith of the Latter-Day Saints, of which I have the honor, under God, of being the founder. Mr. Wentworth says, that he wishes to furnish Mr. Bastow, a friend of his, who is writing the history of New Hampshire, with this document. As Mr. Bastow has taken the proper

Times and Seasons, *Mar. 1, 1842.*

The *Times and Seasons* was published in the complex from May 1845 to Feb. 1846, and the *Nauvoo Neighbor* was published from May 1845 to Oct. 29, 1845, under the direction of John Taylor and business manager **Elias Smith.** This was the fourth and last location of the *Times and Seasons* office (HC 5:193).

John Taylor was born in 1808, married Leonora Cannon in 1833, and was baptized in 1836. He was the third president of the Church, serving from 1880 to 1887.

Elias Smith, son of Asael Smith Jr., was a first cousin to the Prophet. He was born in 1804 at South Royalton, Vermont. He married Lucy Brown when he was 41 and was a bishop in the Nashville (Iowa) Stake before moving to Nauvoo. In Utah, Elias was business manager of the *Deseret News* in the early 1850s, postmaster from 1854 to 1858, editor of the *Deseret News* from 1856 to 1863, and probate judge of Salt Lake County for many years (BiE 1:719–22).

After the Saints were forced to leave Nauvoo in 1846, **Almon W. Babbitt,** Church trustee, lived in this **home** while disposing of property and serving as postmaster in the corner building (BiE 1:284–86; see Site Nos. 45 and 46).

■ **60. Jonathan Browning Home and Gunsmith Shop.** These structures are located on the east side of Main between Munson and Kimball Streets. Kentucky native and convert to the Church at Quincy, IL, **Jonathan Browning** earned a living as a gunsmith. He invented one of the earliest repeating rifles and manufactured many of the weapons the Saints used for self-protection in Illinois.

After Jonathan moved to the West with the Saints, his son **John M. Browning** made many firearms inventions in Ogden, UT, including the well-known Browning automatic rifle. The gunsmith shop includes displays of several weapons and gun-making tools and procedures (BYUS 19, no. 2 [1979]: 201–29). The house is original, but the gunsmith shop has been rebuilt. The two-story **barn** and **log cabin** were reconstructed on their original sites. The barn has **public rest rooms.**

Jonathan Browning home, Nauvoo, IL, before restoration.

■ **61. Sylvester Stoddard Home and Tin Shop.** The **Sylvester Stoddard home** and tin shop is a reconstructed two-story brick home located north of the printing complex, on the west side of

Main Street between Munson and Kimball Streets. Stoddard was born in the early 1800s and joined the Church sometime between 1833 and 1836. He married Almira Knight in 1844. Items sold in the tin shop included nails, buckets, stoves, scales, axes, sheets of tin, hand irons, and stove pipes (OMN 116–17).

Sylvester Stoddard home and tin shop in Nauvoo, IL, before restoration by Charles Allen in 1989–90.

■ **62. David and Patty Sessions Home Site.** The **home** of **David and Patty Sessions** was located on the south side of the NW corner lot of block 108, on the SE corner of Main and Hotchkiss Streets.

David was born in Maine in 1793. He was a farmer (PPM 86). Patty was born in 1795. She married David in 1812 and was baptized in 1834. She was a noted midwife to the legendary number of 3,977 babies and was a "doctor" of herbal medicines. She kept an excellent journal as she traveled west in 1857 with a 50-member pioneer company captained by her son, Perrigrine. She lived in Salt Lake City and Bountiful, dying in 1892 at age 97.

Perrigrine Sessions, Patty and David's oldest son, lived with his wife in a home on the SW corner of Hotchkiss and Hyde Streets near his parents. **Sylvia,** Patty's daughter, married Windsor P. Lyon, who ran the Windsor Drug and Variety Store in Nauvoo (MoC). The Lyons and Sessions lived next to each other.

■ **63. Joseph Knight Sr. Home Site.** The **Joseph Knight Sr. home site** is located on the NE corner of Hotchkiss and Bain Streets. Joseph was born in 1772 and was baptized in 1830. He married Polly Peck, and they had seven children. After Polly's death in 1831 in Missouri, Joseph married Phoebe Crosby in 1833. In 1829 Joseph supplied the Prophet Joseph Smith with food and paper while the Prophet translated the Book of Mormon plates in Harmony, Pennsylvania. A special revelation given through the Prophet to Joseph encouraged him in the work of the Lord (D&C 12). He remained a faithful Latter-day Saint until his death at Mount Pisgah, IA, in 1847 (TAMF 3–5, 183).

■ **64. SCOVIL BAKERY. Lucius N. Scovil** operated a bakery and confectionery store where now a reconstructed single-story brick building is located immediately south of the Masonic lodge on Main Street between White and Hotchkiss Streets. Scovil, born in 1806 in Connecticut, married Lucy Snow in 1824 and was baptized in 1836. The Scovils catered for socials in the Cultural Hall next door. Visitors receive information about the ovens and may sample a free gingerbread cookie (OMN 110–11).

■ **65. MASONIC HALL (CULTURAL HALL).** This imposing three-story brick structure on the SW corner of Main and White Streets was one of the most widely used public buildings in Old Nauvoo. It was dedicated Apr. 5, 1844, as a Masonic lodge under the direction of Hyrum Smith after the Nauvoo lodge's dispensation had been revoked (HC 6:287). It was used as a police headquarters and for at least 30 other different purposes. Each floor had a different function.

The main floor was used for theater productions, musical presentations, and public meetings. The second floor was used for public, Church, and political meetings. The third floor was used as a Masonic lodge and for dances and parties.

The multipurpose use of the building accounts for its current name: Masonic Hall and Cultural Hall. Some Latter-day Saints were Masons before the founding of Nauvoo, but Joseph Smith did not affiliate with Freemasonry until the Nauvoo era. And even then, he attended only two meetings before the cornerstone of the Masonic

Masonic Hall (Cultural Hall), Nauvoo, IL, before restoration.

Masonic Hall (Cultural Hall) after restoration.

lodge was laid (HC 4:550, 552; 5:446; 6:287).

As the Prophet Joseph Smith made his way toward Carthage on June 24, 1844, he met Captain Dunn of the state militia, who asked Joseph to return to Nauvoo and deliver the arms of the Nauvoo Legion. Afterward, the Prophet started toward Carthage again. Stopping in front of the Masonic Hall, Joseph said, "Boys, if I don't come back, take care of yourselves; I am going like a lamb to the slaughter" (HC 6:558).

Elder Adam S. Bennion and Wilford C. Wood remove a copper box from the cornerstone of the Masonic lodge in Nauvoo, IL, on June 24, 1954. The cornerstone had been laid June 24, 1843, by Hyrum Smith. Wood, who purchased the Masonic lodge 31 days before the box was removed, gave the box and its contents to President David O. McKay. It contained original lodge minutes and other items. (Courtesy of Wilford C. Wood)

■ **66. Nauvoo Legion Parade Ground.** A **Nauvoo Legion parade ground** was located on the SE corner of White and Granger Streets (lot 2, block 100) behind the Masonic lodge, where the legion's arms were stored before the armory was built. Other locations that served as parade grounds were the **general parade ground** on the Old Carthage Road, **the stand west of the Nauvoo Temple,** and the **public square** NE of the Temple (HC 7:133–34, 447–48).

Tour Eight: Hyde, South Main, and Parley Streets

Go south on Hyde Street six blocks, west on Water Street one block, north on Main Street two blocks, then east on Parley Street three blocks to Durphy Street.

■ **67. Orson Hyde Home.** The **Orson Hyde home** is a typical two-story clapboard building built in Greek Revival style during the Nauvoo period. It is located on the NW corner of Hyde and Hotchkiss Streets.

Orson Hyde home, Nauvoo, IL. (Courtesy of LDSCA)

Orson Hyde was born in 1805 and baptized in 1831. He married Marinda N. Johnson in 1834 and became one of the original Apostles of the Restoration in 1835. While serving a three-year mission, he dedicated the Holy Land in 1841 for the return of the Jews. In appreciation for his many years of missionary work, the Saints of Nauvoo built this home for his family.

Orson Hyde gave the dedicatory prayer at the public dedication of the Nauvoo Temple, May 1, 1846. He was president of the Quorum of the Twelve for 27 years, the longest anyone has served in this capacity. He died in 1878 at Spring City, UT (ORH).

■ **68. Perrigrine Sessions Home Site.** The **Perrigrine Sessions home** was located on the SW corner of Hotchkiss and Hyde Streets, near the home of Perrigrine's parents, David and Patty Sessions. Perrigrine, born in 1814, was a captain of 50 in a wagon train that went to the Salt Lake Valley in 1847 (MoC 738). He settled north of Salt Lake City in a settlement that took his name, Session's Settlement, and eventually became Bountiful, UT.

■ **69. Lyon Home, Drug, and Variety Store.** A Vermont native, **Windsor P. Lyon** was baptized in of 1832. He arrived in Nauvoo with his wife, Sylvia Sessions (daughter of David and Patty Sessions), and family in 1839. By 1840 he had established a **drug store** in a small log building at 23 Main Street on the SE corner of Hotchkiss and Main Streets. The store building, which doubled as his home, was operated under the name of Windsor's teenage brother, Carlos, and was know as the CW Lyon Store.

By 1843, Windsor had built a large brick home and store just east of the first store and facing Hotchkiss Street. Since the store carried dry goods, groceries, hardware, drugs, medicines, paints, and other items, it was named the **Lyon Variety Store** and was identified by a lion painted on a sign. In his garden, Windsor grew many herbs, such as lobelia, cayenne, and sassafras, from which he made his medicines (HC 5:184; 7:274).

■ **70. John D. Lee Home Site. John D. Lee's** two-story brick **home** was located on the west side of Hyde Street, in the middle of the block between Hotchkiss and Munson Streets (OMN 114–15). Lee was born in 1812 and married Agatha Woolsey in 1833. He was the Nauvoo wharfmaster, a major in the Nauvoo Legion, and an avid temple worker in Nauvoo. He is best known in connection with his involvement in the Mountain Meadows Massacre, for which he was executed in 1877. Lee's Nauvoo house cost him $8,000 to build. He was offered $800 for it, but a committee sold it for $12.50 after Lee went west.

John D. Lee home, Nauvoo, IL. (Courtesy of LDSCA)

■ **71. The Brickyard.** The **Brickyard** is centrally located on the north side of Kimball Street between Partridge and Hyde Streets. It is a reconstruction of kilns and brick-making equipment representing several brickyards operated by the Saints to supply red bricks. When Nauvoo Restoration representatives are present, tourists may purchase souvenir bricks for a small fee.

■ **72. Noble-Smith Home. Joseph Bates Noble,** bishop and justice of the peace in Nauvoo, built this two-story brick **home** and lived in it from 1843 to 1846. It is located near the SE corner of Kimball and Hyde Streets. A carriage house in the rear housed the carriage used by Joseph's wife (HC 7:434).

Joseph, born in 1810 and baptized in 1832, married Mary Adeline Beaman in 1834. He was healed when the Prophet administered to him in July 1839. He performed the marriage of Joseph Smith to his first plural wife of record, Louisa Beaman, Mary's sister, on Apr. 5, 1841. He died in Utah in 1900 (BiE 4:691).

In 1846 the Church, under the direction of Brigham

Young, purchased the home as a residence for **Lucy Mack Smith,** mother of the Prophet. Lucy, her daughter Lucy, her daughter's husband, Arthur Milliken, and their children lived in the home for four or five months. When anti-Mormon tension grew in Nauvoo, they moved to Knoxville, IL, in the late summer of 1846. They lived there for three years before moving to Ramus, IL, and eventually returning to Nauvoo. Lucy lived her last years with Emma Smith and her second husband, Lewis Bidamon, dying in 1855 or 1856 before having an opportunity to head west.

Noble-Smith home, Nauvoo, IL. (Courtesy of LDSCA)

Lucy Mack Smith. (Painting by Sutcliffe Maudsley, circa 1842; courtesy of LDSCA)

■ **73. Snow-Ashby Duplex.** The two-story brick **duplex** of **Erastus Snow** and **Nathaniel Ashby** is near the NW corner of Hyde and Parley Streets. Erastus occupied the portion on the north.

Erastus Snow was born in 1818 in Vermont and baptized in 1833. He married Artemesia Beaman, sister of Mary and Louisa, in 1838. He arranged to build a house in 1843 but sold half his property to Nathaniel Ashby and built a duplex.

Snow-Ashby duplex. (Courtesy of BYUL)

Erastus Snow and

Orson Pratt were the first Latter-day Saint pioneers to visit the Salt Lake Valley, reaching it on July 21, 1847. Elders Snow and Pratt were members of the Quorum of the Twelve Apostles from 1849–88 and 1835–81, respectively (BiE 1:103–15).

Nathaniel Ashby was born in 1805 at Salem, Massachusetts. He was baptized there by Erastus Snow in 1841 and moved to Nauvoo in 1843 (OMN 88–89). Nathaniel had a **cobbler shop** in his half of the duplex.

■ **74. Joseph W. Coolidge Home and Workshop.** This large white frame home, built in 1843, is one of the few frame buildings that have survived from that early period. Located on the NE corner of Parley and Hyde Streets, it was the **residence** of **Joseph W. Coolidge.** He was a member of the Council of Fifty and a Church real estate agent. He also had a shop in his house, where he made window sashes and doors.

Joseph Coolidge sold the home to **Johann Georg Kauffman,** a non-Mormon who placed a German language inscription on the house, which remains to the present. In English it reads, "This house is mine and yet not mine. Who comes after me shall find the same. I have been here, and who reads this will also have been here." In its restored state, the home is used for cooper, potter, and candle-making demonstrations.

■ **75. Foster's Daguerreotype Gallery Site (photo site). L. R. Foster's Photographic Gallery** was located on the east side of the lot, on the SE corner of Parley and Hyde Streets, facing Parley Street. He used the daguerreotype method of photography, which debuted in 1839. Foster's photos were the first ones produced in Nauvoo.

Shown here is the most famous of only two photos of Old Nauvoo. **Charles W. Carter,** an early Utah photographer, copied it from a Foster glass negative. Rowena J. Miller, assistant historian of Nauvoo Restoration, Inc., has identified the buildings in the photo, which was apparently taken between 1845 and 1846 either from the roof of the Gully store on the corner of Parley and Hyde Streets or from the top of Foster's home (CN Nov. 6, 1965, 11).

Nauvoo, IL. (Daguerreotype by Lucian R. Foster, circa 1845; courtesy of LDSCA)

(1) Nauvoo Temple
(2) Possibly Parley P. Pratt's Home and Store
(3) Temple Stand
(4) Amos Davis Home and Store
(5) Robert Foster Hotel
(6) Philo Johnson Home
(7) Samuel Williams Home
(8) Heber C. Kimball Home
(9) Brick Stable (owned by E. Tufts, then Almon W. Babbitt)
(10) Silas W. Condit Home
(11) Albert Brown Home (cabin)
(12) Noble-Smith Yard
(13) Possibly Joseph W. Coolidge Yard
(14) Parley Street

■ **76. Gully Store Site.** The large brick **General Commission Store** and home of **Samuel Gully** was located on the SE corner lot of Parley and Hyde Streets (lot 2, block 141).

■ **77. Simeon Dunn Home.** The **Simeon Dunn** two-story brick **home** is located at the SW corner of Parley and Hyde Streets. Simeon was baptized in 1839 at Van Buren, MO, and moved to Nauvoo in 1841. He was senior president of the Fifteenth Quorum of the Seventy (OMN 168–69).

■ **78. Henry Thomas Home. Henry Thomas's** two-story brick **home** is on the east side of Hyde Street between Parley and Sidney Streets. He was born in 1781, married Esther Thomas in 1808, and was baptized in 1836 (OMN 170).

■ **79. Vinson Knight Early Home Site. Bishop Vinson Knight's** early **home site** was on the NE corner of Hyde and Sidney Streets. He died in 1842, perhaps in this home. His wife, Martha, lived in his newer home on the SW corner of Kimball and Main Streets after his death (see Site No. 56).

■ **80. Edward Partridge Home Site. Edward Partridge's home** was located on the lot at the SE corner of Sidney and Hyde Streets. Edward was born in 1793 and was baptized in 1830. He became the first presiding bishop in the Church when he was called by **revelation** in 1831 (D&C 41:9–11). The Lord likened Edward to Nathanael of old, "in whom there is no guile" (D&C 41:11). At Independence, MO, he was tarred and feathered by enemies of the Church. He was bishop of the Upper Ward in Nauvoo and died at his home May 27, 1840 (BiE 1:218–22).

■ **81. Hiram Clark Home. Hiram Clark's** two-story red brick **home** faces east and is located on the lot at the SW corner of Hyde and Sidney Streets. Hiram arrived in Nauvoo in 1839 and paid $500 for his lot. He was a high priest in the Church (OMN 171).

■ **82. Theodore Turley Home Site.** The **Theodore Turley home site** (log cabin) is located on the west side of Hyde Street in the center of the block between Water and Sidney Streets. Theodore was born in 1801 in England. He married Frances A. Kimberley in 1821 and was baptized in 1837 in Canada. He arrived in Nauvoo in 1839 and became the **first Latter-day Saint to build a log cabin home in Nauvoo.** He was a gunsmith here, served a mission to England with the Twelve in 1839–41, and helped settle San Bernardino, CA, in 1850–51. He died in southern Utah in 1871 (JTT 1, 15, 53).

■ **83. Sidney Rigdon Home and Post Office. Sidney Rigdon's** two-story frame **home** is on the east side of Main, north of the Mansion House, near the SW corner of Main and Sidney Streets. It has a post-Nauvoo-era addition.

Sidney Rigdon home and post office, Nauvoo, IL.

Sidney was born in 1793 in Pennsylvania and married Mary Phebe Brook in 1820. He was baptized in 1830 and became the only first counselor the Prophet Joseph Smith ever had (1833–44). He had been a Reformed Baptist minister before his conversion to the Church. Following his example, many of his followers—Disciples of Christ (Campbellites)—were also baptized into the Church.

The **Nauvoo Post Office** was located in Sidney's home while Sidney was postmaster, and also when George W. Robinson became postmaster in Sept. 1840.

After Joseph Smith's martyrdom in 1844, Sidney returned to Nauvoo from his Pennsylvania home, offering himself as the "guardian" of the Church. The Apostles and nearly all the Saints rejected his claims and sustained Brigham Young, president of the Quorum of the Twelve, as the new leader of the Church. In this home Brigham Young and Orson Hyde discussed Sidney Rigdon's claims to authority (T&S 5:648–49; BiE 1:31–34).

■ **84. Mills Tavern (Hotel).** The south wing of an **early frame hotel** built in 1842 is located on the NW corner of Main and Sidney Streets. While the Saints were in Nauvoo, it was known as Mills Tavern, Masonic Tavern, Loomis Hotel, and City Hotel. It is

Mills Tavern (hotel), Nauvoo, IL. (1935; courtesy of George Strebel)

currently owned by the Community of Christ.

During a court session in the **Red Brick Store** on Feb. 20, 1843, **Joseph Smith** saw two boys fighting in the street by Mills Tavern. He ran to them and immediately stopped the fight. He lectured the bystanders for not interfering and then returned to court. "No body is allowed to fight in this city but me," said the Prophet, who was the mayor (DoJS 307).

Between Mills Tavern and Parley Street to the north, 10 other business establishments and houses stood at one time or another on the west side of the street: Grant and Watt Tailors, George Alley Boots and Shoes, Harris Commission House, Gray Milliners, Mikesil House, Wells Tailor, a small house, a brick house, a bowling alley (1847), and McIntyre Mercantile.

■ **85. RISER BOOT AND SHOEMAKER SHOP.** The recently reconstructed Riser boot and shoemaker shop is a two-story brick building situated near the NW corner of Main and Parley Streets. George C. Riser was born July 16, 1818, at Chornwesthaem, Wurttemburg, Germany. He was baptized Dec. 12, 1842, after a hole was cut in the ice of the Mississippi River at Nauvoo. The day after his baptism, the Prophet and Elder Orson Hyde administered to George's young son, who was near death. The child was miraculously healed (OMN 122–24).

■ **86. DANIEL BUTLER HOME AND COBBLER SHOP FOUNDATION. Daniel Butler's home** and **cobbler shop** was built on the NE corner lot at Main and Parley Streets. The foundation of this two-story brick home and shop still exists.

■ **87. THOMAS MOORE HOME SITE.** The two-story **Thomas Moore** brick **home** was built on the north side of Parley Street between Partridge and Durphy Streets (east side of lot 3, block 123). Thomas was born in 1801, married Mahala Higby about 1825, and is believed to have been baptized in 1842 (OMN 92).

Tour Nine: Durphy and Wells Streets

From the corner of Parley Street and Durphy Street (State 96), go north five blocks on Durphy (named after Jabez Durphy). Just past Ripley Street, turn NE and go up the hill from the "flats" to the "bluffs." At the top of the hill turn left (north) on Wells Street (named after Daniel H. Wells) and go two blocks to Young Street.

■ **88. George A. Smith Home. George A. Smith's home** is located in lot 4, block 123, on the NW corner of Durphy and Parley Streets. George was the son of Patriarch John Smith and was a first cousin to the Prophet. He was born June 26, 1817, and baptized in 1832. He married Bathsheba W. Bigler in 1841. On Apr. 26, 1839, at the temple site in Far West, MO, he was ordained a member of the Quorum of the Twelve at age 21, becoming the youngest Apostle in this dispensation. He served as first counselor to President Brigham Young from 1868–75 (BiE 1:37–42).

George A. Smith home, Nauvoo, IL. This home is sometimes identified as the John Smith home. (Courtesy of LDSCA)

■ **89. Thomas Bullock Home Site. Thomas Bullock's home site** was located on lot 3, block 121, in the north half of the lot. This site was just north of the corner lot on the NE corner of Kimball and Durphy Streets.

Thomas, born Dec. 23, 1816, in England, married Henrietta Rushton in 1838 and was baptized in 1841. He was a clerk to Joseph Smith in Nauvoo, a clerk in the camp of the original pioneers of 1847, and the chief clerk in the historian's office in Salt Lake City. He moved to Wanship, UT, in 1868, died in Coalville, UT, in 1885, and was buried in Salt Lake City. He was the father of 25 children by three wives (BiE 2:599–600).

■ **90. Drainage Ditch.** A drainage ditch ran along the east side of Durphy Street between White and Kimball Streets. At Kimball Street it ran under Durphy Street to the SW, where it emptied into the Mississippi River near the foot of Hyde Street. Drainage ditches such as this one, natural or man-made, drained the marshy land and made Nauvoo more habitable.

■ **91. Winslow Farr Home. Winslow Farr's** two-story brick duplex is located on the NW corner of Munson and Durphy Streets, facing Munson. Winslow was born in 1793 in New Hampshire. He married Olive H. Freeman in 1816, was baptized in 1832, and moved his family to Nauvoo in 1840. Lorin Farr, Winslow's son, lived in a small house behind Winslow's home (OMN 80–81).

Winslow Farr home, Nauvoo, IL. (1994; courtesy of Jim Frederick)

■ **92. Lorin Farr Home Site. Lorin Farr's** single-story brick **home** was located on the west side of Durphy Street, immediately north of his father's (Winslow Farr's) home on the NW corner of Munson Street and Durphy Street (State 96). The **Young Gentlemen and Young Ladies Relief Society,** forerunner to the Church MIA program, held one of its first meetings in this home (HC 5:320–22).

Lorin Farr was born in 1820 in Vermont. He was baptized in 1832, lived with Joseph Smith in Far West in 1838, moved to Nauvoo with his father's family in 1840, and married Nancy B. Chase in 1845 at Nauvoo. Lorin, who came to the Salt Lake Valley in 1847, was the first president of the Weber Stake and the mayor of Ogden for many years (BiE 1:749).

Lorin Farr home, Nauvoo, IL, mislabeled George Q. Cannon residence. (Courtesy of LDSCA)

■ **93. Wilford Woodruff Home.** The **Wilford Woodruff** two-story red brick **home** is on the SW corner of Durphy and Hotchkiss Streets. This 32-by-20-foot federal-style home was lived in continuously from 1844 to its four-year restoration beginning in 1965. It required minimum restoration and was the first Nauvoo building authentically restored.

Wilford Woodruff home, Nauvoo, IL. (1899; courtesy of Jim Frederick)

Wilford was born in 1807 and baptized in 1833. He married Phoebe W. Carter in 1837 in Kirtland, OH. Brigham Young ordained him a member of the Quorum of the Twelve on Apr. 26, 1839, at the temple site in Far West, MO (D&C 118:6), when he was 28 years old. He was one of the greatest missionaries the Church ever had, baptizing more than 2,000 people. He was Church historian, president of the St. George Temple, and fourth president of the Church (1887–98).

Wilford Woodruff issued the Manifesto of 1890 on plural marriage. He was the most prolific journal keeper in the Church, keeping excellent records for 63 years. He even counted the 14,574 bricks in his new home, recording the number in his journal. Because of his missionary labors, Wilford lived in this house only about 64 days. Like most of the Saints, he lived in a log cabin on his lot before building his brick home (HC 4:442; 7:228; JWW 2:337).

■ **94. William Clayton Home Site. William Clayton's home** was on lot 3, block 104, at the NE corner of Hotchkiss and Durphy Streets. Exactly where his house was located on the acre is unknown.

William was born July 17, 1814, in England and was baptized in 1837, becoming one of the first British converts. He arrived in Nauvoo in Dec. 1840. He succeeded Willard Richards as clerk to Joseph Smith. William wrote the hymn "Come, Come, Ye Saints" as he and the pioneers traveled across Iowa in 1846. He was an excellent diary keeper and was a clerk of the original pioneer camp of 1847. He died in Salt Lake City in 1879 (BiE 1:717–18).

■ **95. Jennetta Richards Grave.** The **grave** of **Jennetta Richards** is located on the west side of Durphy Street in the center of the block between White and Hotchkiss Streets. Jennetta Richards was born in 1817 in England. In 1837, she became the first person in England to be confirmed a member of the Church. A year later, she married Willard Richards, who was ordained an Apostle while on his mission.

Jennetta died in Nauvoo on July 9, 1845, at age 27 and was buried about 20 feet SW of the Richards's home on White Street. Gray stones with proper inscriptions were placed both above and below the casket (OMN 75–76).

In 1868, as excavations were being made near the Richards's home, Jennetta's tombstones and coffin were found and moved to the SW corner of the lot. In the early 1900s, the coffin was moved to its present location, which apparently is a part of an **old burying ground.** An appropriate gravestone marks the site (BYUS 31, no. 1 [1991]: 47; NCJ 36).

■ **96. Old Burying Ground.** In the earliest days of Nauvoo, an **old burying ground** was located, literally, on Durphy Street. It covered a square area south of White Street to a point about one-quarter block north of Hotchkiss Street. The cemetery's west boundary was near Jennetta Richards's grave just west of Durphy Street, and it extended east across Durphy into Nauvoo State Park.

Edward Partridge was among those buried here. As preparations were being made to construct Durphy Street, the coffins were removed. Edward, the first presiding bishop of the Church, died May 27, 1840. His remains were reburied in the Old Pioneer Cemetery. No tombstones remain in the old burying ground (NCJ 35–36).

■ **97. Jacob Weiler Home.** The **Jacob Weiler** single-story brick **home** is located on the west side of Durphy Street between Mulholland and White Streets. Jacob, born in 1808, married Anna M. Malin in 1830 and was baptized in 1840. He was a building contractor. To go west with the Saints, he sold his $1,200 house for $200 (OMN 74–75).

■ **98. Elijah Malin Home Site. Elijah Malin's** two-story brick **home** was built on lot 4, block 91, on the NW corner of Ripley and

Durphy Streets. Malin was born in 1774 and married Catherine Essex in 1797 (OMN 74).

● **99. Lutheran Church.** The **Christ Lutheran Church Elca** is located on the SE corner of Wells and Ripley Streets.

■ **100. Amos Davis Store and Hotel Site. Amos Davis's** large two-story **brick store** and **hotel** was located on the SE corner of Mulholland and Wells Streets, directly south of the front of the Nauvoo Temple. Davis also had a store on the NW corner of Mulholland and Page Streets. **Orrin Porter Rockwell** ran a carriage taxi service from the hotel (BYUS 19, no. 1 [1979]: 241–43; OPR 74).

Amos Davis, born in 1813, married Elvira Maria Hibbard in 1837 and was baptized in 1840. He arrived in Commerce in 1836 and was postmaster in 1839. He also ran a store and guest house near the Kimball Landing. His store ledger books, dating from 1839–42, still exist (OMN 40–41; RPJS 256). He was directed by revelation to buy stock in the Nauvoo House (D&C 124:111), and on Mar. 10, 1842, he was found guilty of, and fined for, using abusive language against Joseph Smith (HC 4:549). Amos, who did not go west with the pioneers, died at Big Mound, east of Nauvoo in 1872 (RPJS 256).

■ **101. The Temple Stand, the Stand, the Grove, and the Proposed Canvas Tabernacle.** No building in Nauvoo could accommodate large congregations of Saints until the **Nauvoo Temple** was partially built. During the warm summers of 1839–46, large groups of Saints gathered for meetings in the "open air" (HC 4:1). Smaller groups met in homes or public buildings.

The **temple stand** was the first, and usual, open-air meeting place in Nauvoo from Oct. 1839 to Apr. 1844 and from June 29, 1845, to Apr. 1846 (a total of five years and four months). The **grove east of the temple** was used for 15 months from Apr. 6, 1844, to June 28, 1845. The temple was used occasionally for meetings as early as Oct. 1842 but not on a regular basis until the last year before the Saints left Nauvoo, from Oct. 1845 to Sept. 1846. Occasionally, meetings were held elsewhere (HC 7:391; 6:183–84; JTB; T&S 4:10–11).

The temple stand was usually called simply **the stand** because

View from the area of the temple stand, looking west across the Mississippi River to Montrose, IA. (1935; courtesy of George Strebel)

leaders or speakers sat or stood on a portable platform or stand. The audience, meanwhile, sat on split-log benches or on the grass (HC 5:60). This area was also sometimes called "the Grove" because it was in a small grove of trees that provided shade (HC 5:136). Joseph Smith called the area the "temple stand" because it was located on the brow of the hill (DoJS 244); "near," "by," and "in front of" the temple (HC 5:136, 256, 423; 6:479; JJT 65; DoJS 460); on the temple block; and immediately west of the temple on Wells Street, where the Joseph Smith Academy, formerly the Catholic Saint Mary's Academy and Convent, is located (HC 4:553; 7:223, 432; DHS 1:50, 113).

Chief Keokuk and about 100 Native American chiefs and braves of the **Sac** and **Fox Tribes,** together with their families, were brought from Iowa by ferries in the summer of 1841. Joseph Smith addressed them at the temple stand and told them about the Book of Mormon. The Saints fed the Indians, who in return danced for the Saints (CHC 2:88–89).

At a **conference** held at the temple stand on Aug. 29, 1842, 380 men volunteered to go on missions to preach the gospel and refute John C. Bennett's false statements against the Church. The Saints were happy to see Joseph at the conference because he had been in hiding for three weeks (HC 5:136–39).

Joseph Smith gave a **sermon** here June 11, 1843, on the "Godhead" and on the "object of gathering the Jews." This was the first of three important discourses the Prophet delivered about the Godhead that were later denounced in the *Nauvoo Expositor* on June 7, 1844 (HC 5:423–27).

The **Twelve** delivered their **last discourses** in Nauvoo at the temple stand on Feb. 8, 1846, before leaving for the West (HC 7:580–81; DHS 1:113).

A **proposed canvas tabernacle** that could hold 8,000–10,000 people was to be erected at the temple stand. On Feb. 4, 1845, Orson Hyde was sent to New York City to purchase the canvas. The tabernacle was to be 250 feet long (north to south) and 125 feet wide, and located immediately in front of and joining the temple where Wells Street is now. It was to be 75 feet high with a 45-degree pitched roof. By the time Orson Hyde purchased 4,000 yards of canvas in New York in 1845, the Saints were planning to move west. The canvas was used for tents and wagon covers instead of for a tabernacle (BYUS 19, no. 3 [1979]: 416–21).

■ **102. Nauvoo Legion Arsenal and Officers' Building Sites.** The **Nauvoo Legion Arsenal** and **Officers' Building** were built on the SW corner block of Wells and Young Streets. According to tradition, they were located in the SW corner lot of the block, now a part of the Joseph Smith Academy. The Officers' Building is thought to have been just SW of the Nauvoo Legion Arsenal. In 1888, the arsenal was used as a Catholic convent (HC 7:271).

■ **103. Orson Pratt Home Site. Orson Pratt's home site** was in the south third of lot 1, block 8, of the Wells Addition, which was just north of the center of the block on the west side of Wells Street between Young and Knight Streets, SW of Parley P. Pratt's home.

Orson was born in 1811 in New York state. He was baptized on his nineteenth birthday, Sept. 19, 1830, and later married Sarah M. Bates. He was a great missionary, writer, editor, philosopher, scriptorian and Apostle (1835–88).

Orson advertised in the *Times and Seasons* that he had "Books for Sale" at his home located a "few rods north of the Temple Block" (T&S 2:502; BiE 1:87–91).

John C. Bennett seems to have boarded with Orson Pratt. Bennett was baptized Sept. 1840 and was instrumental in obtaining charters for the city of Nauvoo. He was the first **mayor of Nauvoo,** was **chancellor** of the University of Nauvoo, and was a **major general** in the Nauvoo Legion. He was excommunicated May 25, 1842, for adultery and other causes. He in died Polk City, IA, in 1867 (RPJS 253).

● **104. Catholic Church.** The **Saint Peter and Paul Catholic Church** is on the east side of Wells Street between Knight and Young Streets.

■ **105. Parley P. Pratt Home, Store, and Tithing Office.** The **Parley P. Pratt home, store,** and **tithing office** is located on the SE corner of Young and Wells Streets, one block north of the Nauvoo Temple lot. The large red brick building faces west. The store was also called the Temple Store.

Parley P. Pratt, born in 1807, married Thankful Halsey in 1827 and was baptized in 1830. He wrote extensively during his lifetime, and his autobiography is a classic in Church literature. He was one of the original members of the Quorum of the Twelve, serving from 1835 to 1857 (BiE 1:83–85).

The *Nauvoo Neighbor* of Jan. 24, 1844, advertised the "Pratt and Snow Store," run by Parley P. Pratt and Erastus Snow and featuring cheap dry goods from Boston. "No one need ask for credit, nor waste breath in bantering on the price," the ad said, "as we have but one invariable price for either cash or barter."

The store also served as a **tithing office** (T&S 5:728), and the room over the store served as one of several temporary sites for **temple ordinances** (JJT 35).

Tour Ten: Young and Knight Streets

From the corner of Wells and Young Streets, go east on Young four blocks, south on Robinson one block, and west on Knight four blocks to the corner of Bluff and Knight Streets near the Clark Store and entrance to the Nauvoo Temple Site.

■ **106. Nauvoo Concert Hall (Music Hall) Site.** The **Nauvoo Concert Hall,** a 30-by-50-foot brick building with an arched ceiling, was located on the NW corner of Woodruff (Bluff) and Young Streets (HC 5:368). With encouragement from Joseph Smith, **Pitts Brass Band** director William Pitt erected and dedicated on Mar. 3, 1845, the concert hall for musical concerts of various types (HC 7:363–64, 379, 388). A **quadrille band** composed of brass, stringed, and reed instruments was organized also.

As **Joseph's** and **Hyrum's bodies** were brought from Carthage into Nauvoo by wagons, the brass band led the procession with music at appropriate intervals. As people viewed the bodies, the band played appropriate music outside the house. When the Saints crossed Iowa, the band played for concerts and dances for both Iowans and Saints and was later organized in Utah for a short time.

At the **dedication of the Concert Hall,** a special hymn, written by Parley P. Pratt, was sung. One of the six verses follows:

> Sacred to Truth this Hall shall be,
> While earth and time remains;
> Where the Band and Choir in harmony
> Shall swell their sweetest strains.
> (ThC 1:137)

On Apr. 8, 1845, a grand concert of vocal and instrumental music was held at the Concert Hall. Hosea Stout said, "We were well entertained" from 6–11 P.M. (DHS 1:34).

■ **107. PUBLIC SQUARE.** The **public square** was block 10 of the Wells Addition. It was between Bluff and Page Streets (east and west), and between Young and Knight Streets (north and south). It was used as a **military parade ground** in 1844–45.

After the **Martyrdom** of Joseph and Hyrum Smith, **Gen. Miner R. Deming,** who was in charge of the Carthage Greys, and **Maj. Gen. Jonathan Dunham** of the Nauvoo Legion ordered the Nauvoo Legion to assemble on the public square on June 28, 1844, and admonished them to keep quiet and not let their outraged feelings get the better of them. From this square a council of legion officers went to accompany the bodies of Joseph and Hyrum to the Mansion House (HC 7:133–34).

As mob forces burned the Saints' homes in Sept. 1845, the Saints prepared for battle. **Lt. Gen. Brigham Young** addressed the soldiers and officers of the Nauvoo Legion on the public square on Sept. 17, 19, and 25. Maj. Gen. Charles C. Rich was in charge of the legion. President Young warned the legion to be ready at all times for battle (DHS 1:64).

Gen. J. J. Harden of the Illinois State Militia brought 400 troops to the public square on Sept. 30, 1845, to keep the peace. **Judge Stephen A. Douglas** was also in Nauvoo for the same purpose (HC 7:447–48; DHS 1:64–69).

■ **108. James Hendricks Home.** The traditional site of **James Hendricks's** two-story brick **home** is located on the eastern three-quarters of lot 3, block 5, of the Wells Addition, which is on the NE corner of Young and Bluff (Woodruff) Streets. It is the second house from the corner, going east. James was born in 1808 and married Drusilla Dorris in 1827. He was baptized in 1835, wounded and paralyzed at the Battle of Crooked River on Oct. 25, 1838, and moved to Nauvoo in 1840 (OMN 52–53).

■ **109. Orson Spencer Home Site. Orson Spencer's** two-story brick **home** was on the NW corner lot at Young and Page Streets (western three-fourths of lot 4, block 5, of the Wells Addition). Orson was born in 1802 and married Catherine Curtis in 1830. He was a Baptist minister when he converted to the Church in 1841. He served as an alderman in Nauvoo. After his wife died while crossing the plains of Iowa, Orson brought her body back to Nauvoo for burial. He was **president** of the **British Mission** and in 1850 was the first **chancellor** of the **University of Deseret** in Salt Lake City. He died in 1855 (BiE 1:337–39).

Orson Spencer home, Nauvoo, IL. (Courtesy of LDSCA)

● **110. Presbyterian Church.** The **Presbyterian Church** is located on the SE corner of Young and Page Streets.

■ **111. Howard Coray School Site. Howard Coray's** single-story **schoolhouse** was built on the NW corner of Young and Barnett Streets. Howard was a clerk for Joseph Smith, helping the Prophet compile the *History of the Church* in 1840 (see Site Nos. 33 and 12).

■ **112. The Grove East of the Temple.** The second **open-air meeting place** of the Saints from Apr. 6, 1844, to June 28, 1845, was located in the fourth tier of blocks east of the temple (HC 6:297; 7:432; DoJS Apr. 6, 1844, 463; JJT 65; DHS 1:50). It was also called **the stand,** or **the grove east of the temple,** and was located in a grove of trees that provided shade on hot summer days. It was on a one-acre lot on the SE corner of Knight and Robinson Streets (lot 2, block 16).

Here **Joseph Smith** presented some of his most powerful sermons (IoC 54), including the **King Follett Discourse,** delivered to about 10,000 Saints as a funeral sermon for King Follett during an afternoon session of the Prophet's last conference on Apr. 7, 1844 (BYUS 18, no. 2 [1978]: 179–225). The sermon is one of Joseph Smith's most well-known talks and explains "the character of God" (HC 6:305, 310). Joseph said God "is an exalted man" and that "the intelligence which man possesses is co-equal [co-eternal] with God himself" (HC 6:305, 310; T&S 5:612–17). Speaking of the weather during the conference, Joseph said, "They have been the greatest, best, and most glorious five consecutive days ever enjoyed by this generation" (HC 6:326).

King Follett died Mar. 9 when a bucket of rocks fell on him while he was walling up a well (HC 6:248–49). He was born in 1788 and was baptized in 1831. His Nauvoo home was on the SW corner of Partridge and Samuel Streets.

John Reid, Joseph's lawyer during court trials in June 1830 in South Bainbridge and Colesville, NY, gave a speech in this grove on May 14, 1844, vindicating the Prophet's account of his trials. He said that because of fatigue, he had not wanted to be Joseph's defense attorney, but he decided that he must defend him because the impression struck his mind that Joseph "was the Lord's anointed" (HC 1:89–96; 6:377; T&S 5:549–52).

The Prophet showed **Josiah Quincy,** mayor of Boston from 1845 to 1848, this "beautiful grove" with its seats and platform on May 15, 1844 (FOP 392). The following month, on June 16, Joseph Smith delivered the **Temple Sermon,** 11 days before his martyrdom, "at the stand" during a rainstorm. In this third great discourse on the "character of God," Joseph discussed the "plurality of Gods," stating that "there is but one God—that is *pertaining to us*" (HC 6:473–74).

After the Martyrdom, **Sidney Rigdon** delivered a sermon here Aug. 4, 1844, claiming he had seen a vision indicating that he

(Sidney) should be the new "guardian of the Church" (HC 7:224–26; MS 25:183–84).

Here the **mantle of the Prophet Joseph Smith** fell on **Brigham Young** on Aug. 8, 1844, convincing many of the Saints to follow the **Twelve,** with Brigham Young at their head (HC 7:231–43). Many Saints, like Benjamin F. Johnson, wrote of this miraculous "transfiguration" (MLR 103–104; NCJ 181).

Brigham Young was sustained as **president of the Quorum of the Twelve** at a conference here on Oct. 6, 1844 (HC 7:284–308). This site was also used sometimes as a **parade ground** of the Nauvoo Legion and city police in 1844–45 (DHS 1:7).

■ **113. Charles C. Rich Home Site. Charles C. Rich's** two-story brick **home** was located near the SW corner of Knight and Robinson Streets. Charles was born in 1809 in Kentucky and baptized in 1832 in Illinois. He married Sarah D. Pea in 1838 at Far West, MO. In Nauvoo, he served as a city councilman, regent of the University of Nauvoo, fire warden, high councilor, and member of the Nauvoo Stake Presidency. He served as an Apostle in the Utah Territory from 1849 to 1883 (BiE 1:102–103; OMN 48).

■ **114. Daniel Spencer Home Site. Daniel Spencer's home** was on the lot in the NE corner of Page and Knight Streets (in the south third of combined lots 2 and 3, block 11, of the Wells Addition).

Daniel, born in 1794, married Sophronia Pomeroy and became a prosperous merchant. When he learned about the restored gospel, he closed his establishment for two weeks and shut himself up to study and pray about this new religion. One day, when his son was with him in his study, Daniel suddenly burst into a flood of tears and exclaimed, "The thing is true, and as an honest man I must embrace it; but it will cost me all I have got on earth" (BiE 1:287). He was soon baptized.

Daniel arrived in Nauvoo in 1841 and served on the Nauvoo City Council. He was nominated as **mayor of Nauvoo** in Jan. 1845 to finish out Joseph Smith's term. He was captain of the first 100 families that crossed the plains in the fall of 1847. In the Salt Lake Valley he served on the high council in 1847 and was **president** of the **Salt Lake Stake** from 1849 until his death in 1868 (BiE 1:286–89).

■ **115. Robert Foster Home Site.** The **home** of **Dr. Robert D. Foster** was located on the SW corner of Page and Knight Streets. Robert, born in 1811, married Sarah Phinney in 1837 and was baptized in 1839. He was a prominent citizen in Nauvoo and had considerable property. He was a regent of the University of Nauvoo and a Hancock County magistrate. In 1844 Robert joined a dissident movement led by William Law and helped publish the *Nauvoo Expositor,* which set the stage for the Martyrdom. Although he turned against Joseph Smith, he felt that "Mormonism was true" and seems to have felt remorse for his acts (HC 7:513; see Site No. 120).

■ **116. Old Nauvoo City Jail.** The **Old Nauvoo City Jail** is located in the center of the block immediately east of **Temple Square.** It was built of limestone blocks that came from the ruins of the Nauvoo Temple.

Old Nauvoo City Jail, made from Nauvoo Temple stones. (1978)

■ **117. Raymond Clark Store and Home.** Originally built as a home and store in 1843, this two-story red brick building is currently used as a visitors center for the temple lot. It is located across the street north of the temple block, on the NW corner of Knight and Bluff Streets. **Raymond Clark** ran a general store at this location beginning in 1842. He emigrated with the Saints and served as a bishop at Winter Quarters (MoC 163; OMN 53–54).

Clark store and home, Nauvoo, IL. (1978)

■ **118. Nauvoo Temple Site.** The block where the famed **Nauvoo Temple** stood facing west is bounded by Mulholland, Wells, Knight, and Bluff Streets. **Daniel H. Wells,** not a Latter-day Saint at the time, sold the temple block to the Church at a reduced price. He was born in 1814 in New York state and was baptized Aug. 9, 1846. He was mayor of Salt Lake City 1866–76, counselor to Brigham Young 1857–77, and a lieutenant general in the Utah War of 1856–57.

Under the supervision of architect **William Weeks,** the Saints built the temple by employing volunteer labor and suffering great financial sacrifice (BYUS 19, no. 3 [1979]: 337–60). Construction took more than five years, but the Saints willingly sacrificed because this was the house of the Lord. The cornerstones were laid in an elaborate ceremony Apr. 6, 1841, just a few weeks after Joseph Smith had recorded the revelation (D&C 124:25–44) commanding the Saints to build a temple (HC 4:326–31).

The temple was built of gray limestone from nearby quarries, including those near the north end of Main Street, and of lumber from Wisconsin. It featured Greek architecture, one steeple, and 30 pilasters with sunstone capitals, moonstone bases, and star stones. At its completion in 1846, the Nauvoo Temple was the largest structure in the United States north of St. Louis and west of Cincinnati. It was 66 feet high, 128 feet long, and 88 feet wide. The angel weather vane on top of the belfry was 158½ feet above the ground. The building had three stories and a basement.

Nauvoo Temple. (Photograph of daguerreotype, possibly by Lucian Foster, circa 1845–46; courtesy of LDSCA)

By the fall of 1841, the Saints had completed the basement, including the baptismal font. On Nov. 8, 1841, they dedicated the font and put it to use Nov. 21 (HC 4:446–47, 454). Baptisms, particularly for the dead, which had previously been

Nauvoo Temple. (Daguerreotype by Lucian Foster, circa 1845–46; courtesy of LDSCA)

Nauvoo Temple, from old colored print. (Courtesy of LLUSI)

First published engraving of the Nauvoo Temple, which appeared in Graham's Magazine *in 1848. The article accompanying the engraving explains that the baptismal font was in the basement.*

The Nauvoo Temple. (Painting by C. C. A. Christensen; courtesy of MOABYU)

performed mostly in the Mississippi River, could now be performed in the 12-by-16-foot limestone baptismal font mounted on the backs of 12 oxen, first made of wood, then of stone. As other portions of the temple were completed, they were dedicated and put to use with temporary seats and floor (T&S 4:10–11). The first meeting in the temple was Oct. 30, 1842. The endowment rooms were used between Dec. 10, 1845, and Feb. 8, 1846, during which 5,500 Saints received their endowments.

The **first floor** of the Nauvoo Temple had offices and an assembly hall, with pulpits on both ends, much like the Kirtland Temple. The second floor had offices and was similar to the first floor, and the third floor (attic floor) also contained offices, as well as dressing rooms and endowment rooms. It also had waiting rooms, a garden room, a terrestrial room, and a celestial room (BYUS 19, no. 2 [1979]: 361–74).

The **attic** was used for temple ordinances in the winter of 1845–46. Room No. 1 in the SE corner of the attic was Brigham Young's office because he felt that the SE corner of a temple represented the strongest source of revealed light.

Many **spiritual experiences** took place in the Nauvoo Temple. Thomas Bullock recorded that in a meeting on Mar. 15, 1846, there was speaking in tongues, interpretation of tongues, prophecies, visions, halos around speakers, and the appearance of two men arrayed in priestly garments. Bullock indicated that the meeting was "the most profitable, happy, and glorious meeting I had ever attended in my life" (JTB 61). The glory of God was so bright around the temple that people thought it was on fire (JTB 62).

The Saints who desired to do temple work were privileged to do so by working day and night from Dec. 1845 to Feb. 1846. The Nauvoo Temple was privately **dedicated** by Joseph Young on Apr. 30, 1846. On May 1, 1846, Elders Orson Hyde and Wilford Woodruff dedicated the temple in public services. Additional services were also held May 2–3. By then, most of the Saints had already abandoned their homes and farms in Nauvoo.

The **"Tomb of Joseph"** was a **stone burial vault** built for Joseph Smith on the south side of the temple block. It later became part of a wine cellar (ThC 7:300; HiR 825–26). The **mock burial** of Joseph and Hyrum took place in the vault (HC 6:628). **Caroline,** wife of William Smith, was buried in the Tomb of Joseph on May

Nauvoo Temple ruins. (Steel engraving from sketch made by Frederick Piercy, 1853)

Icarian Building, Nauvoo, IL. The building was made from Nauvoo Temple stones and was located on the SW corner of the temple block. (Circa 1915; courtesy of Gale Bullock)

Archaeological dig at the Nauvoo Temple site looking west at the Icarian piers that ran in a row east and west down the center of the temple. The piers supported interior columns that in turn supported the temple floor. The plastic covers the base of the circular stairwell in the front of the temple. Bricks of the basement floor can be seen at the bottom of this photo. Just beyond the brick flooring is the temple's 30-foot-deep well, covered with an iron grate (HC 4:446). Water for the baptismal font was drawn from this well. (1969)

Archaeological dig at the Nauvoo Temple site looking from SE to NW. The temple well is in the east end of the temple basement and centered north to south (located immediately to the right of the person in this photo). Water from this well was drawn to fill the baptismal font in the center of the basement. Note the plastic tent-like cover over the stairwell base of the circular staircase in the NW corner of the Nauvoo Temple. Archaeologists Virginia and J. C. Harrington directed the final archaeological digs. (1969)

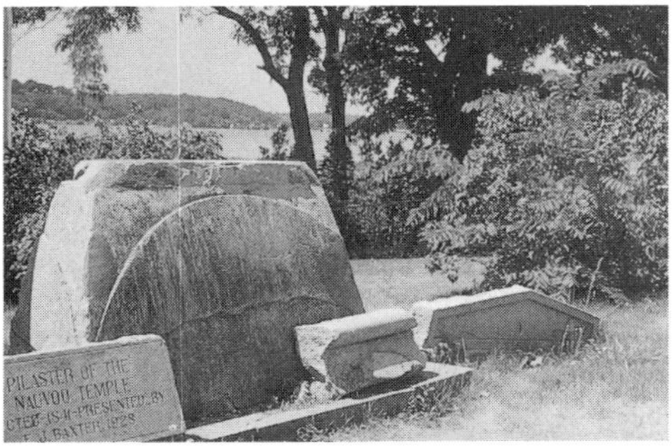

One of thirty original moon-stones that were at the bottom of each pilaster. This one was located by the Joseph Smith Homestead in Nauvoo, IL, in 1999.

Nauvoo Temple bell, located on Temple Square in Salt Lake City, UT.

One of thirty original sunstones that were capstones on top of the pilasters. This one was located at the Nauvoo Temple site in 1999.

Sketch of the Nauvoo Temple baptismal font by Henry Lewis, showing the two stairs leading up to the 15-by-11-foot wide x 7-foot-deep font that rested on the backs of twelve stone oxen, carved by Elijah Fordham of New York City. The temple's basement floor sloped toward the baptismal font in the center of the basement, and water drained from the font toward the south in a twelve-inch square channel (made of flat slabs of stone laid under the brick floor), under Mulholland Street, and into a ravine. (Courtesy of MHSSL)

24, 1845. Her body was later moved to the Smith Family Cemetery (HC 7:418).

Within a few months after the Saints left Nauvoo, the temple fell into other hands, including a socialist group, the **Icarians.** On Feb. 9, 1847, a small fire burned a 16-by-10-foot hole in the roof (HC 7:581), and in 1848, an arsonist, suspected to be Joseph Agnew, set it on fire. In 1850, a tornado toppled one of the temple walls. Local people tore down two walls and used the stone in various buildings in Nauvoo, including the old Nauvoo Jail located in the block east of the temple site.

The Nauvoo Temple Bell was brought to Utah and is located on Temple Square in Salt Lake City (CN July 14, 1985, 5, 13). One of 30 original sunstones, which were capitals atop each of the 30 pilasters, is located on the Nauvoo Temple site. It is believed to be one of only three existing originals. A second is held by a private collector in Provo, UT, and a third by the Smithsonian. The Church reacquired the **temple site** through a series of purchases made by **Wilford C. Wood** beginning Feb. 19, 1937 (ERA Apr. 1937, 226–27). An archeological team excavated the present site (1962–69), revealing the walls, drains, and other features. The temple square was handsomely landscaped, and tour guides were available (ERA Nov. 1963, 974–82). With groundbreaking ceremonies on Oct. 24, 1999, the Church began rebuilding the Nauvoo Temple as an exact replica of the original structure. Construction was completed in the spring of 2002, and the dedication was held on June 27, 2002.

Tour Eleven: Mulholland Street and Old Road to Carthage

From the corner of Woodruff and Knight Streets, go one block west to Wells Street and south one block to the corner of Wells and Mulholland Streets. From here you will be in a position to follow the **Old Road to Carthage.** This road is sometimes called the "Martyrdom Trail," since it is the route taken by Joseph Smith as he made his way 18 (now 22) miles to Carthage on June 24, 1844, three days before the Martyrdom.

In order to find the interesting sites along the way, it is helpful to keep track of your mileage and start near the temple block at the corner of Mulholland and Wells Streets. Read about Site No. 119 *before* leaving this corner, and read about Site Nos. 120–29 as you go east on Mulholland Street. From this point, you are on the **Old Road to Carthage** when you go east through what is now the current Nauvoo business district on Mulholland Street. Go .9 mile east to Winchester Street. Turn south on Winchester and travel .45 mile to Parley Street. Go 1.1 miles east to the parking lot of the **Old Pioneer Cemetery.** If you travel east another .6 mile, you will arrive at the beginning of the Joseph Smith Farm on the south side of the road. The road runs east along the north side of Joseph's farm for .5 mile.

■ **119. Mulholland Street Near the Temple.** Joseph Smith crossed the Mississippi River to go west during the night of June 22–23, 1844, but returned June 23 to Nauvoo, where he spent the night. At 6:30 A.M. on June 24, Joseph and about 25 other people left the "flats" of Nauvoo and went up the hill to Mulholland Street to the "bluffs." Here they paused and looked over the city and the temple then under construction.

Joseph Smith remarked, "This is the **loveliest place** and the best people under the heavens; little do they know the trials that await them" (HC 6:554).

Mulholland Street, Nauvoo, IL, the city's principal business street. (Circa 1899; courtesy of Jim Frederick)

They continued east on Mulholland Street and rode their horses to the scene of the Martyrdom, 18 miles away in Carthage (HC 6:553–60).

■ **120. Dr. Foster's Mammoth Hotel Site.** Dr. Robert D. Foster owned lots 1, 3, and 4 in block 19, just east of Temple Square. **Foster's Mammoth Hotel** was probably located in lot 3 on the NE corner of Mulholland and Woodruff (Bluff) Streets.

Joseph Smith "preached in front of Dr. Foster's Mammoth Hotel to several thousand people" on Jan. 21, 1844. He spoke on "sealing the hearts of the fathers to the children and the hearts of the children to the fathers" (DoJS 442). *The History of the Church* says he preached at the SE corner of the temple, which would be close to the front of Foster's hotel (HC 6:183–85).

■ **121. *NAUVOO EXPOSITOR* BUILDING SITE.** The two-story brick ***Nauvoo Expositor* building** was located in Dr. Robert Foster's lot 3 on the north side of Mulholland Street between Woodruff and Page Streets at about number 1245, where a furniture store is located (HC 6:357).

Dissident Church members who felt Joseph Smith was a fallen prophet united in an effort to destroy both Joseph and the Church through the publication of a bitter, anti-Mormon newspaper called the *Nauvoo Expositor.* Its one and only issue of four pages was dated June 7, 1844. Publishers were William and Wilson Law, Robert and Charles Foster, Frances and Chauncey Higbee, and Charles Ivins (HC 6:430).

The Nauvoo Expositor *building, located on the north side of Mulholland Street (the brick building on the right) at about number 1245. (Courtesy of LDSCA)*

Joseph Smith called the newspaper a "filthy sheet," and the Nauvoo City Council, fearing it could cause the destruction of Nauvoo, declared it a public nuisance and ordered its destruction (TPJS 385). Marshal John P. Green directed the burning of the paper's press, type, tables, paper, and so forth in Mulholland Street on June 10, 1844 (HC 6:453–58; 7:63–64, 130). Two days later Joseph Smith and other members of the City Council were arrested for "riot" (HC 6:448–58). Destruction of the *Nauvoo Expositor* led to the martyrdom of the Prophet.

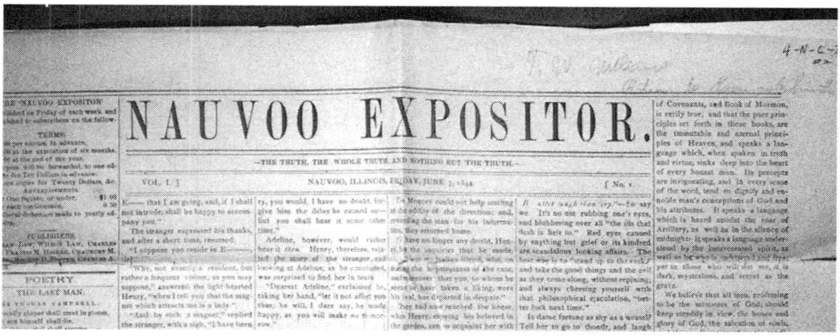

NAUVOO EXPOSITOR.

—THE TRUTH, THE WHOLE TRUTH, AND NOTHING BUT THE TRUTH.—

VOL. I.] NAUVOO, ILLINOIS, FRIDAY, JUNE 7, 1844. [No. 1.

The Nauvoo Expositor, published in Nauvoo, IL.

The *Expositor* attacked Joseph and Hyrum on political, moral, and religious fronts. Its editors opposed the doctrines involved in the temple endowment ceremony, unconditional sealing up to eternal life, plurality of wives, and plurality of gods (Nex).

The **Nauvoo Chamber of Commerce Tourist Information Center** is located just east of the *Expositor* site at the corner of Mulholland and Page Streets.

■ **122. Weld House Museum.** The two-story brick building that houses the office, library, and museum of the **Nauvoo Historical Society** is located on the south side of Mulholland Street (no. 1380) between Page and Barnett. According to tradition, the building was built in the 1840s by a Latter-day Saint and sold to Dr. John F. Weld, whose wife was a member of the Church (OMN 45).

■ **123. Joseph Agnew Home.** The post-Nauvoo period **home** of **Joseph Agnew,** who made a deathbed confession to starting the fire that gutted the Nauvoo Temple on Oct. 9, 1848, is located on the NW corner of Robinson and Mulholland Streets. The **Grub and Ritchie Store** was located here earlier (OMN 46–47).

Joseph Agnew home, Nauvoo, IL. (1985)

● **124. United Methodist Church.** The **United Methodist Church** is on the SE corner of Green and Ripley Streets.

■ **125. East Mulholland Street and the Final Battle Site. Mulholland Street,** the principal business street of Nauvoo, was named after Joseph Smith's scribe, James Mulholland, who helped write the *History of the Church* and who died at age 35 on Nov. 3, 1839 (HC 3:375; 4:88–89).

On June 28, 1844, about 3 P.M., the martyred **bodies** of **Joseph** and **Hyrum** arrived in Nauvoo, met by a great assemblage of Saints a mile east of the Nauvoo Temple on Mulholland Street. Willard

The Battle of Nauvoo was the final battle between enemies of the Church and the Saints remaining in Nauvoo. (Painting by C. C. A. Christensen; courtesy of MOABYU)

Richards, accompanied by Samuel Smith, Artois Hamilton of Carthage, and eight soldiers of the Nauvoo Legion, led the group as a heavy cloud of sadness hung over the city (T&S 5:561; HC 6:626).

The **Battle of Nauvoo,** Sept. 10–14, 1846, was centered on the eastern portion of Mulholland Street about one mile from the temple. Even though most Saints had already fled Nauvoo by the spring of 1846, those remaining agreed to move in 60 days and surrender their arms. But mobs were still not satisfied. Campbellite preacher **Thomas S. Brockman** and approximately 1,000 men, armed with six cannons, were located within "cannon shot" south of Mulholland Street. About 200 Nauvoo citizens, armed with a few homemade cannons, were lined up north of Mulholland Street in a fortification of breastworks. During the ensuing battle, three Latter-day Saints and a dozen or so of Brockman's men were killed. **Daniel H. Wells,** not yet a Church member, was one of the heroes of the battle and later served as the general over the Mormon Militia in the Utah War of 1857–58.

Nauvoo citizens were forced to sign a peace treaty Sept. 16, and on Sept. 17, riotous, drunken mob forces entered Nauvoo, pillaged homes, and forced the remaining Saints to leave on ferries at "the point of the bayonet" (CHC 3:11–22). Within a day or two, the last of the Saints had left Nauvoo, crossed the Mississippi River, set up tents along Sugar Creek in Iowa, and waited for help from Brigham Young and those who had left earlier. These forced-out Saints were the "poor Saints" who had nine babies born in one night and who were fed quails in a miraculous way (BYUS 21, no. 4 [1981]: 441–44; CHC 3:134–36).

■ **126. Old Pioneer Cemetery.** The **Old Pioneer Cemetery,** located on William Marks's farm, is two miles east of State 96 on Parley Street (south of the road 100 yards) and beyond Casper Creek (now Chandler Creek), named after Church member William Casper. The cemetery parking lot is located 2.1 miles from Durphy Street.

On Nov. 1, 1842, Joseph Smith's buggy tipped over as he and his party went down the hill toward Casper's Creek and the cemetery. Frederick G. Williams bruised his cheek, but no one was seriously hurt. The carriage was broken and left there (HC 5:182).

The LDS Church acquired and cleaned the **cemetery,** rededicating it Oct. 7, 1989. The markers are generally in poor condition; nevertheless, it is possible to decipher some of the names on the gravestones. Most of the 1,800 Saints who died in Nauvoo are buried here (CN Oct. 14, 1989, 3–4).

Two small headstones located in the east central part of the cemetery identify three small children of Colonel Windsor P. Lyon, a druggist, and his wife, Sylvia. All three children—Marian, Asa, and Philafree—died under the age of three between 1842 and died 1844.

Bishops Edward Partridge and Vinson Knight are among those buried here (CN Sept. 30, 1984, 11). About 200 headstones have readable names, including William Casper, Richard B. Cormack, James Durfee, Harriet Fuller, Katherine Goodale, Charles Hofheins, Nancy Holbrook, Catherine S. Jackman, Mary Pincock, Artemesia Rich, James Robison, Lucy Scovil, William P. Swartz, Leonora Taylor, James Webb, and Dwight Whitcomb. The cemetery includes a heroic-sized sculpture by Dee Jay Bawden depicting a family burying a loved one.

If you travel from Durphy Street about one mile east on **Parley Street** toward the cemetery, you will pass the area where Mormon sharpshooters led by **William Anderson** hid in the cornfields and were fired upon by mobbers led by Thomas S. Brockman at the head of Mulholland Street (Sept. 10–14, 1846). Captain **Andrew L. Lamoreaux** led the Latter-day Saints with the aid of **Daniel H. Wells** (CHC 3:6–16; ME 237).

■ **127. Joseph Smith Farm Site. Joseph Smith's farm** was located east of Nauvoo on the south side of the Old Road to Carthage, which runs along the north boundary of Joseph's 160-acre farm. The NE corner of Joseph's farm is the SW corner of the intersection identified as 900 E. and 2300 N. From Durphy Street, **mileage readings** going east on Parley Street are as follows: 1.8 miles at Casper Creek, 2.1 miles at the Old Pioneer Cemetery parking lot, 2.2 miles at the section line between the original county survey sections 7 and 8, 2.7 miles at the NW corner of the farm, and 3.2 miles at the NE corner of the "half-mile square farm" on the prairie.

By 1842, Cornelius P. Lott and his wife, Permelia Darrow, managed the farm. David Nye White, senior editor of the *Pittsburgh Weekly Gazette,* visited the Prophet in Aug. 1843 and wrote about the farms on "the Plains":

> Most of the prairie, near Nauvoo, is fenced with turf. A ditch some two feet deep is dug on each side of the fence, and the turf piled up between, making a very good and durable fence . . . broad enough on the top for a foot path. Quite a number of the houses or huts in which the inhabitants on the prairies live, are also made of turf, and covered with clapboards (PJS 1:440).

Joseph Smith's **journal** records some of Joseph's visits to his farm with his family.

> Visited my farm, accompanied by my brother Hyrum (HC 6:35).
>
> Rode out with Emma and visited my farm (HC 5:307, 500).
>
> I rode out to the farm with my children, and did not return until after dark (HC 5:182).
>
> Rode to the farm with my daughter Julia (HC 5:515).

Other entries indicated Joseph worked on the farm:

> Dined on my farm; hoed potatoes, etc (HC 5:58).
>
> Rode on the prairie with my clerk, to show some land to Brother Russell from New York; dined with my farmer, Brother Cornelius P. Lott, and hoed potatoes (HC 5:66).
>
> In the afternoon rode out to my farm, and spent the time plowing, etc (HC 5:183).

As **Joseph Smith** and his party road toward **Carthage** on June 24, 1844, they passed Joseph's farm. He took a good look at it, and after passing it, he turned around several times to look again, at which some of the company made remarks. Joseph said, "If some of you had got such a farm and knew you would not see it any more, you would want to take a good look at it for the last time" (HC 6:558).

■ **128. Nauvoo Legion Parade Ground.** The **general parade ground** of the Nauvoo Legion in the early Nauvoo years was on the Old Carthage Road east of Nauvoo (east Parley Street), just beyond Joseph Smith's Farm.

Joseph Smith recorded in his journal entry of May 6, 1843:

> At half-past nine A.M., I mounted with my staff, and with the band, and about a dozen ladies, led by Emma, and proceeded to the general parade-ground of the Nauvoo Legion, east of my farm on the prairie. The Legion looked well. . . .
>
> The officers did honor to the Legion. . . . The men . . . had made great improvements both in uniform and discipline, and we felt proud . . . [they] are the pride of Illinois (HC 5:384).

After Joseph gave a brief address to the Legion, the Legion marched to the city and disbanded on Main Street about 2 P.M. (HC 5:384). The general parade ground is probably the scene of the **sham battle** of May 7, 1842. Stephen A. Douglas was on hand to witness the battle, having adjourned the district court in Carthage to see the Nauvoo Legion on parade. John C. Bennett was accused of plotting Joseph's death at the battle, and Joseph spoke to the troops afterward (HC 5:3–4; CHC 2:140–47).

■ **129. The Big Field.** The **big field** located six miles SE of Nauvoo on the Old Road to Carthage was a six-mile square, 3,840-acre plot farmed by Church members joined together in the Big Field Association.

On Sept. 5, 1845, 616 Saints at the farm celebrated their bountiful harvest of 60,000 bushels of wheat and corn. John Taylor said they "spent the day most happily, without 'strong drink,' or swearing, or gambling; feasting, as all honest people ought to, to be healthy, upon the simple luxuries that sustain life, with pure water, peace and union, praying and praising God" (JJT 87; HC 7:437–38).

Tour Twelve: Parley and Water Streets

From the Old Pioneer Cemetery or Joseph Smith Farm, return to Parley Street and continue west to Page Street. Go one block south on Page Street, two blocks west on Sidney Street, and one block north on Wells Street to Parley Street. After going north and east in the Nauvoo State Park to visit Site Nos. 135 and 136, continue west on Parley Street to the **Webb Blacksmith Shop** and imagine yourself purchasing a wagon and loading it with all the goods you can take, then traveling west on Parley Street to the **Lower Stone House Landing,** ready to say farewell to your beautiful city and home and be led by God into the wilderness to establish Zion in the tops of the mountains. Finish your tour of Nauvoo by going SE on Water Street to the corner of Main.

■ **130. Hosea Stout Home Site.** From 1844 to 1846, **Hosea Stout's home** was located on the "bluffs" two blocks north of Parley Street, on the SE corner of Gordon and Munson Streets. He had a home on the "flats" before this time (DHS 1:115). (See Site No. 2.)

■ **131. Ezra T. Benson Home Site.** The **home** of **Ezra T. Benson** was two blocks north of Parley Street, on the SW corner lot of block 52 and on the NW corner of Munson and Fulmer Streets. He owned the whole one-acre lot.

Ezra was born in 1811 in Massachusetts. He married Pamelia Andrus in 1832, and they had eight children. He was baptized in 1840 at Quincy, IL, and moved to Nauvoo in 1841. He was ordained an **Apostle** in 1846 and was a member of the original pioneer company in 1847 (RPJS 300–301).

His grandson, **Ezra Taft Benson,** was **president** of the Church from 1985 to 1994.

■ **132. George Laub Home. George Laub's** two-story federal-style brick **home** is located on the SW corner of Parley and Page Streets. George was born in 1814 in Pennsylvania and was baptized in 1842. He was present at the transfiguration of Brigham Young in 1844 following the Prophet's martyrdom. In 1846, he married

Mary J. McGinness in Nauvoo, where he worked as a joiner. He buried his small son in the SW corner of his lot (BYUS 18, no. 2 [1978]: 151–78).

■ **133. Ellis Sanders Home. Ellis M. Sanders's** two-story brick **home** is on the NW corner of Page and Sidney Streets. Ellis was born in 1808 and married Rachel B. Roberts in 1839. He joined the Church in 1843 (OMN 104).

■ **134. William Mendenhall Home.** The **William Mendenhall** two-story brick **home** is located on the north side of Sidney Street about a block west of Page Street. William was born in 1815. He married Sarah Lovell in 1838 and was baptized in 1841. He worked as a brick mason and woodcutter before he left for the West (OMN 105–106).

● **135. Nauvoo State Park.** The **Nauvoo State Park** is seven blocks long east to west and four blocks wide north to south, with Lake Horton in the center. Camping and picnic sites are available to tourists within the park. To enter the park, start on Durfey Street and travel east on Parley Street.

■ **136. Nauvoo Historical Society Museum.** The **Nauvoo Historical Society Museum** is located on the south side of Kimball Street in the Nauvoo State Park. The museum is housed in the two-story brick home that, according to tradition, was built by the Wagoner or Scott family. Alois Rheinburger purchased it in 1850 and built an addition on the original house.

■ **137. Carrington and Lyman Home Sites.** The **Albert Carrington home site** was located on the SW corner lot where Parley and Durphy Streets cross. Albert was born in 1813 and baptized in 1841. He was educated at Dartmouth College. He was a member of the original pioneer company of 1847 and an **Apostle** from 1870 to 1885. In Nauvoo, he was a topographer and surveyor. He died in 1889 in Salt Lake City (BiE 1:126–27).

Amasa M. Lyman lived on this same corner lot in 1842. This was one of several places he lived in Nauvoo. Amasa was born in 1813 and baptized in 1832. He married Maria Louisa Tanner in 1835, served as a member of the Quorum of the Twelve 1842–67, and was appointed a member of the First Presidency on Jan. 20, 1843 (HC 5:255, 264). In 1862 he denied the necessity of the Atonement in a speech in Dundee, Scotland, and was later involved in spiritualism. He was excommunicated in 1870 (RPJS 266–67).

■ **138. Webb Wagon and Blacksmith Shop.** The one-story stone building that housed the **Webb Wagon and Blacksmith Shop** was reconstructed in 1969–70 on the foundations of the original structure on the NW corner of Parley and Granger Streets.

Webb Wagon and Blacksmith Shop, Nauvoo, IL. (1985)

The **Webb Brothers—Chauncey, Edwin, Edward, Pardon,** and **James**—learned to blacksmith in their father's shop in Kirtland. Edwin started blacksmithing in Nauvoo in 1842. By 1843 he was in this "stone-shop" (OMN 129–30). Chauncey worked with Edwin to repair and build wagons for the pioneer trek west. Five of Brigham Young's wagons were manufactured here. After the Battle of Nauvoo in Sept. 1846, the Webbs moved to the West, where they continued in their trade in Ogden, UT.

The bellows, anvils, and other tools used today in the blacksmith shop were used in Nauvoo by the Webb brothers and taken to Ogden when they emigrated. The tools were later donated to Nauvoo Restoration, Inc., by family members and returned to Nauvoo. The shop features blacksmithing demonstrations for visitors.

■ **139. James White Stone House Site.** The **James White** 2½-story **stone house** was built 200 yards NW of the foot of Parley Street. White was born in 1782 in Vermont, moved into this area in 1824, and purchased land from the Indians. He had a thriving riverboat trade. In 1829 he built the first house in what was then called Venus, the first county seat of Hancock County. Venus would later be named Nauvoo. White died in 1836.

Isaac Galland purchased the house from White and lived in it until 1839, when **Sidney Rigdon** occupied it. Saints later purchased this site and other property from Galland.

James White stone house, Nauvoo, IL. (Courtesy of LDSCA)

By 1841 the stone house was known as the **Nauvoo Ferry Hotel** and was managed by Charles Ivins and S. Bennett (T&S 2:502). The nearby steamboat landing was called the **Lower Stone House Landing** (ThC 7:302). The house and site were inundated by Lake Cooper in 1913, which was formed by a dam at Keokuk. The dam made the Mississippi 20 feet deeper at Nauvoo.

■ **140. Maudsley Home Site. Sutcliffe Maudsley** had his **home** in the block just north of block 111 of the Galland Purchase. He was a squatter near the river on property the Church never purchased. His home was located just north of the "projected" Munson Street and west of the "projected" Hills Street.

Maudsley was born in 1809, arrived in Nauvoo from England in 1841, and died in 1881. The first practicing painter in the Church, Maudsley produced the earliest known paintings of Joseph, Hyrum, Emma, and Lucy Mack Smith, and many other prominent Church figures. In 1842, he painted Joseph Smith in full Nauvoo Legion uniform for the Gustavus Hills Map of 1843 (NCJ 252).

■ **141. The Islands.** At least one of two timber-covered **islands** located in the Mississippi River between Nauvoo and Montrose provided **Joseph Smith** with refuge and wood for fuel during the summer of 1842 when he was sought by Missouri authorities. The islands have been under water since Lake Cooper was formed behind a dam at

Keokuk in 1913 that raised the water level about 20 feet. Joseph was in seclusion much of the time from Aug. to Dec. 1842. He spent part of this time in the homes of John Smith, Edward Sayers, Carlos Granger, Newel K. Whitney, and Edward Hunter (HC 5:89–91, 145; LJS 412).

Emma Smith secretly visited the Prophet on an island Aug. 11, 1842. Joseph wrote of her, "My beloved Emma . . . the wife of my youth, and the choice of my heart. . . . Undaunted, firm, and unwavering—unchangeable, affectionate Emma" (HC 5:107; CHC 2:161). Joseph made this and other entries in the **Book of the Law of the Lord** while he was in hiding (CHC 2:160–64).

While in seclusion, the Prophet wrote the **revelation** found in **Doctrine and Covenants** 128, which discusses the doctrine and ordinance of baptism for the dead (HC 5:142–53; CHC 2:151–52).

■ **142. LOWER STONE HOUSE LANDING.** The **Lower Stone House Landing,** also known as Montrose Crossing or Lower Ferry, is located in the Galland Purchase at the foot of Parley Street, 200 yards south of the James White stone house, which at times was a hotel.

This **steamboat landing** is one of at least four in Nauvoo: Nauvoo House Wharf, Lower Stone House Landing, Kimball Landing, and Upper Stone House Landing.

The Saints used these and other landings when they fled Nauvoo to escape persecution. On Feb. 4, 1846, Charles Shumway and family were the first of 18,000 Saints to cross the Mississippi River in the great **exodus** to the West. Police, under the direction of Hosea Stout, superintended the crossing of the river.

Lower Stone House Landing on west Parley Street, Nauvoo, IL.

Ferries embarked almost hourly. Later that month, the river froze and the Saints crossed on the ice (HC 7:580). In recent years a modern ferry service has operated sporadically here.

Paddle wheel steamboat at Nauvoo, IL. (Courtesy of LDSCA)

■ **143. Exodus to Greatness Monument and Pioneer Memorial.** The **"Exodus to Greatness" monument** is located near the Lower Stone House Landing on the east side of the bend in the road. It is dedicated to the memory of the Saints who fled persecution and settled in the Rocky Mountains of the West. Elder Mark E. Petersen of the Quorum of the Twelve gave a dedicatory prayer here Aug. 17, 1978 (CN Feb. 9, 1986, 11).

Renovations on the site were made in 1997 for the pioneer sesquicentennial, and President Gordon B. Hinckley rededicated the site as a pioneer memorial on Apr. 18, 1997 (CN Apr. 26, 1997, 3).

Crossing the Mississippi River on the Ice. *(Painting by C. C. A. Christensen, 1846; courtesy of MOABYU)*

■ **144. Wilson Law Home Site. Wilson Law's** two-story brick **home** was located on Water Street in the NE corner lot where Water Street and Sidney Street cross the "projected" Marion Street (lot 3, block 135).

Wilson was born in 1807. He married Elizabeth Sikes in 1842 and became a Nauvoo city alderman. He became disgruntled with

Joseph Smith, helped organize a dissident church on Apr. 28, 1844, and helped publish the *Nauvoo Expositor,* which led to the martyrdom of Joseph and Hyrum Smith (OMN 137–38).

■ **145. William W. Phelps Home Site.** The 1839 **home** of **William W. Phelps** was located on the NW corner lot of Sidney Street and the "projected" Locust Street. William was born in 1792 and married Sally Waterman in 1815. In June 1831, Joseph Smith received a revelation directing Phelps to assist Oliver Cowdery in printing and writing books for schools in the Church (D&C 55). He published *The Evening and the Morning Star* and the Book of Commandments at Independence, MO. He served on the Nauvoo City Council and, while in Nauvoo, assisted Willard Richards in gathering Church history materials. He was also a scribe to Joseph Smith. In Utah he was active in church and civic affairs. He died in 1872 in Salt Lake City (BiE 3:692–97).

■ **146. Laws "Lower Steam Mill" Site. William and Wilson Law** erected a **steam flour** and **sawmill** in 1842. It was located immediately west of the foot of the proposed Locust Street in the SW corner of Nauvoo and was known as the "lower steam mill." Nauvoo also had an upper steam mill (T&S 3:663–64).

■ **147. Corner of Main and Water Streets.** You may want to conclude your visit to Nauvoo, the "City of Joseph," here. Perhaps no street corner in Nauvoo was more honored with the footprints of Joseph Smith than the corner of Main and Water Streets. Here, between the Prophet's two Nauvoo houses, you walk where Joseph walked and learn where Joseph taught.

Hancock County

In addition to establishing Nauvoo, the Latter-day Saints built several other settlements in Hancock County, IL. **Joseph Smith's** vision of settlement by the Saints was not limited to Nauvoo. On Mar. 4, 1843, he said, "There is a wheel; Nauvoo is the hub: we will drive the first spoke in Ramus, second in La Harpe, third Shokoquon, fourth in Lima; that is half the wheel. The other half is over the river" (HC 5:296).

In his wheel-hub-spoke analogy, Joseph Smith referred to some but not all of the Saints' settlements in Hancock County. The settlement pattern in that county was extensive, including 17 communities. By 1845 there were 34 branches of the Church in Illinois.

Hancock County was created Jan. 13, 1825, from unorganized territory attached to Pike County and named for **John Hancock** (1737–93), first signer of the Declaration of Independence, president of the Continental Congress, and governor of Massachusetts. The county had no seat until 1833, when Carthage became the county seat. Hancock County has an area of 797 square miles. The Mississippi River forms the county's western border. The county is bounded on the north by Warren County, on the east by McDonough County, and on the south by Adams County. Hancock County's towns are small, and its landscape is essentially rural with cornfields interspersed with soybean fields.

The 17 communities that the Latter-day Saints either planned or established in Hancock County may be divided into various categories. Some towns—Ramus (Webster or Macedonia) and Lima—may appropriately be called major colonies. Other settlements—Plymouth, Green Plains, Golden's Point, Yelrome (Tioga), and Camp Creek—may be designated as minor colonies. Other sites may be considered missionary towns, places where the Saints lived among nonmembers, hoping to convert them to the gospel. Such towns were Carthage, Bear Creek, La Harpe, and Fountain Green. Several small settlements surrounded Nauvoo and might be considered Nauvoo suburbs: Stringtown, Mormon Springs, Rocky Run, Sonora, and Davis Mound. The Saints planned one settlement that was never built. This town, to be named Warren, might be called a paper town. Non-Mormon towns included Warsaw and Pontoosuc (ENS Feb. 1986, 62–68).

Note: Not all of these sites are worth visiting. In some cases, there is literally nothing to see. In other cases, the locations are obscure. The travel route follows a natural and convenient pattern that makes a loop around Hancock County, starting and ending in Nauvoo.

■ Stringtown

The settlement known as Stringtown was located three miles east of Nauvoo on State Alt. 2. The remains of an old stone blacksmith shop can still be seen alongside the road on the Lloyd Gerhardt farm, two miles east of the Nauvoo-Colusa High School.

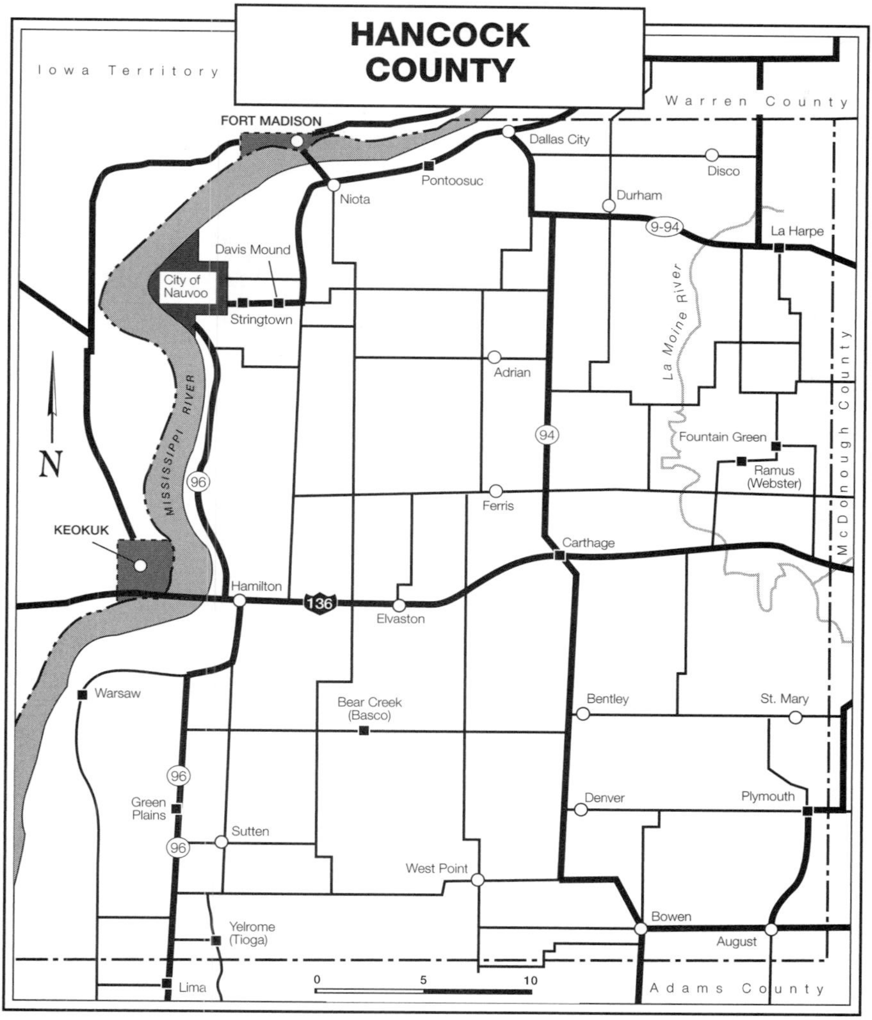

About 75 members, five or six families, resided in this town. They were converts from England who had given all their money for the construction of the Nauvoo Temple in exchange for a few acres of land east of Nauvoo. Since they had no money, they lived on a shoestring; hence, their settlement was called Stringtown (ENS Feb. 1986, 68).

Big Mound

About five miles east of Nauvoo, and .2 of a mile east of Stringtown on the old La Harpe Road (State Alt. 2) is a **landmark** called Big Mound. It is also called "the Mound" and Davis Mound after **Amos Davis,** a Latter-day Saint who built a large home and large barn atop the 50-foot hill north of the road (BYUS 31, no. 1 [1991]: 99, n18). Davis owned a store in Nauvoo and a hotel immediately south of the temple on Mulholland Street (see Site No. 100).

Latter-day Saint settlers in the area of the Mound included **James Jones, John Kay,** and **John** and **William Benbow**. **Joseph Smith** purchased the Mound from Hiram Kimball on June 14, 1842. The Prophet said, "Rode to the big mound on the La Harpe road, accompanied by Emma, Hiram Kimball, and Dr. Richards, and purchased a three-quarter section of land [480 acres] of Kimball, including the mound" (HC 5:25).

Pontoosuc

Pontoosuc is located on State 96, which runs along the Mississippi River, 13 miles NE of Nauvoo and two miles west of Dallas City.

Richard Ballantyne, James Standing, Phineas H. Young and his son **Brigham** were abducted by a mob near Pontoosuc. They were forcibly taken to Pontoosuc, where 50 armed men planned to hold them until some non-Mormons who had been arrested earlier were freed. They were kept in **Jeremiah Smith's** storehouse near the river until the evening of July 13, 1846, when they were taken to a small prairie, where they were threatened with being shot. They were then taken to **William Logan's** house, where they were again threatened. The mob, told the Mormons were near, took the prisoners the next day to Shokoquon and then to an island in the Mississippi. After various other afflictions, the prisoners were released after being held hostage for 12 days (HiR 847–48).

La Harpe

The missionary town of La Harpe is located 25 miles east of Nauvoo and eight miles north of Ramus on State 9–94. The designation "missionary town" is appropriate because La Harpe had already been settled by others and remained largely a Gentile town.

La Harpe is one of the oldest towns in Hancock County. One of the first settlers in the area was **Abraham Brewer,** who arrived in 1830. Major William Smith and Marvin Tryon founded the town in 1836, naming it Franklin. Later it was renamed La Harpe after Bernard de La Harpe, a French adventurer and fur trader in the company of French explorer La Salle.

The earliest Latter-day Saint settler in La Harpe was **Erastus Bingham,** who arrived in 1839. Erastus and other Saints began doing missionary work, and soon the nucleus of a Church branch was formed. Apparently, the most successful missionary was **Zenos H. Gurley,** who reported that he had baptized 52 people in six days (T&S 2:350).

Erastus Bingham, Zenos Gurley, and other Church members succeeded in converting a number of influential members of La Harpe, including **Lewis Rice Chaffin,** an early settler who was instrumental in selecting the name of La Harpe for the new town. Chaffin was one of the town's leading citizens, being a merchant, farmer, landowner, gristmill operator, and postmaster. After joining the Church, he became the object of anti-Mormon persecution. To avoid problems, he ground grain at night for his fellow believers. One night after a mob caught him in the act, one mobster warned, "If you grind a grain of flour for the Mormons, we will blow your brains out!" Chaffin replied, "Let me grind my own toll." The mob retorted, "You have a damned lot to grind" but allowed him to grind all the grain he brought (ENS Feb. 1986, 67).

Dr. George Coulson, another leading citizen of La Harpe, also joined the Church while living there. Dr. Coulson and his family moved to the area in the mid–1830s, built a log cabin on Main Street, and erected a building that later became the first schoolhouse in La Harpe. Missionaries, local Church members, and visiting Church leaders were all welcomed at the Coulson home.

The combination of immigration and missionary work led to the creation of a branch at La Harpe on Apr. 17, 1841. This branch was part of the Ramus Stake, Ramus being less than 10 miles to the south. Church leaders from Nauvoo frequently visited the La Harpe Branch. On Nov. 17, 1841, for example, Elders **Brigham**

Young and **John Taylor** visited. The Saints at La Harpe in turn visited John Taylor while he lay wounded at Carthage in June 1844.

La Harpe, which had a blacksmith shop run by **James Webb,** and other Latter-day Saint settlements in Hancock County served as way stations for missionaries and Church leaders as they traveled. **Charles C. Rich's** group stopped at La Harpe on a return trip to Nauvoo in July 1843. **William Clayton** and **Stephen Markham** stopped here en route to Dixon, where they warned the Prophet of his impending arrest (ENS Feb. 1986, 67–68).

■ FOUNTAIN GREEN

Fountain Green is located 10 miles south of La Harpe on State Alt. 17. After visiting his brother Don Carlos, **Joseph Smith** and his family started for Nauvoo on June 24, 1839. They went to the home of **William Perkins,** who lived near Fountain Green, and were invited to stay. While there, Joseph preached with considerable liberty to a large congregation the next day before he and his family continued their journey (HC 3:378).

■ RAMUS (CROOKED CREEK, MACEDONIA, WEBSTER)

Ramus is located 20 miles SE of Nauvoo and eight miles south of La Harpe. It is eight miles NE of Carthage, the county seat, on State Alt. 4. The town was established by Latter-day Saints and was regarded as an important settlement in Joseph Smith's plans for the area.

Joel H. Johnson and his family were largely responsible for the establishment of Ramus. They had settled in Carthage before Commerce (Nauvoo) was chosen as a settlement location. As a result of missionary work performed by Joel Johnson and others, several families along Crooked Creek joined the Church. Soon the Crooked Creek Branch was organized, and a site for a town, surveyed and platted under the direction of **William Wightman,** was chosen in the fall of 1840. Area residents chose the name Ramus, a Latin term meaning "branch," which may indicate the strong interest early Saints had in ancient languages (T&S 2:573).

Hyrum Smith created the **Ramus Stake** in this beautiful farming area on July 15, 1840, with **Joel H. Johnson** as stake president (T&S 2:222). A meeting house was built by members of the Ramus Stake, which was an unusual practice in the early days when

Webster Community Church, site of an early LDS chapel in Webster (Ramus), IL. (1989)

meetings were held in homes or out-of-doors. This building was one of the first meetinghouses built by the Latter-day Saints. The present Webster Community Church was built in 1897 on the site of the earlier meetinghouse. It is located on the east side of town one block south of State Alt. 4 (SE corner of Second and Elm Streets and directly south of the SW corner of the platted town square, or one block east and one block south of the post office).

The Saints in Ramus were very faithful. Under **William Wightman's** leadership, they deeded Church property in Ramus to **Joseph Smith** (HC 4:467–68). They also donated nearly $1,000 worth of personal property for the Nauvoo Temple (HC 4:469).

Joseph Smith visited Ramus frequently, stopping there en route to other destinations, holding Church conferences, convening Church courts, visiting relatives, and receiving revelations. Perhaps his most celebrated visits occurred in April and May of 1843, during which he recorded D&C 130 and 131.

On Apr. 1, 1843, **Joseph Smith, Orson Hyde,** and **William Clayton** traveled to Ramus. After spending the night at the home of Joseph's close friend **Benjamin F. Johnson,** they held a meeting at 10 A.M. During his remarks, Elder Hyde taught two points of doctrine the Prophet considered false. Elder Hyde taught that the Savior would appear on a white horse as a warrior and that the Father and the Son dwell in the hearts of men. While taking lunch at **Sophronia Smith McCleary's** home, the Prophet informed Elder Hyde that he was going to correct some errors in his sermon. These corrections, given later that day, are found in D&C 130. "When the Savior shall appear we shall see him as he is," the Prophet taught. "We shall see that he is a man like ourselves." The Prophet also taught about knowledge, intelligence, and the laws of heaven. He said the Father and the Son have bodies "of flesh and bones," adding that "the idea that the Father and the Son dwell in a man's heart is an old sectarian notion, and is false" (D&C 130:1, 22, 3; HC 5:323–24).

Joseph Smith returned to Ramus on May 16, 1843. That evening at the Johnson home he gave the family instruction on marriage and the priesthood (D&C 131:1–4). Information found in D&C 131:5 concerning "the more sure word of prophecy" was part of a sermon the Prophet delivered the following morning. The section's remaining verses were given in response to a sermon delivered by Samuel A. Prior, a Methodist minister. William Clayton recorded these things in his diary.

Joseph Smith was athletic, and the Saints living in Ramus saw him not only in his prophetic role but also in his role as a wrestler and stick puller. Joseph liked to wrestle, and he took pride in his prowess in that sport. He also engaged in the frontier sport of stick pulling. On one visit, the Prophet pulled sticks with **Justus A. Morse,** the strongest man in Ramus, and beat him while using only one hand. Later, during the same visit, Joseph wrestled **William Wall,** the most expert wrestler in Ramus, and threw him.

Sophronia and Catherine, two of the Prophet's sisters, lived in Ramus. Earlier, Catherine married Wilkins J. Salisbury, a young lawyer who also practiced blacksmithing in Ramus. He joined the Church in Kirtland but was excommunicated in 1834. Catherine lived here from 1847 until her death in 1900 at age 87. Her gravestone is in the small **Ramus Cemetery** about ¼ mile west of the town center. During the 47 years Catherine struggled as a widow in Ramus, Brigham Young sent $600 to help her (FJS 95–98).

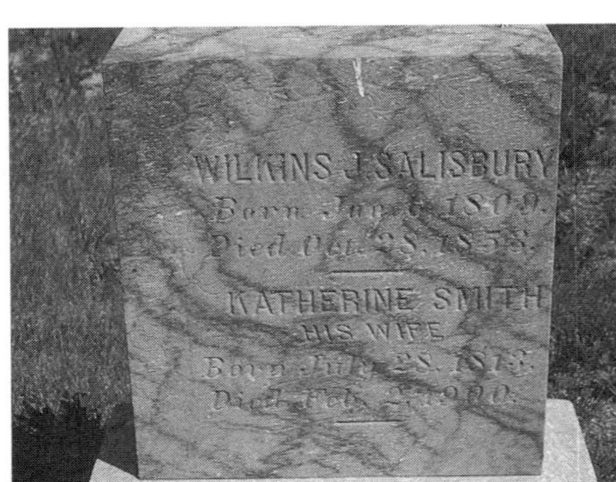

Gravestone of Catherine Smith Salisbury, sister of Joseph Smith, in Webster (Ramus), IL. (1989)

It is commonly believed that all Latter-day Saints left Hancock County in 1846 to begin their exodus to the West. Church records indicate, however, that the last ones to leave Ramus and travel to Utah did so in 1850. It appears that once the large body of Saints had left and the perceived threat from the Mormons was removed, the Saints in Ramus were allowed to live in peace (ENS Feb. 1986, 68).

■ Carthage

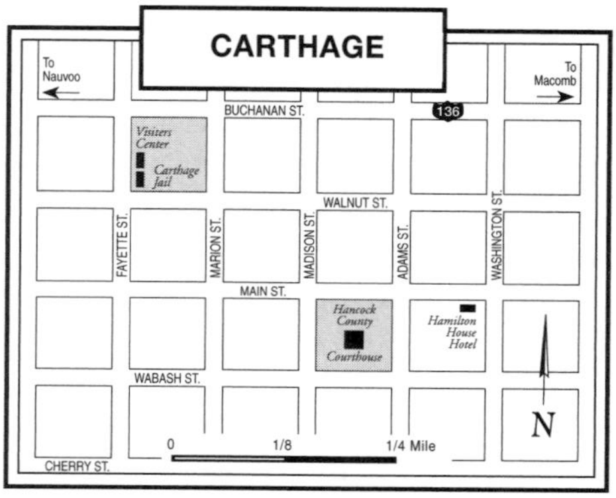

Carthage, the county seat of Hancock County since 1833, is located about 13 miles SE of Nauvoo (23 miles via State 96 and U.S. 136) in the geographic center of the county at the intersection of State 94 and U.S. 136. The town of approximately 3,000 residents is best known as the place where **the martyrdom of Joseph and Hyrum Smith** occurred.

While dining with **Sheriff Jacob Backenstos** and Judge **Stephen A. Douglas** on May 18, 1843, Joseph prophesied that the judge would aspire to the presidency of the United States but that if he ever turned his hand against the Saints, he would feel the weight of the hand of the Almighty upon him. This prophecy was printed in the *Deseret News* on Sept. 24, 1856, and was fulfilled during the election of 1860 (HC 5:393–94; CHC 2:183).

An **anti-Mormon meeting** occurred here Sept. 6, 1843. The citizens resolved to combine against the Saints and their leader, seek extradition of Joseph Smith by Missouri, and refuse to vote for any candidate who supported the Latter-day Saints. A similar meeting was held here Feb. 17, 1844, to devise ways by which the Saints could be expelled from the state.

Carthage Jail is located on the NE corner of Fayette and Walnut Streets, with a parking lot on the south side of State 136. Built 1840–42, the jail is 400 yards NW of the courthouse, but at the time of the murder it was on the outskirts of town. The jail, a 34-by-28-foot stone building, is two stories high with 2½-foot-thick walls. Part of the jail was occupied by the jailer as a residence (ThC 4:306).

Under the direction of **Joseph F. Smith,** the Church purchased the jail on Nov. 5, 1903, for $4,000. It was the first historical landmark purchased by the Church. A historical marker was placed on State 136, one block north of the old Carthage Jail, on Aug. 15, 1935. Later, on Oct. 27, 1963, a Carthage Jail Bureau of Information was dedicated. In 1984 the Church acquired the entire block where the jail is located. A new visitors center and grounds were dedicated in June 1989 (ENS Sept. 1989, 74; CN July 8, 1989, 3).

Carthage Jail, Carthage, IL, being used as a house. (Courtesy of LDSCA)

The martyrdom of Joseph and Hyrum took place in Carthage Jail on June 27, 1844. Joseph had voluntarily traveled here to meet in court on indictments filed by the proprietors of the *Nauvoo Expositor* regarding the destruction of their printing press.

On June 21, 1844, **Illinois governor Thomas Ford** came here to investigate problems. He sent an express to the mayor and city council of Nauvoo, requesting that they send him one or more well-informed, discreet persons, who could lay before him the city council's verdict of the difficulty.

On June 24, 1844, about four miles from Carthage, **Joseph** and **Hyrum Smith** and the group of brethren who accompanied them met a company of about 60 mounted militiamen, sent by Governor Ford, on their way to Nauvoo. Later, upon leaving Nauvoo, Joseph turned to his traveling companions and said, "I am going like a lamb to the slaughter" (HC 6:555). Escorted by Captain Dunn, Joseph's group arrived in Carthage late in the day as prisoners of Governor Ford. As they entered Carthage just past midnight, they were ridiculed by the troops, especially the **Carthage Greys,** who were camped in the public square (CHC 2:250; HC 6:553–60).

Hamilton Hotel, Carthage, IL. (Courtesy of LDSCA)

The **Hamilton Hotel,**

owned and operated by Artois Hamilton, provided lodging for Governor Ford and Joseph Smith's party (OMN 192). It was located on the south side of Main Street, half a block east of the courthouse, across the street from the post office. The hotel operated until 1884.

The **Hancock County Courthouse** is located on Main Street one block south and two blocks east of Carthage Jail. This brick building was the second courthouse built on the square and dates to 1839. Trials for those accused of murdering Joseph and Hyrum were held here in 1845.

Hancock County Courthouse, Carthage, IL. (Courtesy of LDSCA)

On June 25, 1844, Joseph, Hyrum, and 13 others charged with rioting and destroying the press of the *Nauvoo Expositor* on June 10 surrendered themselves to Constable Davis Bettisworth. They were arrested for treason based on a warrant founded upon the oaths of H. O. Norton and Augustine Spencer. The governor and **General M. R. Deming** conducted Joseph and Hyrum in front of the McDonough troops near the courthouse and introduced them as "Generals Joseph and Hyrum Smith." The Carthage Greys refused to receive them (MS 24:357). Joseph prophesied that they would witness scenes of blood and sorrow (HC 6:566). In the afternoon, the Prophet and his party were released on bail until a circuit court judge could hear their case. That evening Bettisworth came to take Joseph and Hyrum to jail to await trial for treason. He produced a mittimus, which Justice Robert F. Smith had signed without conducting a proper investigation, and committed the brethren to the Carthage Jail. They spent the night in the "debtor's apartment" on the bottom floor (HC 6:561–74).

On the morning of June 26, 1844, Governor Ford interviewed Joseph and his party at the jail. Between 100 and 200 of the governor's troops took the men to the courthouse but then returned them to the jail because their hearing was postponed until Saturday, June 29. That evening the Prophet and those with him slept in the upstairs front room of the jail (the jailer's bedroom), and Joseph prophesied to Dan Jones that he would serve a mission to Wales (HC 6:575–601).

On June 27, 1844, Governor Ford left eight men at the jail to guard the Prophet. By mid-afternoon, only four prisoners remained in the jail: **Joseph** and **Hyrum Smith, John Taylor,** and **Willard Richards.** They stayed in the jailer's 16-by-16-foot bedroom, and at about 3:15 P.M., John Taylor sang "A Poor Wayfaring Man of Grief" to cheer up the depressed spirits of the prisoners.

Soon after 5 P.M., a mob of 150–250 men with blackened faces surrounded the jail, forced their way into it, and fired a shower of bullets into the room. Hyrum was killed first by a ball that crashed through the panel of the door and struck him in the face, just left of his nose. John Taylor sprang for the open window opposite the door and attempted to leap out, but a ball struck his watch, forcing him back into the room (HC 7:119–20). Joseph also tried to jump out the same east window but was shot with four balls, falling from the window to the ground below. With the shedding of his blood, the Prophet had sealed his testimony of the establishment of the dispensation of the fulness of times.

John Taylor was severely wounded by four balls, one in his hip. A fifth ball would have passed through his chest had it not been for a watch in his left vest pocket. In his account of the martyrdom, he said the event lasted about three minutes (HC 6:619–21; T&S 5:584–86).

The Prophet Joseph Smith had prophesied regarding Willard Richards that "balls would fly around him like hail, and he should see his friends fall on the right and left, but . . . there should not be a hole in his garment" (HC 6:616–22). Other than a bullet grazing his ear, he escaped unharmed.

After being attacked several times by mobbers on his way to Carthage to see his brothers, **Samuel Smith** arrived during the attack on the jail. **Artois Hamilton** gave Samuel refuge in his hotel.

A mob attacked LDS Church leaders in Carthage Jail, Carthage, IL, killing Joseph and Hyrum Smith. Joseph is seen falling from the window. (Courtesy of LDSCA)

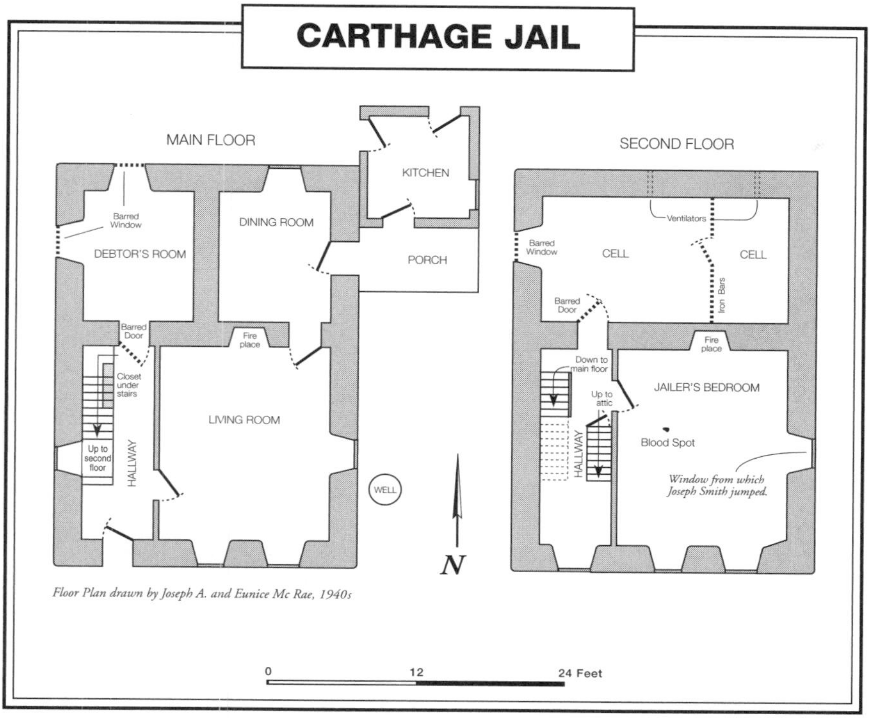

Carthage Jail, Carthage, IL, where the Prophet Joseph Smith and his brother Hyrum were martyred. (Watercolor by Frederick Piercy; courtesy of LDSCA)

Jailer's bedroom in Carthage Jail, Carthage, IL, and the window from which Joseph fell when he was shot by assassins.

John Taylor's watch, which stopped a bullet that could have proven fatal. The hands on the watch indicate the time of the attack at Carthage Jail. (Courtesy of LDSCA)

Stairs leading to the jailer's bedroom in Carthage Jail, Carthage, IL, where Joseph and Hyrum Smith were martyred by a mob after it forced its way up these stairs. (1972)

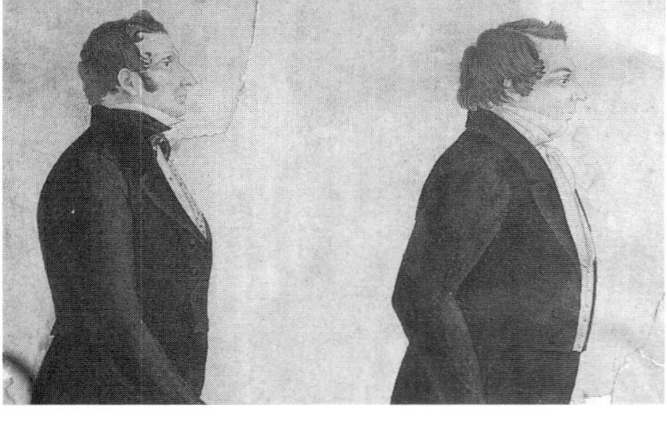

Hyrum Smith and the Prophet Joseph Smith (L to R), in watercolor. (Photo of the original; courtesy of the Wilford C. Wood Foundation, Woods Cross, UT)

After the mob and townspeople fled following the **Martyrdom,** Samuel and Artois went to the jail and had the bodies of Joseph and Hyrum removed to the hotel. Willard Richards persuaded a reluctant Elder Taylor to allow himself to be taken to the hotel, where he remained three or four days after the murder.

At 8 P.M. Elder Richards penned an announcement of the tragedy for the Saints at Nauvoo, and he and Elder Taylor signed it (HC 6:621–22; CHC 2:289–90). Governor Ford returned to Carthage from Nauvoo in the evening, and at 1 A.M. on the public square he advised all present to disperse because he expected the Mormons to burn the town. The people scattered in all directions, and the governor and his posse fled toward Quincy (HC 6:625; CHC 2:291).

Two white horses pulled the wagon that brought the bodies of Joseph and Hyrum from Carthage to Nauvoo on June 28, 1844 (BYUS 19, no. 3 [1979]: 299), under the direction of Willard Richards and Samuel Smith (HC 6:626). A jury acquitted the **murderers** of Joseph and Hyrum on May 30, 1845 (CC 51–54, 75, 97–116, 171–85).

Thomas C. Sharp, an enemy of the Church and editor of the *Warsaw Signal,* was living in Carthage in 1888 and serving as editor of the Carthage *Gazette.* Sharp refused to meet with Elders Andrew Jenson, Edward Stevenson, and Joseph Black when they visited Carthage that year, so the brethren visited with his son instead. He showed them original copies of the *Warsaw Signal* calling for the extermination of the Mormons in Hancock County and a copy of the *Nauvoo Expositor,* which they had not seen before.

■ PLYMOUTH

Plymouth is located 40 miles SE of Nauvoo near the McDonough County line on State 61. **William Smith,** Joseph Smith's brother and an Apostle from 1835 to 1845, settled in Plymouth in 1839. He farmed and kept a tavern (public house) after he was excommunicated from the Church in 1845 (HC 3:377). The Plymouth fire station, just north of the town square, occupies the tavern site. When the Twelve went to England in 1839, William chose to remain on his farm in Plymouth rather than go with them as commanded (D&C 118). In a letter published in the *Times and Seasons* on Dec. 1, 1840, William apologized for not having left on his mission, citing poverty as the reason. He was probably better prepared financially to leave his family, however, than any members of the Twelve who went to England (BiE 1:87).

In 1838, **Catherine Smith Salisbury,** the Prophet's sister, lived here with her husband, Wilkins, who was a blacksmith (HJS 345). **Samuel H. Smith** moved here to manage William's tavern in the fall of 1842. **Joseph Smith** stayed at the tavern on Dec. 27, 1842, as he was traveling to Springfield to stand trial before Judge Nathaniel D. Pope because of an assassination attempt on Missouri governor Lilburn Boggs. Joseph and Elder Willard Richards slept on a bearskin.

On Jan. 9, 1843, Joseph stopped at Plymouth on his return from Springville. At Catherine's home, he talked of Alvin, his deceased brother. Joseph said, "He [Alvin] was a very handsome man, surpassed by none but Adam and Seth, and of great strength." Joseph visited his brother Samuel also. The next day, Jan. 10, the Prophet received a royal welcome in Nauvoo (HC 5:247–48).

■ Bear Creek (Knowlton's Settlement, Basco)

This town is located 21 miles SE of Nauvoo on State Alt. 11, 10 miles east of State 96. It was a missionary town, with a few Latter-day Saint settlers. **Joseph Smith** stopped here on June 5, 1841, while returning to Nauvoo after his visit with Illinois governor Thomas Carlin in Quincy. While staying at Heberlin's Hotel, he was arrested by a sheriff's posse under the direction of Thomas King, sheriff of Adams County, and Thomas Jasper, constable of Quincy. His arrest was on a requisition from Governor Carlin, who planned to deliver Joseph to Missouri authorities (T&S 2:447; HC 4:365, 370–71).

■ Yelrome (Morley's Settlement, Tioga)

Yelrome (Tioga) is located 25 miles south of Nauvoo, three miles north of Lima and two miles east of State 96. **Isaac Morley** was the first Latter-day Saint settler in the area. He and his family were among the thousands of Saints seeking refuge in Illinois after being savagely driven from Missouri in 1839. Yelrome is Morley spelled backward with an extra "e." The name may have come from a Latter-day Saint penchant to spell words backward. Resident **Alpheus Cutler,** from Tioga County, Pennsylvania, may have had something to do with the name Tioga.

The names of the people living in Yelrome in the 1840s (at

least 424 members) constitute a genealogical treasure chest. In addition to the Morleys and Cutlers, the families of Thomas Hickenlooper, Lucy Morley Allen, Orville S. Cox, William Critchlow, Edward Whiting, Enos Curtis, Edmund Durfee, William Garner, Anna N. Gifford, and Solomon Hancock lived there, as did **Eliza R. Snow** in 1843–44 (ENS Feb. 1986, 62–68).

Branch president Isaac Morley was a cooper, employing 12 men making barrels to sell in Quincy. Isaac's daughter, Cordelia, taught school.

Another Latter-day Saint, Frederick Cox, ran a chair-making shop. Members of the Church in Yelrome had many opportunities to hear the **Prophet Joseph Smith** speak. On Sunday, May 14, 1843, the Prophet spoke on "salvation through knowledge." He taught, for example, that "knowledge through our Lord and Savior Jesus Christ is the grand key that unlocks the glories and mysteries of the kingdom of heaven." That night Emma arrived with the carriage, and the next morning they rode home together (HC 5:387–90).

Because Yelrome was isolated and located near anti-Mormon elements in Adams County and the town of Warsaw, the Saints suffered mob attacks. Mobs burned 175 homes to the ground, and on Nov. 15, 1845, **Edmund Durfee** was killed (HOI 287; NCJ 187–88). A marker honoring Edmund has been placed one block south of the United Church, just as the road reaches the south boundary of Tioga. Saints in Yelrome abandoned their town and moved to Nauvoo. No Latter-day Saint buildings remain (HC 7:440; JTB Oct. 24, 1845).

■ LIMA (ADAMS COUNTY)

Lima is located three miles south of Yelrome just over the Adams County line on State 96. A number of Latter-day Saint families settled here after their expulsion from Missouri in 1839, and when the Lima Stake was organized Oct. 23, 1840, **Isaac Morley** was appointed stake president (HC 4:233; ThC 6:404).

Elders Brigham Young and **Heber C. Kimball** started on their missions to England in Sept. 1839 but were too sick and feeble to sit up. **Brother Osmon M. Duel** carried them in his wagon 16 miles to Lima, where another brother received them and carried them about 20 miles more that day (HC 4:10).

Speaking on the Word of Wisdom here on June 11, 1843, **Elder Kimball** stressed the importance of example by saying that every spirit begets its own (HC 5:427–28). **Lorenzo Snow** and **Eliza R. Snow** taught in the school here until Jan. 20, 1844, leaving in Feb. 1844. **Titus Billings,** second counselor to Bishop Edward Partridge from 1837 to 1840, lived here until mobs burned the Saints' homes in 1845.

In Sept. 1845, a messenger reported to Brigham Young that eight houses had been burned by a mob in Lima. The Twelve met in council and decided to advise the Lima brethren to sell their property to the mob and bring their families and grain to Nauvoo (JJT 90).

Several Church members are buried in the **Lima Cemetery,** but no buildings remain in Lima from the Latter-day Saint period.

■ Green Plains

The site is located eight miles south of Hamilton on State 96. Latter-day Saints established an 80-member branch (the Prairie Branch) here after fleeing from Missouri in the spring of 1839. The town disappeared because of a cholera epidemic about the time of the Civil War. Today nothing but farmland exists in the area.

John Smith, president of the Adam-ondi-Ahman Stake (and later of the Zarahemla and Salt Lake Stakes), fifth patriarch to the Church, and uncle to the Prophet, located here about Mar. 1839. He put in a crop of corn, split rails, and performed much hard labor unsuited to the health of a 58-year-old (JSN 144; BiE 1:183). **Joseph Smith** and his family stayed here at his uncle's home on May 9, 1839, while on their way to Commerce (HC 3:349).

The house of **Levi Williams,** a notorious mob leader, served as the post office for the area. It was located six miles SE of Warsaw. Several mob expeditions that were organized to arrest the Saints or destroy their property in Hancock County during the persecutions of 1844–46 originated in this area (EnH 303).

■ Warsaw and Warren

Warsaw, built 1812–14 near two old forts, is located on the Mississippi River 16 miles south of Nauvoo opposite the mouth of the Des Moines River and three miles west of State 96. It was well known in Joseph Smith's day as an anti-Mormon town.

John E. Page, an **Apostle** from 1838 to 1849, located south of here soon after Apr. 26, 1838. The following year he failed to go to England with his brethren of the Twelve (BiE 1:92).

The ***Warsaw Signal,*** the local newspaper, began its anti-Mormon stance with an article that appeared May 19, 1841. Its editor, Thomas Sharp, a bitter enemy of the Church and founder of an anti-Mormon political party in 1841, attacked the Church in print at every opportunity. The Prophet Joseph Smith condemned the *Signal* because of its lies. The paper's print shop was located at 204 Main St. A print shop museum is located nearby at 424 Main St.

Warren, named after one of Joseph Smith's lawyers, was a paper town located one mile south of Warsaw. Willard Richards settled in Warsaw in Sept. 1841 to sell city lots in Warren. Elder **Joseph Fielding** brought a company of 204 British immigrants to Warren on Nov. 24, 1841, but because of hostility from Warsaw residents, the community was not established (HC 4:405, 410, 471). Later, the First Presidency asked the British immigrants to move to Nauvoo. Those who remained in Warren were persecuted (CHC 2:120).

Daniel Avery and his son **Philander** were kidnapped from here Dec. 2, 1842, and carried into Missouri by a company of Missourians assisted by some anti-Mormon Illinoisans (T&S 4:375–76; HC 6:99).

The hard feelings of the Warsaw townspeople continued to grow. Resolutions passed at a mass meeting at Warsaw were presented for approval in Carthage on June 13, 1844, and adopted. Among other decisions, the people resolved to exterminate the leaders of the Church and drive all the Saints into Nauvoo.

On the morning of June 27, 1844, a posse from Warsaw marched toward Carthage but was met by an order from Governor Thomas Ford to disband. Learning that Ford was not in Carthage, approximately 200 of these men hastened there and participated in the attack on Carthage Jail that resulted in the death of Joseph and Hyrum Smith. After the Martyrdom, the murderers met in the Warsaw Hotel (Flemming's Tavern), the brick part of the present building located at 130 Main Street.

When mob violence continued after the Martyrdom, Governor Ford demanded the public's arms at Warsaw in July 1844. Citizens refused to comply with his order, however, asserting that it was absolutely necessary that either the Mormons or the other citizens leave the county. In a letter to the people of Warsaw appearing in the *Nauvoo Neighbor* newspaper on July 31, 1844, he exhorted them to live in peace with the Mormons. He warned them that their course of staying armed, drilling, and insisting that the Saints leave was improper and unwarrantable and would result in his "most determined opposition" (HC 7:214–15).

Northeast of Nauvoo

■ Monmouth

Monmouth, the county seat of Warren County, is located at the intersection of U.S. 34 and U.S. 67, 40 miles south of Rock Island. **Joseph Smith** was brought to Monmouth June 9, 1841, to stand trial on trumped-up charges. The trial was held to determine whether Joseph should be returned to Missouri to stand trial. Six lawyers acted nobly and honorably in behalf of Joseph. **Judge Stephen A. Douglas** liberated him on a writ of habeas corpus (HC 4:364–71; CHC 2:78–82).

■ Knoxville

Knoxville is located 22 miles east of Monmouth on U.S. 150 and two miles SW of U.S. 74. **Lucy Mack Smith** and her daughter **Lucy** moved here from Nauvoo in the late summer of 1846. They lived here three years and then moved to Ramus (WS-R 141).

■ Ottawa

Ottawa is located 75 miles SW of Chicago and two miles south of U.S. 80 at the intersection of U.S. 6 and State 23. **Hyrum Smith** and **Lyman Wight** traveled to Michigan and recruited 22 volunteers for **Zion's Camp.** On their way to Missouri to meet **Joseph Smith's** group, they forded the Illinois River one mile below the village of Ottawa (see map page 242) and had lunch before continuing on to the Vermilion River, where they camped May 22, 1834, after having traveled 33 miles (ZCB 79; JEF).

■ Norway (Fox River Settlement)

Norway is located 12 miles NE of Ottawa on State 71. Fox River Settlement, founded in 1834, is the oldest continuous settlement of Norwegians in North America. In Mar. 1842, Church member

George P. Dykes converted and baptized several Norwegian settlers and organized a branch. In 1844 the Saints here purchased 160 acres and founded the City of Norway (HC 7:312).

This settlement, which included a location for a temple the Saints selected at the Prophet's request, was located three miles SW of present-day Norway. Unfortunately, nothing remains of the original LDS settlement. After the Saints left Nauvoo, this group split into factions, some joining with the Strangites in Wisconsin, some joining the RLDS movement, and some going to Utah in 1849.

■ NEWARK

Newark is located 20 miles NE of Ottawa on State 71. **Elders Wilford Woodruff** and **George Albert Smith** of the Council of the Twelve spoke here May 18–19, 1844, at a conference attended by 33 members of the Newark Branch. The next day at a political meeting to further Joseph Smith's presidential candidacy, the men presented Joseph's views on government (HC 6:400).

■ CHICAGO

Chicago is located on the shore of Lake Michigan at the NE corner of Illinois. It is the point of intersection of several interstate freeways.

Colonel John Wentworth, to whom the famous Wentworth letter was written, resided in this city. He was the editor of the *Chicago Democrat* and printed some impartial items about the Church (T&S 3:790; CHC 2:130–31).

Arthur L. Thomas was born here Aug. 22, 1851. He became the fourteenth governor of the Territory of Utah, serving 1889–93 (ERA Sept. 1901, 801–802).

Egyptian mummies and the **papyrus** from which the book of Abraham in the Pearl of Great Price was translated were exhibited here in Wood's Museum. The mummies are believed to have been destroyed in the Great Fire of 1871 (EnH 646).

Martin Harris, one of the Three Witnesses to the **Book of Mormon,** bore testimony of his angelic visitation to a large number of people at the American Hotel on Aug. 21, 1870 (BiE 1:273).

The **Mormon Tabernacle Choir's** first tour group arrived here Sept. 1893 for the World's Fair, called the Columbian Exhibition. **Evan Stephens** was the conductor. The choir won second place in the musical competition and was awarded $1,000 (CHC 6:242–44). **Presidents Wilford Woodruff** and **George Q. Cannon of the First Presidency** and **Utah governor Caleb W. West** gave addresses at the fair Sept. 9 on "Utah Day."

The **first branch** of the Church in Chicago was organized June 4, 1896, with **Lars F. Soderlund** as president (ChCh 212). **Christian D. Fjeldsted,** one of the first seven presidents of the First Council of the Seventy from 1884 to 1905, was called here on a special mission in 1897 to raise up a branch of the Church that consisted largely of Scandinavians (BiE 1:204).

The Roseland District Missionary Home, 10723 Perry Ave., was dedicated by **President Joseph F. Smith** on Nov. 1, 1913. On Nov. 2, President Smith dedicated the Logan Square Church and mission home on the corner of Wrightwood and Sawyer Avenues (ERA Dec. 1913, 185).

Rapid membership growth in the twentieth century led to the organization of 12 stakes in Illinois with five in the Chicago area by the year 2000 (DNCA 2001–2002, 141).

■ Chicago Illinois Temple

The Chicago Temple is located at Glenview, 23 miles NW of Chicago's city center on Lake Avenue, 5.5 miles west of U.S. 94 (exit U.S. 94 onto Lake Avenue at exit 35A-B going north and exit 34 going south).

The beautiful light-gray marble Chicago Temple with its six spires was the thirty-fifth LDS temple in operation. It was dedicated during 19 dedicatory sessions Aug. 9–13, 1985, with 24,000 members attending from 40 stakes, 12 states, and a portion of Canada, which make up the temple district.

President Gordon B. Hinckley, then the second counselor in the First Presidency, gave the dedicatory prayer. Afterward, he remarked, "I have a feeling that the erection and dedication of this House of the Lord [the Chicago Temple] carries something of a redemption of what happened in the past. It brings together the tradition of Nauvoo and the blessings of today" (CN Aug. 18, 1985, 3).

Other Sites to See in Chicago

1. **Art Institute of Chicago** houses famous paintings and watercolors.

2. **Chicago Board of Trade** is one of the world's largest commodities exchanges.

3. **Sears Tower** was the world's tallest building in the 1990s.

4. **University of Illinois at Chicago** is an architecturally unusual campus.

5. **Grant Park** (lake front) contains **Buckingham Fountain,** a yacht basin, rose garden, band shell, and other attractions.

6. **John G. Shedd Aquarium** exhibits more than 10,000 fish and sea creatures.

7. **Field Museum of Natural History** is a museum of natural sciences.

8. **Adler Planetarium** features three floors of exhibits and a sky show.

9. **Soldier Field** is home to the Chicago Bears football team.

10. **Chinatown** is a picturesque community with gift shops and restaurants.

Plano

The **first headquarters** of the Reorganized Church of Jesus Christ of Latter Day Saints (CC) was located in Plano on U.S. 34, 50 miles SW of the Sears Tower in Chicago. In Jan. 1866, **Joseph Smith III,** son of the Prophet, who was then serving as president of the Reorganized Church, moved here and edited the *Saints Herald* newspaper (LJFS 250–51). Plano was the RLDS Church headquarters from 1866 to 1881. The headquarters was then moved to Lamoni, Iowa. Fourteen general conferences of the RLDS Church were held here.

Prominent RLDS members in Plano, in addition to Joseph Smith III, included Israel Rogers, William Marks, Zenos Gurley (who ordained Joseph III as president of the RLDS Church), and two of Joseph Smith's brothers, Alexander and David, the "Sweet Singer of Israel." The oldest RLDS building, constructed in 1868, is located in Plano at 320 South Center St., adjacent to a modern RLDS meetinghouse.

Elders Orson Pratt and **Joseph F. Smith** visited Plano in 1878 while on a special mission to gather facts of early Church history. Joseph Smith III was not at home, but they were asked to speak in an RLDS prayer meeting (CHC 5:536–58).

■ Sycamore

John E. Page, an **Apostle** from 1838 until his excommunication in 1846, died here in the fall of 1867. The town is located 27 miles NW of Geneva, where state highways 64 and 23 cross (BiE 1:93).

■ Pawpaw Grove

Pawpaw Grove is located 25 miles west of Plano and five miles south of U.S. 30. **Joseph Smith** stopped here for a night in 1843 while in the custody of **Sheriff Joseph H. Reynolds** of Missouri. They were en route to Ottawa, where Joseph was to be tried. The next morning the citizenry gathered in the largest room of the hotel and insisted upon hearing the Prophet preach. Sheriff Reynolds objected and told the people that Joseph Smith was a prisoner and could not be allowed to preach. One citizen, **David Town,** spoke up, calling the sheriff a "damned infernal puke" and telling him to sit down and not interrupt. The Prophet then addressed the company for about an hour and a half on marriage.

The trial was postponed because the judge was absent. While the group was traveling to Nauvoo, a lawyer for Sheriff Reynolds challenged anyone in the group to a wrestling match. Stephen Markham—a huge man and an experienced wrestler who served as a bodyguard to Joseph—took up the challenge. When the lawyer threw him, the Prophet's enemies let out a taunting shout. At the Prophet's urging to "get up and throw that man," 19-year-old Philemon C. Merrill, who was not a wrestler, "arose to his feet filled with the strength of a Samson." Philemon, later a member of the Mormon Battalion, threw the lawyer over his shoulder when Joseph Smith counted to three (ENS Nov. 1986, 30; HC 5:439–53).

■ Amboy

Amboy is located 12 miles SE of Dixon on U.S. 52. On Apr. 6, 1860, **Joseph Smith III,** son of the Prophet, attended a conference of people who believed that he, as Joseph's son, should succeed his father as president of the Reorganized Church of Jesus Christ of Latter Day Saints. Joseph III was sustained as the new prophet and president of the new RLDS Church. A marker is located where this event took place (CHC 5:139). Membership of the church, now known as the Community of Christ, is approximately 250,000.

Palestine Grove

Palestine Grove is located ½ mile west of Amboy, just south of Amboy Road. A few cellar stones on a ridge is about all that remains of the town. In 1848, **William Smith,** the Prophet's brother who had apostatized, declared Palestine Grove to be a new gathering place for the Saints (WS-R 141). He established a periodical called *Zion's Standard* but enjoyed little success here. A second town by the same name is located 85 miles east of Vandalia on State 33, but this is not the original settlement.

Dixon

Dixon is located in Lee County, 75 miles NE of Rock Island, on U.S. 52. **Isaac** and **Davie Hale** and **Elizabeth Wasson,** Emma Smith's brothers and sister, lived eight miles away from Dixon. The Wasson farm is located just outside present-day Amboy. It is on the east side of U.S. 52, just north of the Lutheran church, which is just across the northern boundary of Amboy.

Joseph Smith was accosted by **Joseph H. Reynolds,** sheriff of Jackson County, and **Harmon T. Wilson**, sheriff of Carthage, while visiting the Wassons on June 23, 1843. When they threatened to shoot him, Joseph bared his breast and told them to go ahead, saying, "I have endured so much oppression, I am weary of life; and kill me, if you please" (HC 5:440). The men repeatedly punched their pistols into Joseph's sides, leaving large black-and-blue marks on each side of his body (HC 5:440–42).

Stephen Markham and **William Clayton** rode 212 miles in 66 hours to help the Prophet, but they were restrained by the sheriff's party. About 75 men from Nauvoo went with **Dan Jones** on the ***Maid of Iowa*** up the Illinois River to intercept Reynolds, Wilson, and Joseph's group (HC 5:447). Joseph was taken to Dixon to be tried but obtained a delay and a writ of habeas corpus from the Ninth Judicial District at Ottawa, 60 miles SE of Dixon. While going to Ottawa, Joseph stopped at Pawpaw Grove and gave a discourse on marriage (HC 5:445). While there, his group learned that Judge John D. Caton of the Ninth Judicial District was in New York, so the men headed for Quincy to have the writ of habeas corpus reviewed. They were met on the way by a group of 175 men from Nauvoo who had ridden horseback to rescue the Prophet. The men compelled Joseph's group to go to Nauvoo. When they arrived, city residents greeted the Prophet with cheers, cannons, and the Nauvoo Band. He was subsequently released because of lack of evidence (HC 5:446–74; BiE 1:194; T&S 4:242–43; JD 2:218).

On the evening of June 30, 1843, Joseph reported on his experience at Dixon to the Saints assembled at the grove. "I pulled sticks with the men coming along, and I pulled up with one hand the strongest man that could be found," he said. "Then two men tried, but they could not pull me up, and I continued to pull, mentally, until I pulled Missouri to Nauvoo" (HC 5:466).

■ Freeport

Freeport lies 40 miles NW of Dixon, where State 26 intersects U.S. 20. **J. Wilson Shaffer,** the seventh governor of Utah, was from here. Appointed governor Feb. 1, 1870, Shaffer was determined to rule the Saints but died after seven months in office (ERA Mar. 1901, 323).

■ Fulton City

Emma Smith lived in Fulton City, located 125 miles north of Nauvoo and 38 miles west of Dixon on State 136, for a time after she moved from the Mansion House in Nauvoo. Her apartment was in a large, white, two-story frame house owned by Dr. Daniel Reed and located at the corner of Base and Wall Streets, four blocks from the river (ME 365, n17). Emma's mother-in-law, **Lucy Mack Smith,** also lived here for a while. **William Marks,** previously president of the Nauvoo Stake, also lived in this town and helped persuade Emma to move here.

● Galena

Galena is located in the NW corner of Illinois, 75 miles west of Rockford and along U.S. 20. It is the largest port on the Mississippi River north of St. Louis and the center of trade for the upper Mississippi lead-mining region. During the mid-19th century, 80 percent of all lead mining in the world was conducted in this area. Several Latter-day Saints worked in the lead mines in the Galena area during the construction of the Nauvoo Temple.

Galena residents presented the **President Ulysses S. Grant Home State Historic Site** (no fee) to General Grant after he returned from the Civil War in 1865. This home contains many of his possessions, including White House china and silver. President Grant was the first president of the United States to visit Utah. In Oct. 1875, he was met by President Brigham Young and Sunday School children lining South Temple Street in Salt Lake City to give him a hearty welcome as his carriage passed them (CHC 5:503–506).

Vinegar Hill Lead Mine (fee) is located six miles north of Galena. The museum, containing artifacts of early mining days, offers a guided tour.

East of Nauvoo

■ Good Hope

Good Hope is located 40 miles east of Nauvoo on State 9. **Francis M. Lyman,** an **Apostle** from 1880 to 1916, was born here Jan. 12, 1840. His parents moved their family the following spring. Francis M. Lyman offered dedicatory prayers at the Holy Land on three different dates at three different places in 1902 (BiE 1:136–37).

Francis M. Lyman, an Apostle from 1880–1916. (Courtesy of LDSCA)

■ Walnut Grove

This town is located seven miles NE of Good Hope and five miles north of State 9. **Robert Taylor Burton,** second counselor to Presiding Bishop Edward Hunter (1875–83) and first counselor to Presiding Bishop William B. Preston (1884–1907), stopped here with his father's family in 1838 when they heard of the terrible persecution of the Saints in Missouri. They remained in this branch for about two years.

● Peoria

Peoria is located 115 miles east of Nauvoo and 125 miles SW of Chicago, where I-74 crosses the Illinois River. **Thomas Ford,** governor of Illinois when Joseph and Hyrum Smith were martyred, died here penniless on Nov. 3, 1850 (CC 220–21).

■ Pekin

Hyrum Smith's division of Zion's Camp, composed of 18–21 persons from the Pontiac, Michigan, area, spent nine nights within 18 miles of Pekin while on their way to Missouri in 1834. Pekin, located nine miles south of Peoria on State 29, was a village of 15 houses at the time (ZCB 100). The camp stopped here for several days, meeting with a small branch of about 30 members and having a wagon wheel repaired.

■ Macomb

Macomb, home of **Western Illinois University,** is located 25 miles east of Carthage on U.S. 136. **Samuel Smith,** one of the Eight Witnesses to the Book of Mormon, moved to a rented farm near here in 1839 with his brother **Don Carlos. Joseph Smith** and his family visited Don Carlos here June 16, 1839 (HC 3:377). A **Nauvoo Legion cannon** is mounted in concrete in Macomb's Chandler Park.

■ Colchester

Colchester is located 18 miles east of Carthage on U.S. 136. **Joseph F. Smith** and **Samuel H. B. Smith,** while on their way to Great Britain to fill a mission in 1860, stopped to visit two of Joseph Smith's sisters, **Sophronia** and **Catherine,** who were living here. In 1872 **George A. Smith** visited Joseph's three sisters—Sophronia, Catherine, and **Lucy**—here while on his way to Palestine to dedicate it for the return of the Jews.

Sophronia Smith Stoddard lived here until her death on Aug. 28, 1876. She is buried here in the Mount Auburn Cemetery. Catherine was buried in Ramus.

Lucy Smith, youngest sister of the Prophet, and her husband, **Arthur Milliken,** lived near Colchester for many years. Arthur died here Apr. 23, 1882. He was a drummer boy in the Mormon Militia and had fought in the battle of Crooked River, where he was shot through both legs above the knees, escaping death only by a miracle. Lucy was buried here Dec. 1882. Lucy and Arthur were "received" into the Reorganized LDS Church in 1873 (HiR 190).

Southeast of Nauvoo

■ QUINCY

Quincy is the county seat of Adams County, which was organized in July 1825. It is located 45 miles directly south of Nauvoo where U.S. 24 crosses the Mississippi River, and was named after President **John Quincy Adams.**

Hyrum Smith's division of Zion's Camp stopped at Quincy and ferried across the Mississippi River to camp on the west bank on June 5, 1834 (ZCL 96). Journal keeper Elijah Fordham wrote that the town had 70 houses, 2 inns, and 9 stores (JEF). Hyrum's division crossed the river on Logsden's Ferry near the saw and grist mills, happy to arrive in Missouri.

Joseph Smith and **Brigham Young** crossed the frozen Mississippi River at Quincy as they escaped from their enemies in Kirtland and fled to Far West, MO, in Jan. 1838 (HC 3:3).

Quincy, a town of 2,000 people, was the principal gathering place for the Saints expelled from Missouri in 1838–39. After ferrying across the Mississippi River here, they met with a friendly reception and were relieved from want and possible starvation. **Eliza R. Snow** wrote a poem of gratitude to the people of Quincy that was printed in the *Quincy Whig*, May 11, 1839.

Ezra T. Benson became acquainted with the Church when he moved here in the winter of 1839. He boarded with **Thomas Gordon,** who had been driven out of Missouri, and was soon converted to the Church. **Jonathan Browning,** gunsmith, was also converted in Quincy. On Feb. 25, 1839, the Democratic Association held a meeting here and passed a resolution to help the Latter-day Saints (HC 3:263; EnH 688).

A Church **conference** was held here Mar. 17, 1839, with Brigham Young presiding (Joseph Smith was in Liberty Jail). At this conference, several brethren were excommunicated, including **Thomas B. Marsh,** first president of the Quorum of the Twelve; **John Corrill,** who served as a Church historian in Far West, MO; **Frederick G. Williams,** second counselor to Joseph Smith 1833–37; and **William W. Phelps,** editor of *The Evening and the Morning Star.* William was rebaptized in 1841, and Thomas was rebaptized in 1857. Frederick, who was rebaptized in 1840, made his home in

Quincy, where he died a faithful member of the Church on Oct. 10, 1842 (BiE 1:51–52; CN Oct. 31, 1987, 7).

After spending more than five months in jail, most of that time in Liberty Jail, **Joseph** and **Hyrum Smith** were allowed to escape, arriving in Quincy to join family and friends on Apr. 22, 1839. Joseph stayed here for about 18 days (T&S 1:7; BiE 1:4).

A **general conference** of the Church was held here May 4–6, 1839, with Joseph Smith presiding. During this conference, the membership approved Iowa Territory purchases and the mission of the Twelve to Europe. In addition, **Sidney Rigdon** was chosen to represent the Saints in government at Washington, D.C., as a lobbyist, and **William Smith** was disfellowshipped (BiE 1:87; HC 3:344–48).

A stake was organized in Quincy on Sept. 25, 1840, with **Daniel Stanton** as president (HC 4:233). This stake became a branch in 1841 after most of its members moved to Nauvoo.

On June 1, 1841, Joseph Smith accompanied Hyrum Smith and **William Law,** on their way to a mission in the East, as far as Quincy. While at Quincy, Joseph called on **Governor Thomas Carlin** at his residence. The governor treated Joseph with respect and hospitality, but he made no mention of a former requisition issued by Missouri and endorsed by him for Joseph's arrest (HC 4:364).

On June 5, 1841, Joseph was arrested by Thomas King, sheriff of Adams County. **Judge Stephen A. Douglas** arrived at Quincy that night and set hearing on the writ for June 8, in Monmouth.

Heber C. Kimball, Brigham Young, and others, while on a mission to correct apostate **John C. Bennett's** allegations, preached in the courthouse here on Aug. 17, 18, 1842, against Bennett and other mobocrats. Governor Carlin attended one meeting.

After the Prophet's martyrdom, **Governor Thomas Ford** fled to Quincy on June 29, 1844, and established his headquarters here. The citizens of Quincy convened Sept. 22, 1845, resolving that the Saints should leave Illinois and appointing a committee to confer with Church authorities regarding their intentions about leaving the state (HC 7:451–53; CHC 2:504). **Orrin Porter Rockwell** was jailed here in early May 1846 for shooting **Frank Worrell** the previous fall (OPR 146).

Governor John Wood's 1835 mansion at 425 S. 12th Street is now a museum, displaying several items related to Church history, including the keys of the Nauvoo Temple. Wood, founder of

Quincy and mayor when Joseph Smith was martyred, aided the Saints when they came to Quincy and distributed aid to the Saints on the Iowa plains in 1846 (CN Feb. 18, 1989, 3).

The **town square** (Washington Park), located on the SE corner of North Fourth and Main Street (State 24), is where the Saints camped as they fled from Missouri in 1839. A monument on the south side of the square honors them. One of the seven **Lincoln-Douglas presidential debates** took place here in Oct. 1858.

On Feb. 10, 1989, Mayor Vern Hagstrom gave the **key to the City of Quincy** to Loren C. Dunn of the First Quorum of Seventy. The city declared Feb. 15, 1989, "Latter-day Saints Day" to honor Emma Smith's crossing of the frozen Mississippi River and entering Quincy after fleeing Missouri 150 years earlier (CN Feb. 18, 1989, 3). Emma lived four miles east of Quincy with Judge John Cleveland and his wife, Sarah. Sarah became Emma's first counselor in the Relief Society. Church leaders met at Judge Cleveland's home to decide their future (JWW 1:329–30).

■ Columbus "Mount Hope Stake"

Mount Hope Stake was organized May 27, 1840, at the steam mills in Columbus, 18 miles NE of Quincy, with Abel Lamb as president. The stake was discontinued in 1841 (EnH 545).

■ Payson

Payson is located 10 miles SE of Quincy on State 96. Freedom Stake was organized here on Oct. 27 1840, with **Henry W. Miller** as president (HC 4:233).

One of six Kinderhook plates. (1969)

■ Kinderhook

Kinderhook is located 22 miles SE of Quincy at the intersection of U.S. 36 and State 96. On Apr. 23, 1843, **Robert Wiley** and others claimed to have found six brass bell-shaped plates near here while excavating a large mound. They also supposedly found a nine-foot human skeleton.

Joseph Smith translated a small portion of the Kinderhook Plates but soon lost interest in the project (HC 5:372–84; ENS Aug. 1981, 66–74).

Valley City and Phillip's Ferry (Zion's Camp, Kirtland Camp)

Valley City is located three miles east of Griggsville on County Road 2, where Phillip's Ferry and "ferry landing" were located on the Illinois River. Joseph Smith's division of **Zion's Camp** used the ferry June 2, 1834, for an $8 fee. While camped near here on the morning of June 3, they found in a mound the skeleton of a Lamanite warrior the Prophet identified as **Zelph. Kirtland Camp** also used Phillip's Ferry, camping on both sides of the Illinois River on Sept. 18, 1838 (HC 3:140–41).

Zelph Mound

Zelph Mound (Naples-Russell Mound, number 8, Pike County, IL), one of 120 prehistoric burial mounds located along a three-mile stretch of the Illinois River bluff, is the largest Hopewell culture burial mound ever found. It is located .9 mile south of the center of Valley City and Phillip's Ferry, on the west side of the Illinois River. To reach the mound, first go to Valley City, three miles east of Griggsville on Route 2. In Valley City cross the railroad tracks and travel one mile in a southerly direction, following a dirt road along the Illinois River to a sign marking the Pike County Conservation Area. Park your car and, from this sign, climb .1 mile up the heavily wooded hill west of the road in a NW direction. The unimproved trail goes through heavy brush, and the climb takes about 20 minutes. Archaeologists refer to the

Zelph Mound, looking north. (1989)

Zelph Mound as **Naples-Russell Mound Number 8,** and it is on the National Register of Historic Places.

Joseph Smith and members of Zion's Camp climbed this mound on June 3, 1834. The brethren felt that stones on top of the mound were the remains of three altars erected one above the other centuries earlier (HC 2:79). While on the mound they unearthed a skeleton, which Joseph Smith identified as Zelph, a white Lamanite warrior and chief. An arrowhead found with the skeleton is in the LDS Church vault. Wilford Woodruff placed one of Zelph's thigh bones in his wagon and transported it to Liberty, MO, where it was buried near the home of Colonel Michael Arthur. The next day, June 4, Joseph Smith wrote to Emma that he had been "wandering over the plains of the Nephites" (PWJS 324), indicating that he was in Book of Mormon country.

Eight other mounds are located within .6 miles of Zelph Mound on a north-south line about .2 mile apart. Zelph Mound is located directly west of the .9-mile mark south of the railroad tracks. Six mounds are located 1.1 miles south of the railroad track and .1 mile west of the road. One mound is located 1.3 miles south of the railroad tracks and 145 feet west of the road. Another mound is located 1.5 miles south of the railroad tracks, and 285 feet west of the base of the bluff.

Buffalo Wallow is located west of Zelph Mound on farm land .7 mile up **Church Hollow Road** and 300 feet south of the road. Church Hollow Road comes directly from the old Phillip's Ferry and skirts the north side of the farm. This road may be the one traveled by Zion's Camp in 1834 (HC 2:79–80; BYUS 29, no. 2 [1989]: 31–56; ReSI 97–111).

■ PIKE CITY (MORMONTOWN)

Pike City is located 2.5 miles east of Pittsfield, IL, on U.S. 106. It was a haven for Saints fleeing from Far West, MO, in the early months of 1839 after Governor Lilburn Boggs issued his Extermination Order. Although this was a large settlement, little is known of its history (HSM 293).

Silas Smith settled in Pike City as he was going from Kirtland toward Missouri in the **Kirtland Camp.** On Sept. 24, 1838, while at Elk Fork of the Salt River in Missouri, he learned of the troubles in Missouri. As a result, he and others decided to stay and settle in Pike City, where he presided over the Church, which was organized with a high council (BiE 341–42). He was the son of Asael Smith and Mary Duty, and a brother of Joseph Smith Sr. Silas died in Pike City at age 60 on Sept. 13, 1839. His sons were Sanford, John, and Jesse Nathaniel (BiE 1:316). **William Draper** also served as a leader of the Pike County Branch from 1839 to 1842 (AWD 18–20).

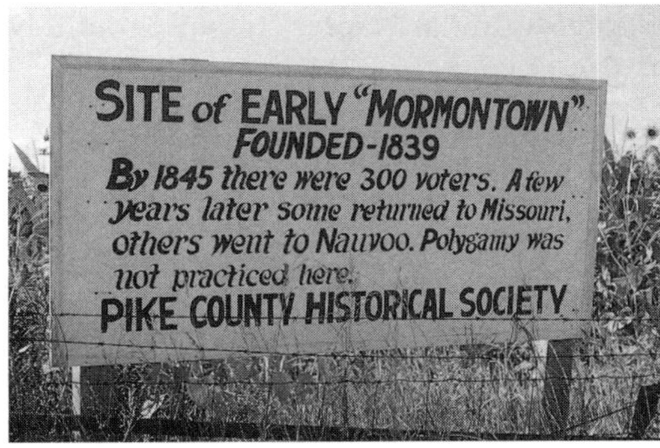

Sign identifying the location of Pike City (Mormon Town), IL. (1975)

In addition to the Silas Smith Family, other Saints who lived here with their families included James Allred (high council member) and wife Elizabeth, Thomas Edwards, William Cooper, Charles Stoddard, Robert Cooper, Chauncey L. Higbee (judge and son of Elias), Elisha Cooper, and David E. Osborne (ADO 10).

Local residents call Pike City "Mormontown," and some Latter-day Saints called it Pittsfield. Nothing remains of Pike City today except bits of pottery and glass fragments scattered in the cornfields. A white wooden sign on the north side of U.S. 36 marks an approximate location.

■ Pittsfield

Pittsfield is located at the intersection of U.S. 54 and State 106, 45 miles SE of Quincy. **Joseph Smith's division of Zion's Camp** had a "noon stop" near here on June 3, 1834. While here, Joseph prophesied that the Lord had revealed to him that a scourge would come upon the camp and they would "die like sheep with the rot." This prophecy was fulfilled when cholera struck the camp (HC 2:80, 106–107, 114–18; T&S 6:788).

Kirtland Camp also went through Pittsfield, camping on a small hill one mile west of town Sept. 19, 1838 (HC 3:141).

■ Atlas (Zion's Camp)

Atlas is located 40 miles SE of Quincy at the intersection of U.S. 54 and State 96. On June 3, 1834, Joseph Smith's division of

Zion's Camp spent the night one mile west of Atlas on the west side of the Sny River. Organized as a military unit with more than 130 men and 25 baggage wagons, they were on their way to Jackson County to repossess land the Saints had lost to mob forces in the fall of 1833. Here a **Colonel Ross** approached **Joseph Smith** and offered to employ 100 men (HC 2:80–82; T&S 6:788). **Kirtland Camp** passed through Atlas on Sept. 20, 1838 (HC 3:141).

When **Brigham Young** and his family left Far West, MO, on Feb. 14, 1839, they stopped here for a few weeks before going on to Quincy, IL (CN May 26, 1934, 7). They stayed here in a **two-story brick house** or **trading post** (restored) on the NW corner of the intersection of U.S. 54 and State 96. Some members of the Heber C. Kimball family also sought refuge here. Other families went east to Pike City (HSM 294).

■ Pike

Pike is located five miles SW of Atlas on the shore of the Mississippi River and on U.S. 54. **Joseph Smith's division of Zion's Camp** stayed here on the east bank of the Mississippi River while ferrying the river June 4–5, 1834 (HC 2:82–83).

Ezra Taft Benson, an **Apostle** from 1846 to 1869, and a man by the name of Isaac Hill laid out this town at the mouth of the Little Blue. Here Ezra built himself a home and a warehouse in the late 1830s, but the place was sickly and he was restless. He left in 1839 and moved to Quincy, where the Saints were gathering. There he was converted to the Church (HiR 133).

■ Vandalia

Vandalia lies 60 miles NE of St. Louis at the intersection of U.S. 40 and U.S. 51. It was the western terminus of the Cumberland Road (the National Road) and was the second state capital of Illinois (1820–39). Abraham Lincoln served his first two terms as state representative in Vandalia. The courthouse that served as the capitol building is a state memorial. In 1838, **John Doyle Lee** received a spiritual witness here of the **Book of Mormon** (JDL 17–31). He joined the Church a short time later in Far West.

● Cahokia

Cahokia Mounds State Park, located south of I-55/70 near St. Louis, has some of the largest earth mounds built by early Indians. The largest mound is Monks Mound, which is 100 feet high and covers 16 acres—three acres more than the great pyramid of Cheops in Giza, Egypt. An excellent museum tells the story of the early Americans.

Monks Mound, Cahokia Mounds State Park, near east St. Louis, IL. (1991)

■ Decatur

Decatur is 39 miles east of Springfield at the intersection of U.S. 51 and U.S. 36. **Joseph Smith** and his division of **Zion's Camp** camped near here May 28–29, 1834 (ZCL 83).

The camp, located nine miles SW of the city center, was one mile south of the Sangamon River and two miles north of Blackland. During military maneuvers on May 29, Heber C. Kimball suffered a sword wound that cut some skin from the palm of his hand.

Joseph Smith said, "At this place I discovered that a part of my company had been served with sour bread, while I had received good, sweet bread from the same cook. I reproved Brother Zebedee Coltrin for his partiality, for I wanted my brethren to fare as well as I did" (HC 2:75).

The **Kirtland Camp** spent the night of Sept. 12, 1838, at the same campsite (HC 3:138–39).

■ Rochester

Rochester is located five miles SE of Springfield on State 29. **Zion's Camp** and the **Kirtland Camp** passed through Rochester on

Sept. 14, 1838. **Wilford Woodruff,** his wife, child, and 53 converts he baptized in the Fox Islands arrived here Dec. 19, 1838, and remained during the winter. The converts were emigrating from Maine to Illinois. Wilford moved to Quincy in the spring, but many Saints stayed in the Rochester area. On Apr. 3, 1839, Wilford escaped serious injury here after being dragged on the ground for about a mile and a half under a wagon (JWW 1:324). He visited here Aug. 10, 1839, on his way to England to serve a mission with the rest of the Twelve (WW 98).

■ Springfield

Springfield, the Illinois state capital, is located at the intersection of I-55 and U.S. 36. **Zion's Camp** generated considerable curiosity when it passed through here without incident May 30, 1834. Zion's Camp members expected trouble here. Spies had been following them and were still pursuing closely, changing their dress and horses several times a day. Zion's Camp camped on the east side of **Spring Creek** three miles west of the center of Springfield near the point where State 125 begins crossing Spring Creek going NW (HC 2:76–77).

Upon reaching Springfield in the fall of 1838, the **Kirtland Camp** stayed in the same place as Zion's Camp (HC 3:139–40). Many in the camp were sick, and money was short. At a camp council, members decided that they should rent houses to take care of the sick, with certain people assigned to remain to care for them. Some of the Kirtland Camp remained in Springfield nearly two years.

Kirtland Camp members **Samuel Mulliner** and wife **Catherine Nisbit** stayed in Springfield. When Samuel went with the **Twelve** to England in the fall of 1839, Catherine did laundry work for Abraham Lincoln to support herself and her husband. Samuel, one of the first two missionaries in Scotland, performed the first baptisms there (ENS Feb. 1987, 26–31).

The Saints who stayed in Springfield were soon organized into a branch presided over by **Joel H. Johnson.** They held meetings in the Campbellite meetinghouse with about 40 members attending. A stake of 300 members was organized in Springfield on Nov. 5, 1840, with **Edwin P. Merriam, Isaac H. Bishop,** and **Arnold Stephens** called as the stake presidency (HC 4:236).

Joseph Smith preached several times while in Springfield

Nov. 4–8, 1839. After hearing Joseph speak, local judge **James Adams** invited the Prophet to his home and became a faithful friend. James later became a patriarch and was one of the first men to receive his endowment in this dispensation, on May 4, 1842. At his friend's funeral, Joseph Smith called the judge "one of the spirits of the just men made perfect. . . . I saw him first at Springfield, when on my way from Missouri to Washington [Oct. 6–8, 1839]. He sought me out when a stranger, took me to his home, encouraged and cheered me, and gave me money. He has been a most intimate friend. I anointed him to the patriarchal power" (HC 6:50–52.)

John C. Bennett went to the **Old Statehouse,** which was the state capitol in Springfield, to secure passage of a bill incorporating the City of Nauvoo. On Dec. 16, 1841, **Governor Thomas Carlin** signed the act incorporating Nauvoo, the Nauvoo Legion, and the University of Nauvoo. The Senate passed the charter without dissent, and the House passed it with only minor dissent. Members of both houses warmly welcomed the Saints. **Abraham Lincoln,** a resident of Springfield and a member of the state congress in Illinois, voted in favor of the act even though he and the Saints had had a misunderstanding during a recent election related to lack of Latter-day Saint support for Lincoln (UHQ [spring 1963]: 91–94). After the final vote, he cordially congratulated Bennett on its passage. During his inaugural address in 1842, **Governor Thomas Ford** called the Nauvoo City Charter objectionable (T&S 4:41) even though it was designed after Springfield's charter (HC 4:239–45; T&S 2:267).

It was in the **Old Statehouse** that Abraham Lincoln delivered his famous "House Divided" speech and where he lay in state before his burial.

Old Statehouse or capitol building, Springfield, IL. (1969)

The home of Abraham Lincoln, located in the center of Springfield at 426 S. 7th Street, is the only home he ever owned. Visitors are welcome (free). **Lincoln's law offices,** at 211 S. 6th Street, were built in 1840 (free). **Lincoln's Tomb** is located about 15 blocks north of the state capitol building (up Spur Street/ State 4) in the Oak Ridge Cemetery (free).

Abraham Lincoln's home in Springfield, IL. (1969)

In Springfield, **Joseph Smith** was commissioned lieutenant general of the Nauvoo Legion by Governor Carlin on Mar. 10, 1841 (HC 4:309–10).

Abraham Lincoln's tomb in Springfield, IL. (1969)

The Lincoln–Herndon Building at 6th Street and Adams was the scene of the trial of Joseph Smith before **Judge Nathaniel D. Pope** Jan. 4–5, 1843. The courtroom is located on the second floor of the building and is open to the public.

Joseph Smith and party arrived in Springfield Dec. 30, 1842, to submit to legal authorities on charges that Joseph was an accessory to the attempted assassination of former **Governor Lilburn Boggs** of Missouri. The trial opened Jan. 5, 1843, in the federal courtroom before Judge Pope of the U.S. District Court. Affidavits were read proving Joseph's presence in Nauvoo at the time of the shooting. **Esquire Butterfield,** the Prophet's counsel, showed why the Prophet ought not to be released to Missouri authorities. On Jan. 5, 1843, Judge Pope acquitted the Prophet (HC 5:220–31, 244; CHC 2:158; DoJS 278–86). Afterward, Joseph Smith met with Judge Pope in the judge's office and explained to him the role of a prophet (HC 5:231–32).

Joseph Smith, Orson Hyde, and John Taylor used the **House of Representatives Hall** for preaching services on Jan. 1, 1843. The hall was filled with Saints, most members of the Legislature (including perhaps Abraham Lincoln), and many others from various state departments. People wanted to see and hear the Prophet.

Stephen A. Douglas, who had previously been friendly to the Saints, delivered his famous speech here June 12, 1857, in which he characterized Mormonism as a "loathsome ulcer of the body politic" and recommended that Congress apply the knife and "cut it out." Douglas' about-face led to the fulfillment of a prophecy uttered by the Prophet Joseph Smith on May 18, 1843. The Prophet told Douglas that if he ever turned against the Latter-day Saints, he would feel the hand of the Almighty upon him. Douglas was twice defeated in his bid for the presidency of the United States (CHC 2:182–92; HC 5:393–94).

George Donner, his brother **Jacob Donner,** and **James Reed** lived here when they received a copy of *Emigrants' Guide to California* by **Lansford W. Hastings.** They organized the ill-fated Donner-Reed emigrant party of 300 wagons that left Springfield for California in 1846 (CN June 13, 1931, 2). Brigham Young and the 1847 pioneers followed the Donner Party's tracks on part of the trail west (JWW 3:226–27; CHC 3:208–209).

The new **state capitol building** was built 1868–87. The dome reaches 361 feet above the ground.

• Lincoln's New Salem State Park

Lincoln's New Salem State Park is located two miles south of Petersburg (20 miles NW of Springfield along State 97). Abraham Lincoln lived here from 1831 to 1837, years that marked a turning point in his life. He was a youngster when he came here in 1831, but when he moved to Springfield in 1837 he embarked on a career of law and statesmanship.

The park has been reconstructed with 23 buildings resembling the old town of New Salem, including timber houses and shops; a carding mill, school, sawmill, and gristmill; and the Rutledge Tavern. In the Onstot Cooper Shop, the only original building, Lincoln studied by the light of a fire made from cooper shavings. A museum contains artifacts of the period (fee), and a statue of

Lincoln by Avard Fairbanks welcomes visitors at the entrance to the village.

■ Dickson Mounds Museum, Havanna, Lewiston

One of the few on-site archaeological museums in the Midwest is located five miles NW of Havana on State 78 (97). The purpose of the museum is to discover and preserve the heritage of prehistoric American Indians (free). An **Indian monument** built and paid for by local Latter-day Saints is located in nearby **Havana.** Twelve feet high and topped by a bronze eagle, it is located near the Illinois River and close to the bridge on the highway going west out of Havana. The Rockwell Indian Burial Mound is located at 500 North Orange (free).

Lewiston, located 35 miles SW of Pekin on U.S. 24, had a small branch of the Church in Dec. 1834 (M&A 1:64).

■ Jacksonville

Jacksonville is located 33 miles west of Springfield on State 78. **Zion's Camp** camped one mile east of the Jacksonville city center on May 31 and June 1, 1834. Members knew where to stop because **Frederick G. Williams** had gone ahead and signaled the location by dropping a pawpaw bush in the road. He then went to Jacksonville to spend the night. On Sunday, June 1, the Saints had two Sabbath meetings. Two hundred townspeople attended, and six elders preached, including Joseph Smith, Brigham Young, Orson Hyde, Joseph Young, Orson Pratt, and Eleazer Miller, all of whom had formerly been preachers for other denominations (ZCL 86–87). Many of the town inhabitants who had come to hear them desired to know who they were. To protect themselves, the brethren mentioned their former denominations rather than admit that they were Mormons. They were introduced using fictitious names, the Prophet's name being "Squire Cook" (ZCL 86; HC 2:77–78; T&S 6:772–73).

The **Kirtland Camp** came through Jacksonville four years later on Sept. 17, 1838. It camped at Geneva, 10 miles SW of Jacksonville and 2.5 miles east of Riggston (HC 3:140).

James Foster, a member of the First Council of the Seventy and a member of the Kirtland Camp, settled here instead of gathering with the Saints in Missouri. He was dropped from the Seventy in Oct. 1844 (BiE 1:192).

■ Rushville

Rushville is located 55 miles NW of Springfield along U.S. 24. **Joseph Smith** and his traveling party started for Springfield from Nauvoo on Dec. 27, 1842, for his trial related to the shooting of former **Missouri governor Lilburn Boggs.** The next day they stopped at a Rushville tavern, and that evening the Prophet visited **Uriah Brown** and his family. After returning to the tavern, Joseph and Hyrum Smith were measured for their height. Both were six feet (HC 5:210).

■ Lovington

Joseph Smith's division of **Zion's Camp** spent the night of May 27, 1834, on the west bank of the Okaw River at a point two miles NW of modern Lovington on State 32 and 50 miles east of Springfield. On this day, Joseph said, "We know that angels were our companions, for we saw them" (HC 2:73). Joseph's encouragement helped dispel the camp's fears.

Kirtland Camp spent the night of Sept. 11, 1838, at the same campsite. Many in the camp were sick (HC 3:138).

■ Oakland

Zion's Camp spent the night of May 26, 1834, one mile west of the Embarras River, which is three miles west of modern Oakland on State 133 about 30 miles west of the Indiana border.

When the brethren found three prairie rattlesnakes in camp, the Prophet said, "Let them alone—don't hurt them!" Joseph "exhorted the brethren not to kill a serpent, bird, or an animal of any kind during our journey unless it became necessary in order to preserve ourselves from hunger" (HC 2:71).

Mob threats caused anxiety in Zion's Camp near Oakland, and when moon reflections appeared to be campfires, there was a "call to arms" (HC 2:70–73).

Zion's Camp and Kirtland Camp in Illinois—1834 and 1838

LaMar C. Berrett and Donald Q. Cannon

Zion's Camp was a Latter-day Saint expedition of 200–228 members, including some women and children (ZCB 263–80), called by revelation (D&C 103) that left from the Kirtland, OH, and Pontiac, MI, areas to rendezvous in Missouri during May–June 1834. **Joseph Smith** organized the Kirtland contingent of about 200 people, and **Hyrum Smith** and **Lyman Wight** organized a smaller group of 21 people primarily from Pontiac, MI. They met at the Allred Settlement on Salt Creek in eastern Missouri to continue on to Clay County in western Missouri. Their purpose was to redeem Zion, support the Saints who had been forced from their homes in Jackson County, help Church members get back their lands and homes, and try to establish peace in Jackson County.

From Kirtland, Joseph's division traveled south toward the Cumberland Road, or National Road, which the division used for 133 miles from Springfield, OH, to Indianapolis, IN. This distance was 16 percent of the total 800 miles. A summary of dates, camps, and events in Illinois follows.

Hyrum Smith's Division of Zion's Camp in Illinois—1834

CAMP	DATE (1834)	MILES (Approximate)
■ **CALAMICK CREEK (INDIANA)**	**MAY 17–18**	**23**

On May 17, Hyrum's division of Zion's Camp crossed the state line between Indiana and Illinois and camped for the Sabbath on Calamick Creek, immediately south of **Chicago Heights**. The camp members had traveled through marshes and saw a great many snakes. At the end of the day, their feet were very sore and blistered, and their stockings were wet with blood. They posted sentinels every night in response to spies who were continually striving to steal their horses or otherwise harass them. On Sunday, May 18, a meeting was held during which the brethren partook of the sacrament of the Lord's supper. Elijah Fordham wrote in his journal, "Truly the Lord is with us, all things go smoothly and we are rejoicing" (JEF; HC 2:68).

■ **HICKORY CREEK**	**MAY 19**	**30**

After making a long 30-mile hike through prairies and marshes this day, the 20–25 members of Hyrum Smith's division of Zion's Camp were tired when they arrived at their campground on the east side of Hickory Creek. Their camp was located two miles west of today's Harlem Avenue and one mile south of what now is U.S. 30, eight miles SW of Chicago Heights and south of Chicago (JEF).

■ **DES PLAINES RIVER**	**MAY 20 (WEST SIDE)**	**18**

The camp's horses got loose in the morning, which made the camp late in starting. The company eventually caught the horses but lost some brethren for a while in the process. Afterward, the division traveled five miles down Hickory Creek, crossed the creek at a sawmill, and then went to the Des Plaines River, which was several rods wide. The men camped near modern **Rockdale** at a point about nine miles NE of modern Channanon and 2.2 miles SW of the point where Washington Street crosses the Des Plaines River in

Joliet. They camped along the river where they crossed, which is about .1 mile east of U.S. 6 (JEF).

■ Illinois River (north of modern Seneca) — May 21 — 33

After an early breakfast before sunrise and a prayer by Hyrum Smith, the division went eight miles and crossed the Du Page River at a gristmill (Channahon). The camp then traveled 25 miles following today's U.S. 6, crossing a miry prairie before camping. All were tired.

■ Vermilion River — May 22 — 33

A man who lived near the camp had 240 head of cattle with 40 calves. Elijah Fordham recorded in his journal: "Had plenty of milk, quite refreshed, called the place 'Eminence and Glory,' for much provision was there and the place was beautiful." The camp then continued its journey "over delightful prairies and groves of timber" (JEF; spelling and punctuation modernized).

Elijah Fordham recorded, "At noon forded the Illinois River, a mile below the village of Ottawa, a delightful situation" (JEF). After traveling 33 miles, the division crossed the Vermilion River and camped on the west side of the Vermilion River for the night. The men got milk for six cents a quart in the morning; they paid six cents per fresh pail that night (JEF).

■ Crow Creek — May 23 — 26

The men went 20 miles up the Illinois River and stopped at Robert's Grove for lunch, where they saw stone coal (JEF).

■ Earl Residence — May 24 — Unknown

The brethren were all in good health as they began their journey this day, but by noon, Samuel Bent was taken ill with malaria. He felt better in the afternoon, so the men continued their journey. They stopped for the night near a spring shaded by willows. A Latter-day Saint couple named Earl visited the camp. The location of the Earl residence is unknown, but author James L. Bradley suggests that the Earls were probably members of the Pleasant Grove

Hyrum Smith's Division

Zion's Camp, Illinois

1834

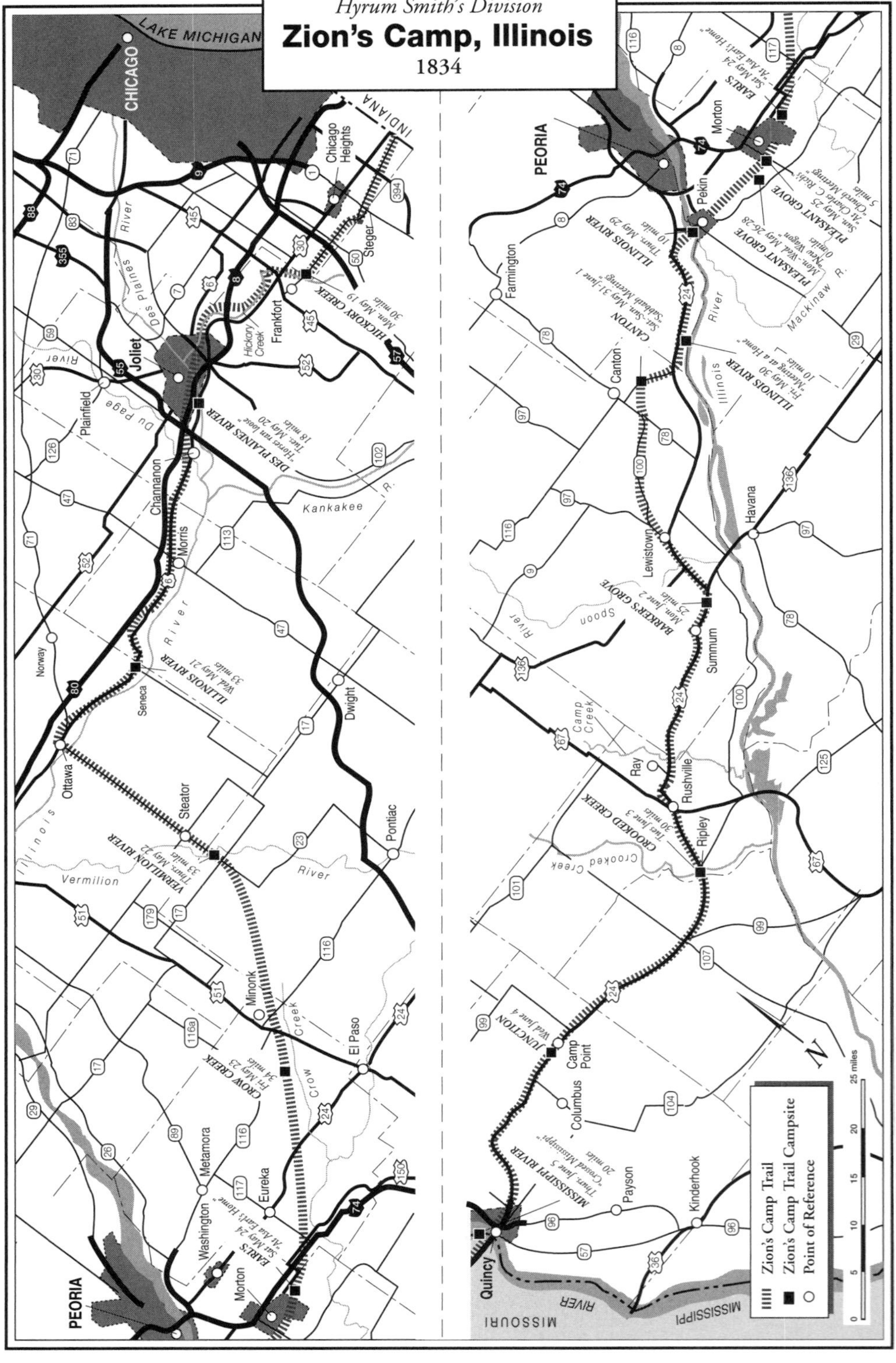

Joseph Smith's Division

Zion's Camp, Illinois
1834

Kirtland Camp, Illinois
1838

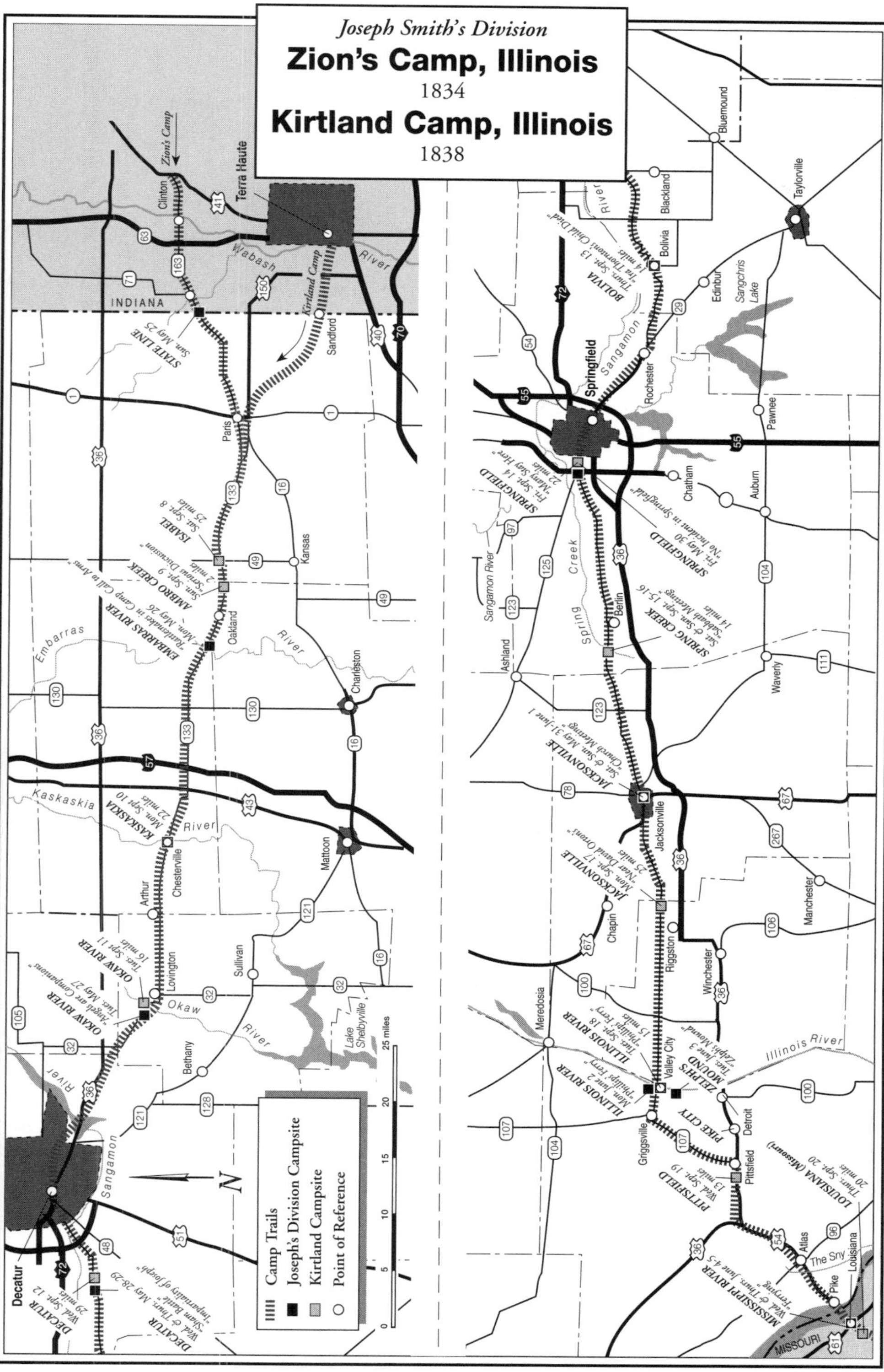

Branch. Bradley has found names or references to 16 branches of the Church west of New Portage, OH, and east of Clay County, MO, during the years surrounding 1834 (ZCB 81; JEF).

■ **Pleasant Grove** **May 25** **5**

The division went about five miles to Charles C. Rich's home and the Pleasant Grove Branch of the Church, where the brethren held meetings in the morning and evening. Elijah Fordham wrote, "The Church rejoiced to see us" (JEF). Charles C. Rich's home was 2 miles NE of Pleasant Grove, 10 miles east of Pekin, IL, and 10 miles SE of Peoria. Pleasant Grove was about 2.5 miles south and 1 mile east of Groveland on the road toward Allentown. Groveland was settled in 1827 and had a post office until 1835. It was located 2 miles north and 1 mile west of Tremount, in section 2 of Elmgrove Township.

Charles C. Rich was a member of the Quorum of the Twelve from 1849 to 1883. He was one of the prominent leaders in settling the Bear Lake region of northern Utah. Rich County is named after him.

■ **Pleasant Grove** **May 26** **0**

The division did not travel this day. Sisters washed the camp members' clothes, which were grimy with sweat and trail dust (JEF).

■ **Pleasant Grove** **May 27** **0**

Lyman Wight, a leader in Hyrum Smith's division, held religious meetings about five miles from Pleasant Grove (JEF).

■ **Pleasant Grove** **May 28** **0**

Lyman Wight "purchased a larger wagon and a yoke of cattle in the place of the little wagon," wrote Elijah Fordham (JEF). While the camp was in the area of Charles C. Rich's home near Pekin, Brother Rich decided to join the contingent. He was only 24 years old and had been baptized two years before (JCL 95–96).

■ **Illinois River (west side, near Pekin)** **May 29** **10**

The camp "took leave of the brethren [Brother Earl and the other Saints] and went almost to the village of Pekin on the Illinois River and broke one wheel of the big wagon. [We] went to Pekin [and] engaged a man to mend it. Pekin is a new place, has a large steam grist mill and a steam saw mill and about 15 houses. We crossed the Illinois and camped, having traveled 10 miles," wrote Elijah Fordham (JEF).

■ **Illinois River (west side)** **May 30** **10**

Elijah Fordham recorded that the camp "waited till most night for the wagon to be finished. Got on about 10 miles and camped under the bluff on the road to Canton. Held meeting at a house. Brother [Hyrum] Smith and [Lyman] Wight spoke. Timber, bad roads" (JEF).

■ **Canton (four miles east)** **May 31** **10**

The roads were bad on the way to Canton. Brother Fordham wrote, "This region is infested with the caterpillar and grasshopper. The woods look like winter with here and there a tree with leaves on that they won't eat, making a strange appearance. Road to Lewiston. Camped about four miles east of Canton" (JEF; spelling modernized).

■ **Near Canton (four miles east)** **June 1** **0**

This was a normal Sabbath day with rest, a prayer meeting, and the sacrament of the Lord's Supper. Elijah Fordham said the division "had a good season. Bro. Colby sick. All the rest well and in good spirits as ever" (JEF).

■ **Near Summum (four miles NE)** **June 2** **25**

The camp traveled through groves and prairies. Elijah Fordham wrote, "Forded Spoon River, a rapid stream—three rods wide—at Barker's ford [near Duncan's Mills]. Went on five miles towards Quincy [IL], our course being between Canton on the right and Lewistown. Traveled 25 miles" on the route of what later became U.S. 24 (JEF).

■ **CROOKED CREEK (LAMOINE RIVER)** **JUNE 3** **30**

Elijah Fordham recorded this day: "Went on from Barker's Grove towards Quincy. Traveled 15 miles. The length of a prairie, along without a road a few rods from the Mormon Road and did not know it got into the Mormon Road. Forded Camp Creek. Went on. Forded Crooked Creek. This creek can't be forded in high water. It is a mad stream. Camped [near or at the modern town of Ripley]. Colby better, Aurelia sick, having traveled 30 miles this day. Heard from Brother Joseph and his troops, about 300 of them [more like 200]. All smart and hearty-looking men. Heard from Jackson County. They [mobs] have burned all the [Saints'] houses and keep guard all the time" (JEF).

■ **CAMP POINT (JUNCTION)** **JUNE 4** **24**

Moving this day toward Quincy, the brethren arrived at the junction of the Mormon and Quincy Roads, two miles east of Camp Point, where they camped. Charles C. Rich gave the prayer at the end of the day. The Mormon Road toward Carthage is State 94 today.

■ **MISSISSIPPI RIVER, MO** **JUNE 5** **20**

From Camp Point to Quincy, IL, the division had a good, dry prairie road. Elijah Fordham wrote, "Quincy is considerable of a place, about 70 houses, 2 inns, 9 stores, [and] an open square in the center, [which] looks well. Got lead for six cents a pound. Crossed the Mississippi about a mile wide at this place, full of islands and a strong current" (JEF).

While in Quincy, the camp straightened a bent wagon axle, crossed to the west side of the Mississippi River at Logsden's Ferry, and camped on the shore. The brethren were glad they had finally reached Missouri. Elijah Fordham wrote, "Advise all brethren to cross at his [Logsden's] ferry. He is friendly" (JEF).

■ **SALT RIVER (MONROE COUNTY, MO)** **JUNE 6** **24**

Brother Fordham recorded that the camp "crossed the bottom lands" and "forded the North and South Fabius rivers. Passed through the village of Palmyra, a thriving place of 100 houses, a goodly number of stores, many houses of brick. Passed on to the nine-mile prairie on the road to Salt River and camped within four miles of the branch of the Church in the area of James Allred's farm" (JEF).

■ **ALLRED SETTLEMENT (SALT RIVER BRANCH)** **JUNE 7–8** **4 AND 0**

In the mid-afternoon, the Joseph Smith division of Zion's Camp arrived at the Allred settlement, selected as the predetermined rendezvous point for the camps. Hyrum Smith's division had traveled about 600 miles from Pontiac, MI, while Joseph Smith's division had traveled about 900 miles from Kirtland, OH. From the Allred Settlement, one of the larger Latter-day Saint settlements between Kirtland, OH, and Independence, MO, the two divisions traveled together as they made their way toward Liberty, MO.

The Joseph Smith division camped on James Allred's farm near a good spring of water. Some Zion's Camp members stayed for a time on James Ivies' farm, located nearby.

Hyrum Smith's division arrived at the Allred settlement in time for Sabbath day meetings on June 8. They had traveled four miles during the day. At long last, the two divisions were together, happy to have arrived only one day apart. They rested and made preparations for a long march and possible military action in Jackson County, MO. Joseph Smith's division numbered about 170. Hyrum Smith's division numbered about 20 when it arrived, but 15 more men joined the ranks at the Allred settlement. When the camp left for Missouri, it totaled about 205 men, with a few women and children. Camp members were between the ages of 10 and 50.

While at the Allred settlement June 7–12, the combined camp

worshiped on the Sabbath, relaxed, repaired wagons, washed clothes, reorganized its numbers into companies of 10, held military training, made a flag, and recognized Joseph Smith as commander-in-chief. Lyman Wight was named general of the camp, and Hyrum Smith was selected as captain (HC 2:88).

Lyman Wight and Parley P. Pratt contacted Governor Daniel Dunklin to see if the governor was prepared with troops to help Zion's Camp in its efforts to restore the Jackson County Saints to their homes and property. Dunklin failed to support the Saints as he had promised, thwarting one of the main purposes of Zion's Camp.

■ **ALLRED SETTLEMENT (SALT RIVER BRANCH)** **JUNE 12** **13**

After forming its line of march, Zion's Camp went 13 miles before camping on a muddy prairie. On the way to Liberty, in Clay County, camp members preached the gospel to small Latter-day Saint branches and to others interested in hearing the elders. Zion's Camp normally held religious meetings on the Sabbath, and members said personal and public prayers daily. The camp went as far as Liberty, MO, before being struck with cholera. It was disbanded shortly thereafter and returned to Kirtland, OH (HC 2:84–93; JEF; for more details on the Zion's Camp march, read HC 2:61–150).

Joseph Smith's Division of Zion's Camp in Illinois—1834

	Camp	Date (1834)	Miles (Approximate)
■	**Springfield, OH, to Indianapolis, IN**	**May 18–21**	**133**
■	**Indianapolis, IN, to State line (near Blanford, IN)**	**May 22–24**	**75**

Enemies had threatened Joseph Smith's division of Zion's Camp by telling camp members that they would never be allowed to pass through Indianapolis, IN. But the Prophet Joseph Smith told the camp "in the name of the Lord, [that] we should not be disturbed and that we would pass through Indianapolis without the people knowing it. When near the place [on May 21, 1834] many got into wagons, and, separating some little distance, passed through the city, while others walked down different streets, leaving the inhabitants wondering 'when that big company would come along'" (HC 2:70).

On May 24, Joseph's division passed over the Wabash River at Clinton and pushed on to the state line, camping in Edgar County, IL, at a point about eight miles west of the Wabash River and 1½ miles west of the Indiana-Illinois state boundary. This area is in present-day Blanford, IN, but within Illinois.

While waiting for a ferry at the Wabash River, the Prophet instructed Zion's Camp members in the proper manner of kneeling for prayer (many had been assuming unseemly positions). "When we kneel to pray, we should be in a graceful position such as could not cause a disgusting impression to arise in the mind of any spectator," he said (ZCB 80–81). The next day, May 25, the camp did not move or have any religious meetings. This was the first time since leaving Kirtland that the camp held no meetings on the Sabbath. Members spent the day washing, baking, and so forth (HC 2:70).

■ **EMBARRAS RIVER** **MAY 26** **27**

On May 26, camp members felt they were guided by angels. When Heber C. Kimball asked Joseph Smith the identity of a certain stranger, the Prophet replied that it was John the Beloved, who was on his way to the ten tribes in the north (ZCB, 85). Finding drinking water was a real problem this day as the brethren traveled across the Illinois plains and past pools of stagnant water. When they came to the house of William Wayne, the only settler in the vicinity, they found a well, which they called "one of the greatest comforts that we could have received, as we were almost famished, and it was a long time before we could or dared to satisfy our thirst" (ZCB 86).

When they arrived at the Embarras River, two miles west of Oakland, they had an encounter with three prairie rattlesnakes at their campsite. The men were about to kill the snakes, but the Prophet intervened: "Let them alone—don't hurt them! How will the serpent ever lose his venom, while the servants of God possess the same disposition, and continue to make war upon it? Men must become harmless, before the brute creation; and when men lose their vicious dispositions and cease to destroy the animal race, the lion and the lamb can dwell together, and the sucking child can play with the serpent in safety" (HC 2:71). "The men carefully picked up the snakes on sticks and carried them across the creek" (ZCB 86–87).

Joseph taught the brethren that they should not kill a serpent, bird, or animal of any kind during their journey unless it became necessary to preserve their lives. Joseph often spoke about this subject. One day while watching a squirrel on a tree, he took a gun, shot the squirrel, and passed on, leaving the animal on the ground. Orson Hyde picked up the squirrel and said, "We will cook this, that nothing may be lost." The Prophet recorded, "I perceived that the brethren understood what I did it for, and in their practice gave more heed to my precept than to my example, which was right" (HC 2:72).

Later that day in the evening, a one-horse buggy entered the firelight of their camp. Parley P. Pratt and Amasa Lyman had arrived with a dozen new recruits from the branch of the Church in Eugene, IL. They were warmly welcomed by the Prophet and assigned to their quarters (ZCB 87)

The Kirtland Camp also camped near the Embarras River. On

Sept. 8, 1838, the group camped 15 miles west of Paris and five miles east of Oakland. On Sept. 9, the Kirtland Camp camped two miles SW of the small town of Isabel and five miles east of the Embarras River.

■ **OKAW RIVER** **MAY 27** **15**

Zion's Camp traveled about 15 miles and camped on the Okaw River at a point two miles NW of modern Lovington. Joseph said, "We know that angels were our companions, for we saw them." The Prophet's encouragement helped dispel fears (HC 2:73).

■ **DECATUR** **MAY 28–29** **29**

The camp was located this day and the next about nine miles SW of the center of Decatur City, near the Sangamon River, two miles north of Blackland. On the afternoon of May 29, the Prophet proposed that the camp be divided into thirds and hold a sham battle for diversion. In receiving a charge, Heber C. Kimball grasped Captain Lewis Zobriski's sword, and in endeavoring to take it from him, cut the skin from the palm of his hand. Joseph Smith called the camp together and cautioned the men to be more careful in the future so as to prevent further injury (HC 2:74–75).

The Prophet discovered that the cook had served sour bread to part of his company while he had received "good, sweet bread." Joseph reproved Brother Zebedee Coltrin for this partiality. "I wanted my brethren to fare as well as I did," he said (HC 2:75).

The Kirtland campground of Sept. 12, 1838, was in the same place Zion's Camp stayed May 28–29.

■ **SPRINGFIELD** **MAY 30** **33**

On this day, the division camped on **Spring Creek,** three miles from Springfield, the capital of Illinois. Frederick G. Williams and Almon W. Babbitt, in disguise, went to Springfield ahead of the camp to get gunpowder and gauge public sentiment. The Prophet wrote, "Our appearance excited considerable curiosity, and a great many questions were asked. The spies who had followed us so long pursued us very closely, changing their dress and horses several times a day" (HC 2:76).

When many of the camp's horses were seized with colic and bloat on this day, Ezra Thayre administered medicine mixed in a quart stone bottle. The medicine, which contained cayenne pepper, water, and tobacco, "would almost invariably cure a sick horse in a few minutes." Brother Thayer called his medicine "18 by 24" (HC 2:76).

Joseph Smith recorded, "A brother came to see us with the news that my brother Hyrum had passed on west the day before with a company, about fifty miles north of us, saying, 'He has a fine company, and they all look mighty *pert.*'" This unnamed brother gave Joseph Smith a hundred dollars to help Zion's Camp on its way (HC 2:77)

■ JACKSONVILLE MAY 31–JUNE 1 30

On May 31, the camp traveled about 28 miles and camped on a small stream of water approximately one mile east of Jacksonville, where the men found a pawpaw bush in the road. Frederick G. Williams had dropped the bush as a signal for Zion's Camp to stop for the night and pitch tents (HC 2:77). Jacksonville had a population of about 800 residents.

The next day, Sunday, Zion's Camp held an outdoor meeting, which attracted about 200 townspeople and others from the surrounding area. The Prophet Joseph Smith, introduced as "Squire Cook," spoke first. He was followed by Elder John Carter, who had formerly been a Baptist preacher. Five more elders spoke in the course of the day, all of whom were former preachers for different denominations: Joseph Young, Brigham Young, Orson Hyde, Orson Pratt, and Eleazer Miller (ZCL, 86–87). The townspeople asked many questions throughout the day, "but none could learn our names, professions, business, or destination," the Prophet wrote. "And, although they suspected we were 'Mormons,' they were very civil" (HC 2:78).

■ ILLINOIS RIVER (MODERN VALLEY CITY) JUNE 2 25

The division traveled about 25 miles this day. The brethren crossed the Illinois River on Phillip's Ferry at a cost of $8 for the whole group and then made their camp on the west side of the river.

Their enemies had threatened that they would not cross the Illinois River, but they were ferried without any difficulty (HC 2:79).

■ **ILLINOIS RIVER (VALLEY CITY)** **JUNE 3** **0**

One of the most interesting and unique events of Zion's Camp took place this day while Joseph Smith's division was camped on the west side of the Illinois River at Valley City. The Prophet and members of Zion's Camp climbed a burial mound near the Illinois River. They dug into the mound and found a skeleton that Joseph Smith identified as "Zelph," a white Lamanite warrior and chief. An arrowhead found with the skeleton is in the LDS Church vault. Wilford Woodruff placed one of Zelph's thigh bones in his wagon and transported it to Liberty, MO (HC 2:79–80; BYUS 29, no. 2 [1989]: 31–56; ReSI: 97–111; T&S 6:787–90; ZCB 111–15). (For details on this site, see Zelph Mound, page 228; see also Valley City and Zelph Mound Map, page 243.)

That same day, the Prophet Joseph Smith stood on a wagon wheel and delivered to the members of Zion's Camp a prophecy. He said the Lord had revealed to him "that a scourge would come upon the camp in consequence of the fractious and unruly spirits that appeared among them, and they should die like sheep with the rot; still if they would repent and humble themselves before the Lord, the scourge, in a great measure, might be turned away; but, as the Lord lives, the members of this camp will suffer for giving way to their unruly temper" (HC 2:80). This prophecy was considered fulfilled when some Zion's Camp members died of cholera near Liberty in Clay County.

Zion's camp continued to travel southwest from the Illinois River, going through Pittsfield about noon and ferrying across the Sny River about a mile west of Atlas. The brethren camped for the night on the west side of the river near Atlas, which is five miles NE of the Mississippi River.

■ **MISSISSIPPI RIVER (EAST BANK)** **JUNE 4** **25**

The Prophet's division of Zion's Camp traveled five miles from the Sny River to the Mississippi River, where the men camped on its east banks and began ferrying across the mighty Mississippi. Only one small flatboat ferry was available, which cost them $16 per company of 12 men. Some of the men found eggs on Mississippi River sandbar. Joseph Smith told the men the eggs were snake eggs and warned the brethren against eating them. Some of the men, assuming they were turtle eggs, ate them anyway and were sick the next day (HC 2:82–83).

■ **LOUISIANA, MO** **JUNE 5** **1**

It took all day to finish ferrying men, horses, wagons, and belongings across the Mississippi River, more than a 1½ miles wide, and land at the village of Louisiana, MO. Some went into the dense forest as a company to offer up fervent prayers that God would spare their lives and permit them to return to their families. They felt that their prayers would be answered. While some were ferrying, others were hunting and fishing (HC 2:82–83).

■ **ALLRED SETTLEMENT (SALT RIVER BRANCH)** **JUNE 6–12** **40**

Eager to get to their destination, Joseph Smith's division of Zion's Camp left early in the morning of June 6 and traveled 40 miles in two days to reach the Allred Settlement. (See Zion's Camp and Kirtland Camp maps, pages 242–243.) The men arrived in the mid-afternoon of June 7. The next day, Hyrum Smith's division arrived at the Allred Settlement and made camp near the large spring of water on James Allred's farm. The rendezvous site was also known as Salt River Branch (ZCB 130). The members of Zion's Camp were thrilled to be in Missouri, where the Church had many members willing to fight for their rights, if necessary.

The approximately 225 adult male participants of Zion's Camp, along with some women and children, spent five days preparing for their journey from the Salt River Branch to Clay County. They underwent military training, washed, mended, blacksmithed, wrote, cooked, and performed jobs to help them prepare for the last nearly 300 miles of laborious travel.

About the General Editor

Dr. LaMar C. Berrett, the general editor of the six-volume work *Sacred Places* and an author in volume two, is a professor emeritus of Church history and doctrine at Brigham Young University. He was born and reared in Riverton, UT, and served as a rifleman and platoon runner in the Second Infantry Division of the United States Army during World War II. While serving, Dr. Berrett spent 110 "combat days" in Belgium, Germany, and Czechoslovakia during the Battle of the Bulge. He later served a mission in the Southern states, where he served as a counselor to the mission president. He has since served in many positions in the Church, including stake clerk, high councilor, bishop's counselor, and bishop. He was a member of the Church Historical Arts and Sites subcommittee for three years, and was the president of his family genealogical organization for 25 years.

Dr. Berrett received a bachelor's degree in business from the University of Utah. He went on to earn a master's degree in Church history and philosophy and a doctorate in educational administration from BYU. Following nine years as a seminary teacher, Dr. Berrett joined the BYU faculty, teaching at the university for 29 years and serving as the chair of the Church History Department for nine years before his retirement in 1991.

He has researched, written, and directed many TV and video productions for use in the classroom. He is the author of several books, including the much acclaimed *Discovering the World of the Bible*. He conducted a comprehensive aerial photography project in 1978, which involved infrared photography of significant Church history sites from New Hampshire to Salt Lake City. He has also conducted numerous Church history travel tours and has hosted more than 150 tours worldwide.

Dr. Berrett has written more than 50 percent of the text of *Sacred Places*, and with the help of other contributing authors, he created all of the exact-scale, never-before-published maps appearing in the series, and he took all photographs unless otherwise noted.

A lifetime of researching the history of The Church of Jesus Christ of Latter-day Saints has been to Dr. Berrett a "soul-satisfying labor of love."

Dr. Berrett and his wife, the former Darlene Hamilton, reside in Orem, UT. The couple has nine children.

About the Authors

Keith W. Perkins is a professor emeritus of Church History and Doctrine at Brigham Young University. He holds degrees from Arizona State University and Brigham Young University, where he joined the faculty in 1975 after teaching in the Church Educational System in Salt Lake City, UT, and Tempe, AZ. Before retiring in 1999, Dr. Perkins served as chair of the Department of Church History and Doctrine, acting associate dean of Religious Education, and director of Electronic Texts in the Religious Studies Center. He is married to the former Vella Crowther, and they are the parents of six children.

Donald Q. Cannon is a professor of Church history and doctrine at Brigham Young University. He holds degrees from the University of Utah and from Clark University, in Worcester, MA. Dr. Cannon joined the faculty at Brigham Young University in 1973 after having taught history at the University of Southern Maine. He has served as the associate dean of Religious Education in addition to other assignments at Brigham Young University. An accomplished author and researcher, Dr. Cannon is married to the former JoAnn McGinnis, and they are the parents of six children.

ABBREVIATIONS USED IN PHOTO CAPTIONS

BYUL	Brigham Young University Special Collections.
LDSCA	Archives Division, Church Historical Department, The Church of Jesus Christ of Latter-day Saints, Salt Lake City, UT.
LLUSI	Lovejoy Library, University of Southern Illinois.
MOABYU	Brigham Young University Museum of Art.
MHSSL	Missouri Historical Society, St. Louis, MO.
PRC	Campbell, Robert. "Gen. Joseph Smith Addressing the Nauvoo Legion" (painting), 1845. LDS Museum of Church History and Art, Salt Lake City, UT.
RLDSLA	Library-Archives and Museum, Reorganized Church of Jesus Christ of Latter Day Saints (The Community of Christ), World Headquarters, Independence, MO.
USHS	Utah State Historical Society, Salt Lake City, UT.

BIBLIOGRAPHY

ADO Osborne, David. "Biography of David Osborn Senior." LDS Church Archives, Salt Lake City, UT.

AES Stevenson, Edward. "Autobiography of Edward Stevenson" (holograph), 17 September 1895. LDS Church Archives, Salt Lake City, UT.

AL *Autumn Leaves* (published monthly for youth of the Reoganized Church of Jesus Christ of Latter Day Saints). Lamoni, IA: Herald Publishing House, January 1888–December 1929.

APPP Pratt, Parley P. *Autobiography of Parley P. Pratt.* 4th ed. Salt Lake City: Deseret Book, 1938; see also Classics in Mormon Literature edition, 1985.

ARM Backman, Milton V., Jr. *American Religions and the Rise of Mormonism.* Salt Lake City: Deseret Book, 1965.

ATM — *Among the Mormons.* Edited by William Mulder and A. Russell Mortensen. New York: Alfred A. Knopf, 1958.

AWD — Draper, William. "A Biographical Sketch of the Life and Travels and Birth and Parentage of William Draper, Who Was the Son of William Draper and Lydia Luthrop Draper." Typescript. Special Collections, Harold B. Lee Library, Brigham Young University, Provo, UT.

AWF — Foote, Warren. Autobiography. LDS Church Archives, Salt Lake City.

BiE — Jenson, Andrew. *Latter-day Saint Biographical Encyclopedia: A Compilation of Biographical Sketches of Prominent Men and Women in The Church of Jesus Christ of Latter-day Saints.* 4 vols. Salt Lake City: A. Jenson History Company and the Deseret News, 1901–36.

BLAS — *Biographical Sketch of the Life of Luman Andros Shurtliff.* Typescript. Special Collections, Harold B. Lee Library, Brigham Young University, Provo, UT.

BLS — Snow, Eliza R. *Biography and Family History of Lorenzo Snow, One of the Twelve Apostles of The Church of Jesus Christ of Latter-day Saints.* Salt Lake City: Deseret News, 1884.

BYAM — Arrington, Leonard J. *Brigham Young: American Moses.* New York: Alfred A. Knopf, 1985.

BYUS — *Brigham Young University Studies.* Published quarterly at Brigham Young University, Provo, UT.

CC — Oaks, Dallin H., and Marvin S. Hill. *Carthage Conspiracy: The Trial of the Accused Assassins of Joseph Smith.* Urbana: University of Illinois Press, 1975.

CHC — Roberts, Brigham H. *A Comprehensive History of the Church of Jesus Christ of Latter-day Saints.* 6 vols. Salt Lake City: The Church of Jesus Christ of Latter-day Saints, 1930.

ChCh — *Church Chronology.* Comp. Andrew Jenson. Salt Lake City: Deseret News Press, 1914.

CN — *Church News.* Salt Lake City: The Church of Jesus Christ of Latter-day Saints, 1936–.

CR — Conference Reports of The Church of Jesus Christ of Latter-day Saints. Salt Lake City: The Church of Jesus Christ of Latter-day Saints, 1898–.

DHS — Stout, Hosea. *On the Mormon Frontier: The Diary of Hosea Stout.* Edited by Juanita Brooks. 2 vols. Salt Lake City: University of Utah Press, 1964.

DLJN — Nuttall, L. John. Diary. 4 vols. Typescript. Special Collections, Harold B. Lee Library, Brigham Young University, Provo, UT.

DNCA — *Deseret News Church Almanac.* Published biennially in Salt Lake City by the Deseret News in cooperation with the LDS Church Historical Department, 1974–.

DoJS — Smith, Joseph. *An American Prophet's Record: The Diaries and Journals of Joseph Smith.* Edited by Scott H. Faulring. Salt Lake City: Bookcraft, 1954–56.

EJ *Elder's Journal of the Church of Latter Day Saints.* Kirtland, OH, October 1837–December 1837; Far West, MO, July–August 1838.

ELDSH Garr, Arnold K., Donald Q. Cannon, and Richard O. Cowan. *Enclyclopedia of Latter-day Saint History.* Salt Lake City: Deseret Book, 2000

EMS *The Evening and the Morning Star.* Published in Independence, MO, June 1832–July 1833; Kirtland, OH, December 1833-–September 1834.

EnM *Encyclopedia of Mormonism.* Edited by Daniel H. Ludlow et al. 4 vols. New York: Macmillan, 1992.

ENS *Ensign.* Published monthly by The Church of Jesus Christ of Latter-day Saints, Salt Lake City, UT, 1971–.

ERA *Improvement Era.* Published monthly by The Church of Jesus Christ of Latter-day Saints, Salt Lake City, 1897–1970.

FJS McGavin, E. Cecil. *The Family of Joseph Smith.* Salt Lake City: Bookcraft, 1963.

FOP Quincy, Josiah. *Figures of the Past from the Leaves of Old Journals.* Boston: Boston Brothers, 1883.

FWR *Far West Record: Minutes of The Church of Jesus Christ of Latter-day Saints, 1830–1844.* Edited by Donald Q. Cannon and Lyndon W. Cook. Salt Lake City: Deseret Book, 1983.

HBY "History of Brigham Young." Manuscript. LDS Church Archives, Salt Lake City, UT.

HC Smith, Joseph, Jr. *History of The Church of Jesus Christ of Latter-day Saints.* Edited by B. H. Roberts. 7 vols. 4th ed. Salt Lake City: Deseret Book, 1965.

HiR Jenson, Andrew. *The Historical Record.* 9 vols. Salt Lake City: Andrew Jenson, 1882–90. (Subtitle: *A Monthly Periodical Devoted Exclusively to Historical, Biographical, Chronological and Statistical Mattters.)* Originally published as a monthly periodical; later issued as a nine-volume set (vols. 5–8 republished with a separate title page: *Church Encyclopedia, Book I).*

HJS Smith, Lucy Mack. *History of Joseph Smith by His Mother, Lucy Mack Smith.* Salt Lake City: Bookcraft, 1958.

HOI Ford, Thomas. *A History of Illinois, From Its Commencement as a State in 1814 to 1847.* Chicago: S. C. Griggs & Co.; New York: Ivison & Phinney, 1854.

HR Backman, Milton V., Jr. *The Heavens Resound: A History of the Latter-day Saints in Ohio, 1830–1838.* Salt Lake City: Deseret Book, 1983.

HSM Kimball, Stanley B. *Historic Sites and Markers Along the Mormon and Other Great Western Trails.* Urbana: University of Illinois Press, 1988.

IBMW Anderson, Richard Lloyd. *Investigating the Book of Mormon Witnesses.* Salt Lake City: Deseret Book, 1981.

InD Noall, Claire A. *Intimate Disciple: A Portrait of Willard Richards,*

Apostle to Joseph Smith, Cousin of Brigham Young. Salt Lake City: University of Utah Press, 1957.

IoC — Jenson, Andrew, et. al. *Infancy of the Church.* Salt Lake City: N.p., 1889. Special Collections, Harold B. Lee Library, Brigham Young University, Provo, UT.

JD — *Journal of Discourses.* 26 vols. London: Latter-day Saints' Book Depot, 1854–86.

JDL — Brooks, Juanita. *John Doyle Lee, Zealot, Pioneer-Builder, Scapegoat.* Glendale, CA: Arthur H. Clark Co., 1961.

JEF — Fordham, Elijah. "Journal of Elijah Fordham." In "Journal History," 8 June 1834. LDS Church Archives, Salt Lake City.

JES — Snow, Erastus. Journal. LDS Church Archives, Salt Lake City.

JGAS — Smith, George A. Journal. LDS Church Archives, Salt Lake City.

JGL — Laub, George. "Journal of George Laub." *BYU Studies* 18, no. 2 (winter 1978): 152–78.

JH — Journal History of The Church of Jesus Christ of Latter-day Saints. Manuscript. LDS Historical Department Library, Salt Lake City, UT.

JHC — Coray, Howard. Journal. LDS Church Archives, Salt Lake City, Utah.

JI — *Juvenile Instructor* (variation of the title *The Instructor;* see ThI).

JJM — Murdock, John. "Journal of John Murdock." Typescript. LDS Church Archives, Salt Lake City, UT.

JJOD — Duke, Jonathan Oldham. Journal. Special Collections, Harold B. Lee Library, Brigham Young University, Provo, UT.

JMH — *Journal of Mormon History* (published annually). Ogden, Utah: Mormon History Association.

JPS — Sessions, Patty. Journal. LDS Church Archives, Salt Lake City, UT.

JSFM — Hill, Donna. *Joseph Smith, the First Mormon.* Garden City, NY: Doubleday, 1977.

JSK — Anderson, Karl R. *Joseph Smith's Kirtland: Eyewitness Accounts.* Salt Lake City: Deseret Book, 1989.

JSN — Anderson, Richard L. *Joseph Smith's New England Heritage.* Salt Lake City: Deseret Book, 1971.

JTB — Bullock, Thomas. Journal. Handwritten. LDS Church Archives, Salt Lake City, UT.

JTT — Turley, Theodore. "Biography and Autobiography of Theodore Turley." In the *Theodore Turley Family Book.* N.p., 1978.

JWHJ — *John Whitmer Historical Association Journal* (published annually). Lamoni, IA: The John Whitmer Historical Association, 1981–.

JWW — Woodruff, Wilford. *Wilford Woodruff's Journal, 1833–1898.* 9 vols. Edited by Scott G. Kenney. Midvale, UT: Signature Books, 1983.

KEQR — *Kirtland Elders' Quorum Record 1836–1841.* Edited by Milton V. Backman Jr. and Lyndon W. Cook. Provo, UT: Grandin Book, 1985.

LHCK — Whitney, Orson F. *Life of Heber C. Kimball, an Apostle; the Father and Founder of the British Mission.* Salt Lake City: Kimball Family, 1888; 5th ed., Salt Lake City: Bookcraft, 1974.

LHJ Hancock, Levi. *Life Hancock Journal.* N.p., 1983. Special Collections, Harold B. Lee Library, Brigham Young University, Provo, UT.

LHPD "Life History of Philo Dibble, Sr." In *Pioneer Journals.* N.p., 1969. Special Collections, Harold B. Lee Library, Brigham Young University, Provo, UT.

LJFS Smith, Joseph Fielding. *Life of Joseph F. Smith, Sixth President of The Church of Jesus Christ of Latter-day Saints.* Salt Lake City: Deseret Book, 1938.

LJS Cannon, George Q. *The Life of Joseph Smith, the Prophet.* Salt Lake City: Juvenile Instructor Office, 1888.

LLS Romney, Thomas C. *The Life of Lorenzo Snow, Fifth President of The Church of Jesus Christ of Latter-day Saints.* Salt Lake City: Sugarhouse Press, 1955.

M&A *Messenger and Advocate.* Kirtland, OH: The Church of Jesus Christ of Latter-day Saints, 1834–37.

ME Newell, Linda King, and Valeen Tippetts Avery. *Mormon Enigma: Emma Hale Smith.* Garden City, NY: Doubleday, 1984.

MHBY *Manuscript History of Brigham Young, 1801–1844.* Edited by Elden Jay Watson. Salt Lake City: Smith Secretarial Service, 1968.

MLR Johnson, Benjamin F. *My Life's Review.* Independence, MO: Zion's Printing and Publishing Co., 1979.

MoC *Membership of The Church of Jesus Christ of Latter-day Saints, 1830–1848.* Comp. Susan Easton Black. 50 vols. Provo, UT: Brigham Young University, Religious Studies Center, 1984–88.

MS *Millennial Star.* Liverpool: The Church of Jesus Christ of Latter-day Saints, 1840–1970.

NCJ Miller, David E., and Della S. Miller. *Nauvoo: The City of Joseph.* Edited by David H. Miller. 2d ed. Bountiful, UT:Utah History Atlas, 1996.

Nex *Nauvoo Expositor.* 7 June 1844 (one edition only).

NWG Roberts, Brigham H. *New Witnesses for God II: The Book of Mormon.* (Manual for Young Men's Mutual Improvement Association.) 3 vols. Salt Lake City: George Q. Cannon & Sons, 1903–06.

OMKM Holzapfel, Richard Neitzel, and T. Jeffery Cottle. *Old Mormon Kirtland and Missouri: Historic Photographs and Guide.* Santa Ana, CA: Fieldbook Productions, 1991.

OMN Holzapfel, Richard Neitzel and T. Jeffery Cottle. *Old Mormon Nauvoo, 1839–1846: Historic Photographs and Guide.* Provo, UT: Grandin Book, 1990.

OPJ Pratt, Orson. *The Orson Pratt Journals.* Edited by Elden J. Watson. Salt Lake City: E. J. Watson, 1975.

OPR Schindler, Harold. *Orrin Porter Rockwell: Man of God, Son of Thunder.* Salt Lake City: University of Utah Press, 1966.

OPW Kimball, Heber C. *On the Potter's Wheel: The Diaries of Heber C.*

Kimball. Edited by Stanley B. Kimball. Salt Lake City: Signature Books in association with Smith Research Associates, 1987.

ORH — Barron, Howard H. *Orson Hyde: Missionary, Apostle, Colonizer.* Bountiful, UT: Horizon, 1977.

PJE — *The Prophet Joseph: Essays on the Life and Mission of Joseph Smith.* Edited by Larry C. Porter and Susan Easton Black. Salt Lake City: Deseret Book, 1988.

PJS — Smith, Joseph. *The Papers of Joseph Smith.* Edited by Dean C. Jessee. Salt Lake City: Deseret Book, 1989–.

PPM — Esshom, Frank. *Pioneers and Prominent Men of Utah.* Salt Lake City: Utah Pioneers Book Publishing, 1913.

PWJS — Smith, Joseph. *The Personal Writings of Joseph Smith.* Edited by Dean C. Jessee. Salt Lake City: Deseret Book, 1984.

RBS — Launius, Roger D., and F. Mark McKiernan. *Joseph Smith Jr.'s Red Brick Store.* Western Illinois Monograph Series, no. 5. Macomb, IL: Western Illinois University, 1985.

ReSI — *Regional Studies in Latter-day Saint Church History, Illinois.* Provo, UT: Department of Church History and Doctrine, Brigham Young University, 1994.

RoOW — Wight, Orange L. "Recollections of Orange L. Wight." Typescript. Special Collections, Brigham Young University, Provo, UT.

RPJS — Cook, Lyndon W. *The Revelations of the Prophet Joseph Smith: A Historical and Biographical Commentary of the Doctrine and Covenants.* Provo, UT: Seventy's Mission Bookstore, 1981.

RSM — *Relief Society Magazine.* Salt Lake City: The Church of Jesus Christ of Latter-day Saints, 1915–69.

RTF — *Restoration Trails Forum.* Independence, MO: Restoration Trails Foundation 1974–February 1980.

SMPM — Talmage, James E. *The Story of "Mormonism" and the Philosophy of "Mormonism."* Salt Lake City: Deseret News, 1920.

T&S — *Times and Seasons* (published monthly in Nauvoo, IL), 1839–46.

TAMF — Hartley, William G. *They Are My Friends: A History of the Joseph Knight Family, 1825–1850.* Provo, UT: Grandin Book, 1986.

ThC — *The Contributor* (published monthly in Salt Lake City). Deseret News Press, 1879–96.

ThR — *The Return* (published monthly, semimonthly for the Church of Christ, by Ebenezer Robinson). David City, IA (Richmond, MO; Independence, MO; Denver, CO), January 1889–October 1900.

TWP — *Truth Will Prevail: The Rise of The Church of Jesus Christ of Latter-day Saints in the British Isles, 1837–1987.* Edited by V. Ben Bloxham, James R. Moss, and Larry C. Porter. Cambridge: The Church of Jesus Christ of Latter-day Saints, 1987.

UHQ — *Utah Historical Quarterly.* Salt Lake City: The Board of Control, Utah Historical Society, January 1928–.

Wex — *The Women's Exponent.* Salt Lake City: The Church of Jesus Christ of Latter-day Saints, 1872–1914.

WM	Tullidge, Edward W. *The Women of Mormondom.* New York: Tullidge and Crandall, 1877.
WS-R	Rudd, Calvin P. "William Smith: Brother of the Prophet Joseph Smith." Master's thesis, Brigham Young University, 1973.
WW	Woodruff, Wilford. *Wilford Woodruff, History of His Life and Labors.* Edited by Matthias F. Cowley. Salt Lake City: Bookcraft, 1964.
ZCB	Bradley, James L. *Zion's Camp, 1834: Prelude to the Civil War.* Salt Lake City: Publishers Press, 1990.
ZCL	Launius, Roger D. *Zion's Camp: Expedition to Missouri, 1834.* Independence, MO: Herald Publishing House, 1984.

Index

Note: Italicized page numbers indicate photographs or illustrations; bold-faced page numbers indicate maps.